Small Dogs, Big Hearts

Praise for This Book

Small Dogs, Big Hearts is an invaluable treasure of information. . . . It includes every aspect of puppy care from infancy through adulthood. It is precise, beautifully written, and easily understood by both the professional dog exhibitor and the owner of a beloved family pet. Every person who contemplates purchasing a dog or who has a dog should own this book.

—Victor Joris, AKC Toy Group Judge

Darlene Arden has come up with an informative book which, just like the little creatures that inspired it, manages to be of serious intent and at the same time entertaining. A thorough instruction manual for small dogs in general, it delves into the breed-specific joys and idiosyncrasies of these mini-sized canine charmers as well.

—Lilian S. Barber, Author, *The Italian Greyhound, 21st Century*

"For anyone who has owned a small dog, the best book ever written has been written by Darlene Arden."

—Martha Smith, *Providence Journal Bulletin*

"At last, we have a book devoted to toy dogs written by an authority on toy dog care. . . . This book would be a worthwhile addition to any dog fancier's library."

—Glenna Fierheller, *Dogs in Canada*

"Darlene Arden's new book demonstrates that small dogs can be well-adjusted bundles of joy in the hands of knowledgeable owners."

—Rosemary Herbert, *The Boston Herald*

Arden's breezy, unassuming portrait of the Rodney Dangerfields of dogdom captures everything from their blue-collar feistiness to their charming insouciance."

—Ranny Green, *The Seattle Times*

"Arden does an impressive job sniffing out facts peculiar to small dogs, from housebreaking to house manners."

—Steve Dale, "My Pet World," *The Chicago Tribune*

"A fascinating, comprehensive book about the care and nurturing of small dogs by an author who argues successfully that the needs of toy dogs are vastly different from those of their bigger counterparts."

—Betty Harrison, *The Atlanta Journal-Constitution*

Small Dogs, Big Hearts

A Guide to Caring for Your Little Dog

Revised Edition

Darlene Arden

Howell Book House
Published by Wiley Publishing, Inc., Hoboken, New Jersey

For general information on our other products and services or to obtain technical support please contact our Customer Care Department within the U.S. at (800) 762-2974, outside the U.S. at (317) 572-3993 or fax (317) 572-4002.

Wiley also publishes its books in a variety of electronic formats. Some content that appears in print may not be available in electronic books. For more information about Wiley products, please visit our web site at www.wiley.com.

Library of Congress Cataloging-in-Publication Data:

Arden, Darlene.
Small dogs, big hearts : a guide to caring for your little dog / Darlene Arden.-- Rev. ed.
p. cm.
Includes index.
ISBN-13 978-0-471-77963-6 (paper: alk. paper)
ISBN-10 0-471-77963-6 (paper: alk. paper)
1. Dogs. 2. Toy dogs. I. Title.

SF427.A73 2006
636.7--dc22

2006008512

Printed in the United States of America

10 9 8 7 6 5 4 3

Second Edition

Book design by Elizabeth Brooks
Cover design by Wendy Mount
Book production by Wiley Publishing, Inc. Composition Services

For Marcia Polimer Abrams, my mother, my best friend, my treasure, my *everything*, who made all things possible. When the gift is so great, the loss is beyond devastating. It is unimaginable. Unfathomable. I will never stop loving you and missing you. You are my heart. This book is for you with all my love.

Contents

Part IV • What Sets Them Apart

Foreword

At last, a definitive book on the inimitable and often underappreciated Toy dog. While they may take up less space than some of their larger cousins, these wonderful creatures are all dog to the core. They occupy an important place in the canine scheme of things, except in a transistorized form.

I love all dogs. And cats. And lemurs. And—well, anything with a leg on each corner. (Actually, I must include a couple of dear three-legged friends as well.) But there has always been an especially soft spot in my heart for the little guys—the "portables."

As a kid growing up, we had dogs of all shapes and sizes, but there was always at least one Pekingese. I learned early on to appreciate those remarkable little lion dogs, not only for their valor, but for their great sense of humor. They taught me a lot. Often unfairly portrayed as a yappy little monster on the lap of some unpleasant dowager lady, the Pekingese got a bad rap. In reality, he is a survivor. A veterinarian friend once told me that a Peke makes a great patient because in a bad situation he will set his jaw and fight to live, where many other dogs will give up.

Pekes are my hang-up. This fine book covers the whole spectrum of Toy dogs—some similarities, many differences—and points the way to bring out the best in them all. They really are a nation unto themselves. Darlene Arden understands this and loves them for it.

So will you.

Betty White
Brentwood, California

Acknowledgments

Writing is a solitary endeavor, but it is not accomplished in a vacuum. I am most grateful to those who have given so generously of their knowledge, experience, and expertise. This book could not have been realized without them.

My deepest thanks to the veterinarians, both here and abroad, who shared their expertise, as well as to the small dog breeders and owners, and the breed clubs, whose web sites have also been of invaluable help. You know who you are, and you know that I am appreciative. With special thanks to my dear friend, Raymond Russo, DVM, MS, AAVN, president of Kingston Animal Hospital, Kingston, Massachusetts.

An enormous thank you to Beth Adelman, who gracefully wears the hats of editor and friend.

And to Ch. Cap'n Ebenezer of Woodridge. Always my Neezie.

Introduction

The ever-growing popularity of small dogs that I predicted when I wrote *The Irrepressible Toy Dog* has certainly come to pass. More and more people are downsizing but want to have a dog. A small one fits neatly into their more mobile lifestyle, which usually includes a smaller home and perhaps an apartment instead of a house with a yard.

But even I had no way of knowing that celebrities would begin to carry small dogs everywhere as if they were fashion accessories instead of living, breathing, sentient beings who deserve love and respect. They are not handbags or bracelets. Little dogs have needs—just as larger dogs have needs. And they're still not right for everyone.

Small dogs have very special needs in many areas and are in a class by themselves. They're charming, intelligent, loving, and, yes, manipulative. Bred down from larger canines to be portable companions, they are dogs nonetheless. The difference is that they have a different perspective on the world. All dogs twenty pounds and under view the world from the vicinity of your ankles. Everything appears huge to them, and this affects them in many ways.

Toys have been around for a very long time; they're probably some of the earliest domesticated dogs. Small dogs were probably the ones who started the entire process of having pets in the home.

My personal odyssey into Toys began with one Yorkshire Terrier puppy. He fulfilled the promise of his bloodlines and became an AKC Champion, but, more than that, the intelligent little fellow more than fulfilled his role as a companion. Ch. Cap'n Ebenezer of

Woodridge walked into my life on four paws and wrapped himself firmly around my heart, where he will live forever.

Unfortunately, small dogs have earned an unfair reputation. There's no reason for them to become the neurotic little wimps or miniature terrorists they're reputed to be. A Toy dog can be a character without becoming a caricature. The small dog should be a happy, fun companion. However, he also occasionally needs protection from the larger breeds and from unruly children and will need to be gently and positively obedience trained, just like any other dog. Every dog is happier and better adjusted when he knows what is expected and what his place is within the family. And every dog can be an ambassador for all dogs when he's well-mannered.

In the years since I wrote *The Irrepressible Toy Dog*, I've learned more and more about our small companions, and I've become even more convinced that training must be gentle and positive. It has been confirmed that aggression begets aggression and has consequences that may not immediately rear their ugly heads at once, but will eventually.

Pekingese

Courtesy of Rose Marchetti

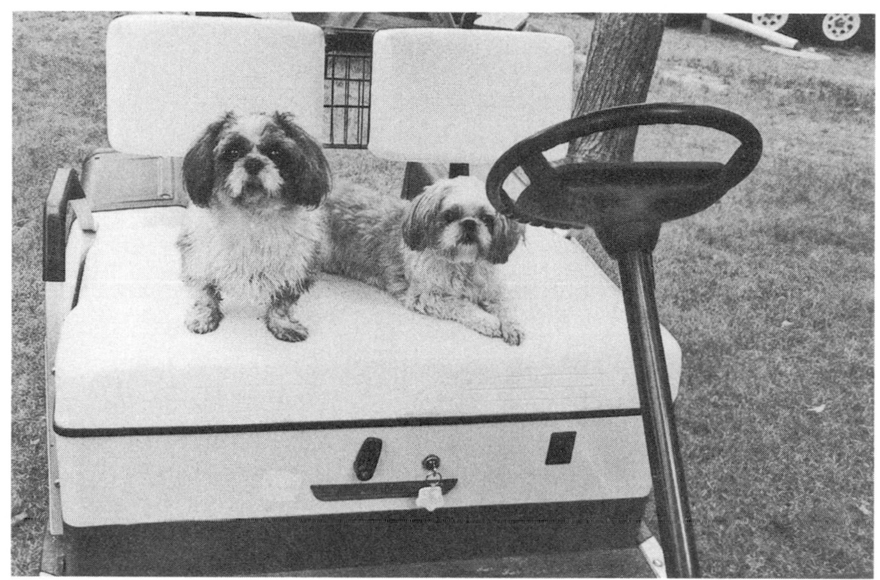

Shih Tzu

Courtesy of Barbara Lees

Although the breeds in the American Kennel Club's Toy Group are the ones primarily thought of as Toys or small dogs, many from other groups, such as Non-Sporting and Miscellaneous, and those recognized by other registries, fall into this category by biology. The information contained in this book most assuredly pertains to them as well. Breeds that come immediately to mind are the Bichon Frise, French Bulldog, Lhasa Apso, Löwchen, Bolognese, Cairn Terrier, Miniature Dachshund, Boston Terrier, Schipperke, and Parson Russell Terrier. There are also many dogs of mixed heritage whose owners will find this book beneficial.

Toy dogs develop differently than larger breeds and have different requirements. Proper development of these little dogs begins early on and moves through the periods of adjustment to their new homes. Because of their diminutive stature and long life, they also have different medical needs and dietary considerations.

The information you'll find here will also be helpful if you are adopting an older pet. When adjusting to a new home, adult dogs should be treated like puppies to aid in the transition. You *can* teach an old dog new tricks—it just takes longer.

These dogs have been called everything from "little fluff balls" to "barking bedslippers." Unfortunately, they're often overlooked by large dog owners, even within the dog fancy. One breeder complained that when a Toy dog wins Best in Show, those with large dogs say, "Oh, the little mutant dog won."

Let me state unequivocally that these are not "little mutant dogs." Small dogs quickly win over anyone who meets them, and their owners cross all cultural and socioeconomic lines from childless couples to grandparents, from truck drivers to celebrities. And as baby boomers downsize from home to apartment, condo, or mobile home, they're downsizing to portable companions as well, enjoying the benefits of a lot of dog in a little body. It's time the Rodney Dangerfields of the dog world were given the respect they deserve.

Part I

The Very Beginning

Cavalier King Charles Spaniels

Courtesy of Bressler West ©

Chapter 1

The Toy Neonate

If you think the Toy dog is small when he's full-grown, think about how tiny he is when he's first born. Breeding these fragile, palm-size handfuls of life is best left to experienced, responsible breeders, because the tiny size that makes them so irresistible also makes them so vulnerable. Breeding small dogs can often be heartbreaking.

Toy mothers usually have very small litters, and that presents its own set of problems. Puppies need other puppies to keep themselves warm and calm—and later to play and socialize with. Singleton pups are usually given a stuffed animal to cuddle with as a substitute littermate, but the pup's breeder must also work extra hard to socialize an only puppy.

Caring for the New Puppy

The newborn Toy weighs mere ounces. Their very small size means it's more difficult even for a veterinarian to treat them than to care for a larger breed pup who may weigh a pound. Weight is a factor in other ways, too. If a fourteen-ounce puppy begins to lose weight, it can certainly be serious but not immediately life-threatening. Toy puppies, however, don't have much extra weight to lose, and they dehydrate rapidly. A pup who is failing to thrive, or one

Cavalier King Charles Spaniels

Courtesy of Bressler West ©

with fading puppy syndrome who is rapidly losing weight, doesn't have the extra ounces he needs to struggle back. Toys simply don't have the reserves that larger puppies have.

Responsible breeders are extremely vigilant with tiny puppies. Since weight gains are slight in small dogs, the breeder must set up a weighing program to check whether the puppies are growing sufficiently. One veterinary neonate expert recommends weighing Toy pups each day during the first week of life, every other day during the second week of life, three times a week during the third week, and two or three times a week thereafter. Weighing is the most sensitive indicator of how the young puppy is doing.

Although weighing is very important and should never be bypassed, experienced breeders can tell when puppies are failing to thrive just by handling them. Even though two pups may be the same size, when the puppies are in the breeder's hands, the one who isn't doing well will feel much lighter. This is one of many reasons why Toy puppies should be handled while they're in the nest.

They should, in fact, receive a great deal of gentle handling from the day they're born, from a variety of family members, so that they will learn the smell and feel of human hands and realize there are many differences among people. Generally, puppies who have had to be hand-raised and hand-fed are more people-oriented than those raised by their mothers who received little handling.

It's important to note, though, that hand-raised pups can grow more aggressive as they are weaned because mothers inhibit forceful sucking earlier than humans do when hand-raising. Humans inadvertently encourage a lack of self-control, so the dog is more likely to learn an inappropriate behavior of pulling and biting to get what he wants. The point is that puppies need a combination of both the mother's and the breeder's attention.

But if the mother falls ill or dies, the total responsibility for round-the-clock feeding (usually every two hours) and caring for these tiny scraps of life will fall to the breeder.

Problems Nursing

No two litters are alike, so it's always wise to expect the unexpected. Anticipating problems is part and parcel of breeding small dogs. The experience of knowing what's normal, what looks normal, and what feels normal is invaluable. There are general rules but not all puppies will follow them, so the breeder must use common sense.

For example, when the puppy is nursing, the breeder must be able to tell if he is actually getting nourishment or simply going through the motions. Sometimes a puppy is born with one or more physical defects that make it impossible for the pup to thrive. Because Toys are so small, it isn't easy to pry open the mouth of a three- or four-ounce neonate to see if he has a cleft palate. It requires good lighting, and probably an extra pair of hands holding a flashlight, to peer into that tiny mouth and look very carefully, because any defect is very difficult to see.

The really thriving puppy is robust, and is in constant motion. Invariably, when nursing, thriving puppies will go to the rear nipples where there's more room, will be aggressive in their nursing activity, and will grow very rapidly. The pup who is not as robust wastes a lot of time, takes forever to find the nipple, doesn't seem to nurse at a steady rate, and seems to fall behind the other littermates.

If a pup is being pushed aside by his littermates and doesn't have an opportunity to nurse, he will lose weight and lose ground. Often these puppies require supplemental

Cavalier King Charles Spaniels

Courtesy of Bressler West ©

feeding with an eyedropper, bottle, or feeding tube. This, however, can create its own problems, such as aspiration pneumonia from inhaling milk into the lungs.

Care is needed with supplementation because many commercial puppy formulas tend to cause loose stools and don't provide enough calories for a small dog. One of the oldest tricks used by breeders is to supplement the formula with goat's milk because it's well tolerated by puppies with weakened stomachs.

Another old trick used by breeders during the first two or three days is to give a weaker puppy, and sometimes the mother, a few drops of "raw liver juice," the bloody liquid from raw liver. It contains erythrocyte (red blood cell) maturing factors, which the pups are lacking.

Low Blood Sugar

Toy puppies are predisposed to low blood sugar (hypoglycemia) and can go downhill with incredible speed. That's because tiny puppies, especially Toys, don't have a lot of fat stores and their liver isn't geared up to make glucose easily yet, simply because of their age. The classic signs of hypoglycemia are weakness and a drunken-type gait. If it gets progressively worse, the puppies will fall over and have small seizures.

Hypoglycemia is highly treatable; the key is recognizing it. The treatment is fairly easy: If the animal isn't conscious and can't eat, the next best thing is to lift up his lip and put sugar water, Karo syrup, or something similar right on his gums. It will be rapidly absorbed into the bloodstream. Feed the puppy once he's up. A veterinarian would give the puppy dextrose intravenously and then make sure he starts eating.

Hypoglycemia, while always serious, only becomes life-threatening when owners and breeders aren't paying attention to their dogs; the puppy's in trouble, they go off to work, and the pup can be dead by the time they get home. Or the blood sugar drops so low that brain metabolism is impaired, and there is irreparable damage. Is it any wonder that responsible Toy breeders are so vigilant with their pups?

A Healthy Environment

Breeders change their clothes and remove their shoes when they come home so they won't carry any germs to the puppies. Everything gets scrubbed and disinfected because sometimes puppies will pick up a viral infection.

The puppies must also be kept warm, because neonates can't regulate their own body temperature. Pups are kept in a small area so they can't crawl too far from their mother and get chilled. If a Toy puppy gets chilled, he can die, and these little ones shiver more because they're more often cold. To add a little warmth for the first two or three days, many breeders will put a heating pad underneath one corner of the whelping box. (The heating pad, however, must not be allowed to overheat and burn the puppies.) This allows the pups to move to another corner if they get too warm (this can be just as dangerous as getting too cold). Some breeders cover most of the whelping box with a blanket, as well.

A sick or injured pup can be wrapped in a blanket to keep him warm. When he is chilled, protective reflexes such as breathing may stop, since a pup's brain center is not fully developed yet. Consequently, the breeder will have to know how to administer mouth-to-nose resuscitation.

Vaccines

Although puppy shots may seem like a routine procedure, in fact more and more controversy has been stirring up around vaccinations for all animals. Vaccines prevent deadly diseases, but they can also create problems. Occasionally puppies will have an allergic reaction to either their first or second vaccination, and pups have reportedly died after combination vaccinations. Sometimes the pup will get through the first shot just fine, but his face or paws will swell up after the second. This has led some breeders to insist upon giving the parvovirus shot separately from the combination that includes kennel cough, hepatitis, leptospirosis, and distemper.

But there's further concern regarding the combination vaccines. Vaccination schedules for both dogs and cats have been revised after extensive reviews by the American Animal Hospital Association and the American Veterinary Medical Association. These groups have concluded that vaccinations should be geared to the dog, the owner's lifestyle, and the place where they live, which will affect a puppy's exposure to various diseases. Rabies vaccine is required by law in the United States.

There are a lot of factors to weigh when you are trying to assess the risk of giving any vaccine. Whenever you immunize a dog or a cat, the animal, the vaccinating agent, and the environment all play a role in how the animal will respond. A vaccine may fail to immunize an individual animal because maternal antibodies are still present in his body. There are also genetic and health reasons why a vaccine may fail or even be dangerous. For example, the animal may be sick, and a sick dog doesn't respond as well to vaccination as a healthy one.

Then there's the animal's environment. If a dog is in a high-stress environment—for example, in a shelter where the volume of infectious agents is high—he can still become infected even after being vaccinated and immunized. Immunization can be overwhelmed by high concentrations of an organism.

As for the vaccine agent itself, is it a modified live virus or a killed virus vaccine? Is it a bacterin? Newest are the recombinant vaccines. Created from the organism's DNA, these don't require an adjuvant to activate them. All these factors affect the efficacy, and the safety, of any vaccine. There are many other questions, as well, about how virulent the organism is and how the vaccine is prepared. All of these things are basically determined by the manufacturer of the vaccine.

For all these reasons, all vaccines should be decided with your veterinarian on a case-by-case basis, after careful discussion.

Leptospirosis

A major question in the vaccine debate concerns leptospirosis, a highly contagious disease that attacks the kidneys. Leptospirosis is a unique kind of bacterin similar to the spirochete organisms that cause Lyme disease and syphilis.

Because a killed leptospiro organism is used in the vaccine, it needs something to boost its immunizing power. To do this, a protein, usually called an adjuvant, is added to the vaccine. The adjuvant is extremely inflammatory and immunogenic—biochemically it can be toxic when given to a small dog. Very likely it's this adjuvant that's causing the problem with the lepto vaccine in small breeds.

In the United States the lepto vaccine is usually given as part of a combination to protect against distemper, adenovirus (hepatitis), parvovirus, and parainfluenza. In the old combination shot, the lepto vaccine comes in a liquid form and is mixed with freeze-dried forms of the other vaccines. It's a matter of convenience that veterinarians use it and breeders buy it that way; half the dosage is lepto plus diluent, the other half contains all of the freeze-dried material. To give the shot you have to use all the diluent, administering a whopping dose of adjuvant to the small dog. And while the little dog needs as much of the actual organism to protect against the virus as the big dog, all that adjuvant can be dangerous. The smaller the breed, the greater the risk.

If a small dog has a reaction to the leptospirosis vaccine, he will usually collapse within twenty minutes after getting the shot and go into allergic shock, called anaphylaxis. Unfortunately, this is usually when the dog and owner are in the car, headed home in traffic. The dog might recover on his own or he might not—it depends on the individual.

The recommendation of Dr. Richard Ford, a professor of Medicine at North Carolina State University's College of Veterinary Medicine, is to either skip the leptospirosis vaccine or to use saline to dilute it for the small breeds. Although Ford says he would not be concerned about the vaccine if the adjuvant were not present, vaccines using killed organisms don't work very well without adjuvants.

So what is the risk of not using the vaccine? Actually, it's not all that great. Leptospirosis is spread via the urine of infected animals, usually wild animals. Certainly, urban dogs have a lower risk of contracting it.

In addition, there are more than two hundred serotypes of leptospirosis, yet veterinarians vaccinate for only a few of them. Half of the lepto cases in the United States are caused by serotypes for which veterinarians don't even vaccinate, and the duration of immunity probably isn't more than three or four months.

When considering environmental factors and leptospirosis, think about whether the dog is likely to be exposed to stagnant water, rodent urine, or wild animal urine. These are not common exposures for Toy breeds, which is why not many Toy dogs are seen with leptospirosis.

In cases where Ford would choose to give the vaccine, as a general guideline he would not administer it until the dog is older than 4 months. But all the variables discussed previously affect any risk assessment, which is why general veterinary guidelines are not always best for an individual animal. There are some animals who have minimal risk and would do just fine never being vaccinated; there are others who certainly should be vaccinated.

Occasionally, there are concentrated outbreaks of leptospirosis. This might be of some concern to the owner of a show dog or a show prospect puppy. Because lepto is transmitted from the urine of an infected dog through the mouth or broken skin of the susceptible dog, it's highly transmissible. With literally hundreds of thousands of organisms excreted in the urine of an infected dog, there's a very good opportunity for dogs who are infected to transmit it to other dogs, which is why veterinarians will suddenly see many cases where there hadn't been any. Such outbreaks are frequently transient. They are also generally not among show dogs who are well cared for and spend their lives predominantly indoors.

Most of the cases that are dealt with in an isolated outbreak are likely caused by a serotype for which the dogs are not being vaccinated, so there's probably very little value in rushing to immunize a dog, even if a few cases break out in your area.

Dogs are at risk of getting leptospirosis if they're kenneled outside, if they go on regular walks in the woods, or if they have access to stagnant water, rodents, and other dogs' urine that might be infected. For the show dog owner who would like to take added precautions, it might be wise to avoid public exercise pens. Even though the risk is minimal, there's no harm in being cautious.

Other Vaccination Issues

You may be surprised to learn that very little research has been done on how long immunity lasts after any single vaccine. While annual vaccinations were long the default, nobody actually knows if dogs need yearly booster shots. Ford doesn't think it's right to vaccinate dogs for distemper every year because there's too much data that shows they're immune for at least three or four years following a single dose at 16 weeks of age. There is also some evidence that rabies immunizations are good for at least two or three years.

Another vaccination issue is who gives the shots. While the average pet owner is strongly advised to leave this to their veterinarian, experienced breeders can and often do vaccinate their own dogs. However, it must be done correctly or the dog will be in trouble.

Correctly means the right timing between all the puppy shots, plus the right technique in giving the injection, plus handling the serum correctly so that it does not spoil or lose its potency.

Vaccinations are recommended three to four weeks apart during the puppy series. Puppies only need to be vaccinated three times. The new vaccines have all been modified, and the veterinarian can stop giving them when the puppies are about 12 weeks old. Under absolutely no circumstances should a pup be vaccinated closer than two weeks apart, because the risk of an adverse reaction (also known as an adverse event) is significantly higher when you do.

Building the Bond

One veterinarian noticed in his practice that small dogs seem less opportunistic with their owners and more protective of them than other dogs. The Toys also seem to form unique bonds with their owners, while the bigger dogs seem more amenable to living with whoever will take care of them. This may come about as a result of the greater dependency small dogs have on their owners because of their size; while larger dogs might feel more capable and self-reliant, small dogs always need the specific humans they have come to love and trust.

Small dogs go through the same developmental processes as other dogs, but they seem to be a little bit slower in their development, which is why they need so much more attention during the growth period. Breeders have observed, for example, that the motor skills of small dogs develop later than those of larger breed pups. On the other hand, small dogs tend to live longer than the giant breeds and to age slowly and gracefully—as opposed to larger dogs, who have a shorter middle age and tend to go downhill very fast.

There's no question that Toy puppies should go to their new homes at a later age. According to one veterinary expert, the longer you can wait to place a puppy in his new home, the better off the puppy is, as long as he's being handled daily.

Handling Toy puppies right from the start, when they're less than a day old, not only enables them to get used to human touch early on, but also builds the bond of trust between dog and human. This is the start of socialization.

As an adult, the well-socialized female raising litters of puppies will be a better mother and her puppies will readily accept being handled because they learn about that from their mother. It's not critical to handle the neonate pups for very long; very gently picking them up and putting them back down will be adequate in those first days. But it's extremely important to start handling them early and progressively increasing the time as they grow older. Dogs socialized this way are happier. You can see the spark in their eye, they'll prance when they run, they won't be snappy, and they won't try to bite people. They're so used to being handled that it's a normal, natural part of their lives.

A puppy sitting winsomely in a pet store cage, raised in a commercial breeding facility, and shipped to the store right after weaning, is unlikely to ever have experienced this early human contact. Consequently, he is unlikely to relate to humans in the same way as a dog who has had an early introduction to the human-animal bond.

The Start of Housetraining

Small dogs are notoriously difficult to housetrain, which is why I've devoted chapter 4 entirely to this subject. But the process can and should begin with very young pups, so we'll get started here.

Initially, breeders start housetraining their puppies by setting up their sleeping place in two sections: one with disposable bed pads or papers and the other with a soft towel or blanket. (Care must be taken, because puppies can injure or bury themselves in loose towels or blankets. They'll also wrap shredded edges of towels around themselves and choke.) Most puppies will begin to housetrain naturally when they're given a space that's big enough to move away from their sleeping area, because dogs naturally do not want to soil their nest. This is the true beginning of housetraining.

Puppies should not be allowed to sit or sleep in their own waste matter. When puppies are commercially raised in cages or by inexperienced pet owners, and are not given the opportunity to move to another area to avoid soiling their nest, they are likely to be more difficult to housetrain because they haven't had the opportunity to stay clean. Sadly, puppies raised under those conditions only learn to go on the paper, sleep on the paper, and live on the paper. They have no frame of reference for cleanliness.

Many Toy breeders believe the introduction to housetraining should start when the puppies are 3 weeks old. This is when Toy puppies are beginning to get their legs under them and are physically able to move to a separate potty area. It's also when the puppies are developing the instinct to relieve themselves away from the nest. Some breeders say if you don't start this process at the critical age of 3 weeks, housetraining will not be as easy when the puppy is older and the real housetraining process begins.

One thing is certain: When a puppy is ready to be housetrained, you will have to remember that he is a dog like any other. Many Toy dog owners don't seriously housetrain because they're not as upset by the small output from a small dog. They'd be a lot more likely to get down to serious business with the pup if he were a Great Dane leaving large piles and pools of waste around the house. But if you don't take the business of housetraining seriously, you'll always be finding upsetting accidents that can only end up making you angry at your dog—although you'll really have no one to blame but yourself.

More Socialization

All dogs benefit from thorough socialization, but the Toys fairly blossom. To facilitate the process, Toy breeders often move the puppy playpen to either the family room or the kitchen when the pups are 2 or 3 weeks old. This enables the pups to see a maximum number of people. Most of those passing through the room will usually stop and talk to the pups and give them an extra loving pat, which gives the puppies added confidence around people. The sights, sounds, and smells of a more active area of the house will also stimulate these puppies socially and increase their sensory awareness.

It's important to spend as much time as possible with the puppies once they're on their feet. They need a lot of socializing from the twenty-first through the forty-fifth day, which seems to be a crucial time for socializing small dogs. Everything they see and do as puppies will remain with them for the rest of their lives, and it is imperative to make sure their experiences are positive.

Puppies should be raised to expect the unexpected. Virtually everything should seem normal and nothing should be terribly startling. If the household isn't noisy, then a radio or

Yorkshire Terriers

Courtesy of Linda Grimm

television should be playing so the puppy will experience various sounds. If the puppy is raised in a very quiet household and someone makes a loud noise when he's older or when he moves to his new home, the puppy will leap back because he is so startled. Small dogs should learn to calmly experience all phases of typical household life, and their senses should be stimulated as they begin to get up and walk away from the nest.

It's important to introduce them to a lot of different things, including contrasting colors and people of all shapes and sizes, to enable each puppy to develop into an outgoing dog who will see new things as exciting and want to explore them. For example, if the pup doesn't usually see people with beards or glasses, introduce him to someone who looks like that, even if you have to ask someone to wear a false beard or put on a pair of eyeglasses.

If the puppy is afraid of someone with a beard, rather than encouraging the pup to approach that person, go up and talk to the person yourself if you know him, perhaps pat the person and let the puppy see that you're not coming to any harm. Ignore the pup until he thinks this looks interesting and goes over to inspect the individual himself. The pup can be given a small food reward when he approaches the person.

While much of this socialization can be done by a puppy's new owner if the dog is a larger breed, with Toy dogs the responsibility falls to the breeder, because the Toys leave home so much later. The first 12 weeks of a puppy's life are considered a crucial socialization period, and all those weeks should be spent with the breeder.

In fact, research now shows that puppies of all sizes should, ideally, remain with mom and littermates until they're 12 weeks old. But the breeder must do the proper socialization during this time. If they don't, the puppy will never be as socially adept and as good a companion as he could be. Puppies who are not properly socialized can turn into fear biters later on in life. Additionally, the mother has much to teach her puppies when she is around to interact with them for a longer period of time. She will often initiate play and will teach them the intricacies of canine body language—skills they practice with their littermates.

Problems experienced in puppyhood can suddenly rear their heads once more in the adult or geriatric dog. A condition such as geriatric-onset separation anxiety can seemingly come from nowhere, yet just as a human may flash back to childhood, an elderly dog can develop an unwanted behavior from a negative early-age experience. The well-socialized puppy is on his way to becoming a well-socialized, well-adjusted adult.

Chapter 2

Early Puppyhood

By 7 or 8 weeks of age, puppies should be in the kitchen or family room with other dogs and family members. Everyone must keep a careful eye on them to make sure nobody steps on them or that a larger dog does not accidentally injure them. Despite the Toy's self-image as a larger dog, throughout their lives small dogs are especially vulnerable to accidental injury and even death. But a litter of active puppies are especially liable to get underfoot and have not yet learned how to look out for themselves.

Remember that these little dogs have a different vantage point. They are somewhere around ankle height, so a human swooping down on them can be startling if they're not conditioned early to this sort of behavior. The very act of swooping down or leaning over a dog can appear to the dog to be a dominant gesture.

If the puppies have names, it's important to use them and to treat the pups as the little individuals they are. Their personalities will be different, and they should be treated accordingly. One breeder I know likes to make up little songs to sing to her dogs. They probably enjoy it as much as she does.

Early Training

When you bring a dog into your home, you're responsible for giving her care and also for her training. And the younger the dog is when training is started, the better she will be for the rest of her life.

Hopefully, more breeders will develop more challenging environments for their puppies starting at about the age of 3 weeks, when they are beginning to use their senses. Sensory development improves with exposure to challenges, which means providing all sorts of safe stimuli for the puppies. The breeder, and later you, should set up a play area with a variety of things such as barriers and toys, making it more complex as the puppies get older. A safe puppy agility course will expose them to a variety of experiences and prepare them to be adaptable. You can often find used children's slides, playhouses, and similar items at garage or yard sales. These can make fun things for young pups to explore.

Chihuahuas

Courtesy of Susan Payne

Unfortunately, too many people think a Toy dog isn't a real dog. Of course, she's a real dog, she's just in a smaller body! While it's fun to treat Toys as the cuddly lapdogs that they are, it's extremely important to remember that they are also dogs, that they have four on the floor, and they can use them! From the time the puppies are walking away from the nest, these little ones should have lots of new experiences, ways to use up their extra energy, and an opportunity to exercise their minds as well as safely exercise their little bodies.

Exercise is not only good for small dogs; they really do enjoy it. The important thing to note here, however, is that you must do this with a cautious eye to ensure that the dog is safe, especially outdoors. Toy dogs are so small that they can be targets for other animals, especially larger dogs who, particularly in the case of sighthounds (such as Greyhounds), might see them as prey.

Holding your dog will not necessarily keep her out of harm's way when it comes to larger dogs. Many Toys have been snatched from their owner's arms and killed. This is not to say that all large dogs will behave this way, but it's better to err on the side of caution, since you are responsible for your dog's life. Unlike the European countries, in the United States not everyone gives their dog basic obedience training, and some dogs are not under their owner's full control at all times. If we had a better tradition of training, life would be much easier. Nevertheless, the important thing is to maintain a calm demeanor so that your concern isn't telegraphed to your dog. You want to instill confidence.

Small dogs are very people-oriented. Because they're often in your lap the way a cat would be, or up near your face sharing hugs and kisses, they bond and interact in a very special way. There's something quite different about a portable dog who goes everywhere with you and spends so much time close to you being cuddled, held, and carried. But beware of too much cuddling and carrying. That will create exactly the kind of spoiled little wimp or monstrous little terrorist you're trying to avoid!

Introducing Children

Some breeders use their grandchildren to socialize their puppies. These children have usually been raised around dogs and know how to behave gently with them. But generally, small dogs are too fragile for small children. Older children whom you're sure will be gentle should be carefully introduced to puppies, and any interaction must be monitored.

Poodles

Courtesy of Brenda Ferner

Children under the age of 7 don't understand that they can inflict pain. They can also accidentally drop a small dog. Children are usually raised with stuffed animals, and their overzealous handling of small dogs, who look like animated stuffed toys, can cause both physical and psychological damage to the dog. It's best to have small children sit on the floor if they're going to interact with the dog, and you must keep a close eye on both dog and child.

Just because the dog is a Toy doesn't mean she won't bite if provoked. She has teeth and her only means of defense is to clamp down when she is experiencing pain. Children are most often bitten because they inflict pain and the dog has no other way to respond.

Interestingly, it has been observed that if small dogs haven't met children while they're still young puppies, they seem more wary of children than are larger dogs. This is partly because while physical play might be fine with a Golden Retriever puppy, it won't be with a Toy. Children don't realize how loud and scary they can seem and how frightening it can be when they gush and swoop down on a small dog. That can be very frightening for the Toy dog, because in the animal's mind, there's no event that would have elicited the sudden change in the child's behavior. Consequently, these always seem like out-of-context behaviors. Even a large dog would have trouble understanding such circumstances.

To a dog, a small child can sound and act like a wounded animal. But while a wounded animal will signal submission, a child will not. The response of the dog might be somewhat aggressive in these situations. Careful supervision will ensure that everyone is safe and having fun. This issue encompasses responsible parenting as well as responsible dog ownership.

Pride and Groom

Grooming should begin when the mother stops taking care of the pups, which is usually at 5 or 6 weeks old. (Sometimes the mother stops caring for the pups much earlier, and the breeder then becomes responsible for stimulating them to relieve themselves and cleaning them up afterward—yet another reason to leave breeding to people with experience!)

Grooming is another example of how early experiences with the breeder will be reflected in the dog as she grows. If the various aspects of grooming are introduced early and gently and you continue in that vein, there shouldn't be any of the struggles sometimes associated with grooming sessions, especially in the coated breeds such as the Yorkshire Terrier, Shih Tzu, and Maltese, which require more extensive coat care.

It's important to plan a regular grooming schedule rather than doing it whenever you can fit it in. If grooming is done regularly, the pup will know what to expect, and there's far less chance of her coat matting to the point where it's painful to groom.

Get the puppy accustomed to the process to make sure that it's a happy experience. Talk to her while you're grooming, reassuring her that brushing is fun and oh, how good she looks with her coat shining so nicely! This can be the perfect time to relax and bond even more closely as you gently brush and comb the coat.

Get the puppy accustomed to having you check her body for fleas and ticks. The dog may not have fleas and ticks now, but the examination will get her used to the procedure. New flea-control medications given monthly are safe for small dogs 8 weeks of age and older. These monthly flea-control products are also safe for geriatric dogs. It isn't always prudent to spray chemicals directly on a dog, so the monthly preventives have become quite common.

Begin teaching your puppy to accept having her teeth cleaned. Small dogs are notorious for dental problems (more about that in chapter 9), and dirty teeth can cause serious health problems such as heart disease and kidney disease. Using a rough cloth wrapped around your finger, gently wipe your puppy's teeth. You can eventually use a special doggy toothbrush and toothpaste, but never use human toothpaste, because it will foam and frighten the puppy. Every small dog, not just show dogs, should learn to stand on a grooming table. You may prefer to groom your pet dog while she's on your lap, but grooming and blow-drying after a bath are accomplished a lot more easily on a grooming table. The dog should be happy and comfortable there. Another benefit is that if the puppy learns to stand quietly on a table, she will be much more easily examined at the veterinarian's office and won't find the experience so foreign. Both your dog and your veterinarian will benefit from this early training.

The breeder can begin table training when the puppy is about 4 weeks old. Initially, the pup should be cradled in the breeder's arm while on the table to prevent her from jumping or accidentally falling to the floor. A little bit of light brushing can also be done to get her accustomed to the feel.

If you're planning to show the dog, the grooming session is also a good time to teach the puppy to stack (stand properly for examination by the judge). This can be accomplished in a very low-key manner, gently telling the pup to Stand and Stay.

The puppy should never be left alone on the grooming table. All dogs should be carefully monitored so they don't get into trouble. One misstep and your dog can be on the floor with, at the very least, a broken limb. If you use a grooming noose (a loop of leash used to hold the dog standing on the table), the dog can hang herself. Be sure to exercise caution and common sense.

Stroking the puppy's feet once a week without doing any nail trimming will begin to accustom her to having her feet handled, as a prelude to having her nails trimmed. The breeder will begin trimming the tips off the puppy's nails when she's 3 weeks old—even earlier if the bitch is showing any indication of scratch marks. The nails can be trimmed while the puppy is cradled in the breeder's arms. Some breeds are more sensitive about having their feet touched, and waiting until a puppy is several months old before starting to regularly trim the nails will probably only result in a squirming, unruly creature who will detest having her feet touched—making nail trimming something both she and you will dread. Nail clippers should be introduced slowly so the puppy doesn't become fearful of them. Clipping the nails while talking quietly and reassuringly to the puppy should be done in a good light, so you can be sure to avoid the quick, the blood vessel inside the nail. If you do happen to nick the quick, use a styptic pencil or styptic powder to stop the bleeding. Cornstarch also works in a pinch.

Ear cleaning begins when a puppy is about 4 to 5 weeks old. Check your puppy's ears to be sure they're clean. You can wrap a tissue around your finger and put it in the ear just a little way. Never push anything into the puppy's ear. Have your veterinarian show you the proper way to check and clean your little dog's ears.

The proper routine is usually to check teeth, eyes, ears, nails, and anal glands. This is also the routine used when dogs are being prepared for the show ring, but every dog should be checked in this manner. Your dog's breeder or veterinarian can show you how.

The occasional bath (more frequent for show dogs) begins in puppyhood. Put cotton in puppy's ears to keep water out and use a no-tears puppy shampoo. Don't use shampoos for humans; canine shampoos are specially balanced for a dog's pH. A hypoallergenic canine shampoo is best. Gently massage the shampoo into puppy's coat, starting at the head and being careful to avoid the eyes. Use warm but not hot water and make sure you rinse out all traces of shampoo. You'll want to use a cream rinse on long-coated Toys, and it should also be thoroughly rinsed out.

Gently dry the puppy, first absorbing the excess water in a towel. If a blow dryer is necessary, make sure it's on a very low setting and don't concentrate the air on one area for very long. You don't want to burn delicate skin and you do want to be certain this is a positive experience. Lots of love and reassurance will help make it so.

The Name of the Games

Tossing a toy for the puppy to chase will accustom her to physical exercise, provide some mental stimulation, and further develop the human-animal bond. This is also a good time to teach her "drop it," the command to release a toy she is holding. You can teach her "trade you!"—swapping the toy for something of a higher value, perhaps another toy or a tasty food treat. It will not only teach her to retrieve, but she'll also learn to drop things on command; this will come in handy if she picks up something that could be hazardous to her health. It's

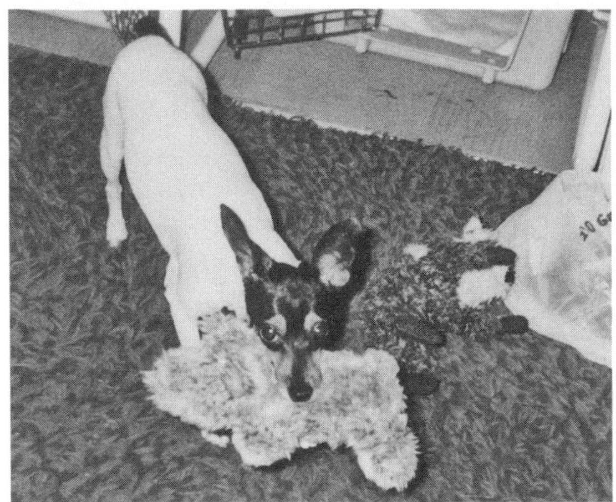

Toy Fox Terrier

Courtesy of Anne Gendron

also a nice time to begin to introduce a few more games that will ease the puppy into doing things that will serve her in good stead throughout her lifetime.

One of the games you can play with your Toy pup while she's sitting on your lap is a variation of one you would play with a child. This is perfect for dogs who hate to have their feet touched, and will eventually make nail trimming much easier. Simply put, it's a canine version of This Little Piggy. Yes, you use all the same words and, with the puppy lying on her back or sitting on your lap, go toe by toe on one of the pup's hind feet. By the time you get to the last toe you'll realize that a dog only has four toes, not five. The solution? Fake it! Pretend there's another toe. Lightly tickle the puppy's tummy while saying, "This little piggy cried wee, wee, wee all the way home!" and end with a kiss or a pat. Then play with the other hind foot.

It's a silly, fun game, but one with a serious purpose. One dog I know enjoyed this game so much that when she was asked if she wanted to play This Little Piggy, she'd either lie on her back and wave her legs or she'd stick a paw in her owner's hand. The obvious lesson was that having her feet held was pleasurable. Nail cutting was just something else that involved having her paw held for a brief period of time.

Another amusing game that will also accustom your dog to having her feet touched is a very gentle version of Pat-a-Cake. Again, the dog is on your lap. Gently holding the front paws, move them slightly but don't pull them together. Playtime should be a happy experience for both puppy and owner.

Many people play tug-of-war with their pups, but did you know that this is the beginning of aggression training? It teaches the dog to pull things away from you, to disregard your commands, to be protective of her possessions around you, and to believe she can get what she wants by being physical. An additional consideration is that these little ones can be injured because they're so easily swung around at the end of a pull-toy, which can also pull a small dog's teeth out of alignment. Find a better game to play with your puppy or dog.

Communication: Beginning the Learning Process

Toy puppies are no different from other dogs. They want to please you, but they need to learn how to do that. You must remember that they don't speak English and don't yet understand enough of it when you speak. Yelling at your puppy will only confuse her.

Imagine going to a foreign country where you are unable to speak the language and people can't understand you. They begin to speak louder in their own language. Now you are becoming more and more confused, as they are speaking even louder in their own language. Finally, they're yelling, and you're upset. You want to understand, they want you to understand, but without a common language it's difficult.

That's pretty much how the puppy feels. It doesn't matter how loudly you speak or how much you yell, you're only going to confuse and upset her. You have to show her what you want her to do and then praise enthusiastically—using a higher tone of voice, which dogs like—when the puppy does the right thing, so she will understand that she's done something right. Understanding begins here. Love and praise speak volumes. And patience is not just a virtue, it's an indispensable training tool.

Training should be based on rewards or the withdrawal of a reward, which can be food or a toy or a loving pat—whatever your particular dog responds to. There's no need for choke chains, prong collars, or cruel training methods of the past, such as punishing the dog for not doing something. Replace negatives with positive reinforcement. Returning to old aversive training methods is akin to going to a doctor or a veterinarian who is still using twenty-five-year-old medical methods. If puppy is chewing on something she shouldn't have, replace it with something the pup can have and, as soon as she begins to play with or chew the allowed replacement, enthusiastically tell the dog how good she is. You can also teach her the "trade you!" game, replacing what you don't want her to have with something of higher value (to her) that is acceptable to you. This, along with teaching her to "leave it!" can come in handy on a walk if she picks up something she shouldn't have.

Ouch!

Every puppy will eventually try to use her teeth to get your attention. Don't allow it. Those needle-sharp little teeth might not feel as painful as those of a larger breed puppy when they're biting your fingers or toes, but this is behavior you definitely don't want to reinforce in any size dog. Make a short noise such as "uh!" and substitute a toy for your body part, then praise the pup when she begins to play with the toy.

Who's Training Whom?

Small dogs are very intelligent little characters. Don't underestimate them. It won't take them long to figure out that they can get you to do their bidding. Many Toy owners have been found fetching for their manipulative little dog. One small dog liked to throw her ball down the stairs. Of course, she wouldn't dream of retrieving it; she'd simply bark until her owner went down the stairs to get the ball. As soon as it was returned, the game would begin again. Needless to say, the owner tired of that version of fetch long before the dog did.

Behind that cute little face is a mind like a steel trap, and once these dogs begin to learn, they will learn how to outsmart you. It's important to establish your leadership early on. Otherwise, your little Toy puppy can grow up to be a very controlling dog.

Early puppyhood is the time to shape house manners. It's not fair to let a puppy get away with something that you would never allow an adult dog to do. How is the dog supposed to know when a behavior is allowed and when it isn't?

As cute as the Toy puppy is—and that's *really* cute—as Fran Lebowitz wrote in *Social Studies,* "No animal should ever jump up on the dining room furniture unless absolutely certain that he can hold his own in the conversation." Although lots of owners are convinced that their dog does add something to the conversation, a small dog could accidentally break a limb in a flying leap, and your dinner guests might frown on seeing your little darling eye to eye across their dinner plates.

Table scraps are never a good idea, anyway. They can lead to health problems, including pancreatitis, and chocolate can be lethal to a dog. But these clever canines will have you wrapped around their little paws in no time, and you'll be sharing your meal if you're not careful.

Treats and Treatments

This is a good time to introduce ice cubes. They're safe, fat-free, calorie-free, and fun for the puppy to lick or chase around the floor. Not only is this a cool, refreshing treat, but if your

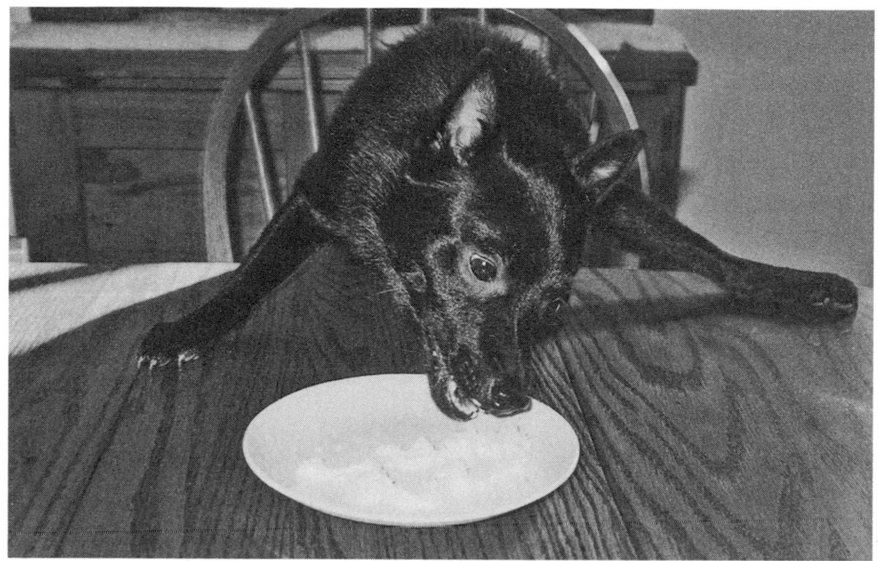

Schipperke

Courtesy of Judith Swan

dog becomes ill and your veterinarian tells you to remove the water dish and replace it with ice to slowly introduce fluids and keep the dog hydrated, the ice cubes won't be a foreign substance. They're something familiar and fun.

If you have two or three metal water dishes, you can keep them in the freezer during the summer. Your dog can lick the ice, and as it melts she'll have ice water to drink. When it's completely melted, refill it with fresh water, pop it into the freezer, and give her one of the other water dishes that's been in the freezer. You can continue to rotate the dishes in this manner. It's another way to help her keep cool.

You may want to occasionally liquefy a small amount of ice cream and put it into a syringe with the needle removed. Using your finger, gently form a pocket on the side of the puppy's mouth and give her the ice cream just the way you would administer liquid medication. This enables the puppy to experience the technique for getting liquid medication as something enjoyable, and will make administering medication much easier if you have to do it later on.

Chapter 3

Homecoming

Because, as a rule, small dogs take longer to develop, a Toy puppy goes to his new home much later than a larger puppy. It's unusual for a responsible breeder to send a puppy off before the age of 3 months, unless it's to an experienced Toy dog owner. Even under those circumstances, a pup would never be sent to his new home before the age of 8 weeks. Although the pup's new owner may be missing some early bonding time, the breeder should be developing the human-animal bond, and that love of humans can be transferred to the new owner.

Because the critical window of opportunity for socialization closes at 12 weeks, it's important to make sure your puppy's breeder has been doing the proper socialization. When a puppy comes to you at 12 weeks, it's easy to transfer the bond but difficult to make up for a lack of socialization. Dogs from rescue groups and shelters bond with their new owners in their "forever homes" at a much later age, but fearful, undersocialized dogs may always have some behavior problems.

There's also a broad weaning age range for small dogs, and each individual pup must be considered. At least some will nurse until they're between 8 and 10 or even 11 weeks old, while others are weaned by the time they're 5½ weeks old. The older age for weaning isn't really about nutrition, it's about behavior. Remember that the longer a puppy can stay with his mom and littermates, the better the start he'll have in life, since he'll learn so much from them about being a dog.

A smooth transition from the breeder's home to yours is the obvious goal. The puppy will be leaving everything that's familiar in his young life: mother, littermates, the humans in the household, as well as the household itself with its very distinctive sights, sounds, and smells. This tiny puppy is being pulled away from everything that has made him secure and taken by strangers to totally unfamiliar territory. No matter how loving you are, you must realize that this can be either a traumatic experience or a wonderful new adventure. It's entirely up to you.

While the transition is difficult for any puppy, it is perhaps more so for the Toys because everyone is a giant from their extra-small vantage point. If you only come up to people's ankles, what does the world look like?

The Matchmaker

Communication between breeder and owner will go a long way toward making sure the transition is a smooth one. It's imperative to educate the new owners as much as possible *in advance*, even before they've seen the pup for the first time.

The education begins the day you start searching for your puppy. The responsible breeder won't allow potential new owners, or any other outsider, for that matter, to touch the pups before they've had their first shots. Puppy buyers will sometimes go from one kennel to another, and germs can be easily spread that way. Don't be surprised if a breeder asks if you've been around any dogs the day you visit. You may have been kissed by a dog whose saliva can carry disease to a fragile pup.

And do be prepared to be thoroughly screened by the breeder, because the person responsible for creating that little life will want to ensure that he's going to a good, responsible, loving home. In turn, you should expect to see at least one house dog and one of the puppy's parents, so you can screen the breeder's dogs for health, temperament, and overall good care.

Good breeding includes breeding for temperament, but the puppy and, ultimately, the adult dog is the result of a combination of nature and nurture. The breeder, who knows the personalities of each of her puppies, should talk to every potential new owner to learn about their lifestyle and expectations in order to make the right match. The wrong personality match of pup and new owner will not produce a happy outcome. One pup might be particularly rambunctious, for example, while another might be an introvert. The person looking for a gentle lap companion shouldn't have the rambunctious puppy, because he will grow into a dog that person will never be able to handle.

This is another reason why breeders spend countless hours observing their puppies. The breeder must also observe you, the buyer, and ask a lot of questions about your life that may seem personal. But the best breeders are also good matchmakers, and their goal is to make a match that lasts for the dog's entire life.

An ethical breeder will always take a puppy or dog back if you can't keep him. The last thing anyone wants is for a dog they bred to end up as another statistic in an animal shelter. This is especially important because the experience is particularly difficult for a small dog. The loud echoing of the kennels, the barking, the sense of loss and being alone is magnified for a small dog who is used to being held and relating closely to humans. The little one will usually be fearful in that atmosphere. A dog who would not normally bite may easily do so out of fear.

Fortunately, small dogs tend to be easy to adopt out, and they don't stay in shelters very long. But it's important to get a small dog into a foster home until a permanent home is found.

And speaking of shelters, if you're adopting your puppy or dog from one, or getting one from breed rescue, remember that making the transition to your home, as well as socialization and housetraining, will be accomplished in the same way. It will just take a little longer with an older dog. You want to build an unbreakable bond with your dog. Love and patience are the keys to living with any dog or puppy. And by adopting, you'll have the added satisfaction of saving a life.

The Best Vet

Before you bring your dog home, be sure you have a veterinarian who knows and likes small dogs. Not every veterinarian is a good Toy dog veterinarian. Your vet must either be familiar with your Toy breed or want to know more about him, and exhibit a genuine interest. Small dogs respond best to a veterinarian who moves slowly and gently during an examination. They are not dog: generic. Many of the Toy breeds have special problems not found in other dogs (more about that in part III). You must find someone in whom you have absolute faith and confidence before you entrust them with this life for which you are now responsible.

The dog's breeder will want to know if you have a veterinarian who is good with small dogs and accustomed to handling them. You may want to use the same veterinarian the breeder is using, if you both live in the same area. You might ask someone with Toys who lives nearby which veterinarian they use, if they're happy with that person, and if their veterinarian seems to understand small dogs.

One of the better ways to find a veterinarian is to contact a major veterinary referral hospital in your area for a recommendation. They have to be cautious about such recommendations, but they can suggest veterinarians who have sent Toys and other small dogs to their hospital who have been thoroughly worked up diagnostically.

You should check out the veterinarian's clinic in advance, taking a tour of the facility. Does the waiting area look and smell clean? Of course there will be some odor, but if it looks and smells dirty, the rest of the facility may be, too. Use your eyes and nose and trust your senses and instincts. Does the clinic have weekend and evening hours? What about emergency services? Payment plans? Is the staff well trained and friendly? Keep in mind that a clinic certified by the American Animal Hospital Association (AAHA) will have been evaluated and found to meet the high standards set by that organization.

Talk with the veterinarian. Finding a veterinarian is like finding a pediatrician for a child, only in this case the patient will never be able to verbally tell the doctor where it hurts. So you want someone who's not only tuned in to a dog's body language but with whom you can communicate easily about everything from treatments to cost. The vet should be more concerned with an animal's well-being than with their self-promotion or ego. They should not be insulted if you ask about getting a second opinion. And someone who runs in and out of the office and isn't paying much attention or doesn't have much patience is not going to be a good candidate to care for your dog.

Preparing the Puppy Layette

Have a puppy layette ready well in advance of the day the puppy comes home. Make sure you have already read one or two books about the breed, because it helps in the adjustment process if you know what to expect before you bring your puppy home. Each breed has its own particular characteristics, and each breed is genetically "programmed" to grow into an adult who behaves and reacts in a certain way. For example, Yorkies and Silkies and several other breeds are Toys, but it doesn't mean that they're not also Terriers. They will still have the same traits as their larger counterparts, and those traits will affect their behavior and training. With a dog of mixed heritage, it may help to try to guess, from the way he looks, what breeds might be in his background. This will help you better understand him.

A good clicker training book or two should also be in your collection, and you should familiarize yourself with clicker training before you bring the puppy or dog home.

Safe Toys

The federal government doesn't have safety standards for pet toys. The pet-product industry has no safety regulations either—they simply assume the manufacturers are making safe products—so it's up to you to choose toys as carefully as you would for a human child.

Play toys should have no loose parts that puppies can chew off. Check for eyes and other small parts that could be easily removed and swallowed. Be especially aware of easily removed squeakers, because small dogs really love to "kill" those kinds of toys, and the squeakers are easily swallowed when the toy is ripped open.

Since your puppy might be teething, or may just be mouthy, you'll want toys that aren't easily destroyed. Also, pups tend to swallow whatever they chew—another reason you want something durable. Really soft toys that can be destroyed can also be swallowed. For this reason, toys should be made from nontoxic materials.

Be sure to buy toys that are specifically made for dogs. Avoid letting your puppy chew on tennis balls. Not only does the fuzz, which puppies can choke on, come off, but the inside of a tennis ball can be lethal; the puppy can also choke on it, and the filling of some older tennis balls can be toxic. Why take a chance?? And be sure to supervise the puppy's play session with any new toy to make sure he's not going to get into trouble with it.

The Crate

The crate is both a training device to help with housetraining (see chapter 4) and a safe haven. Buy a crate that the pup can comfortably stand up and turn around in when he's full grown. A crate should never be used as a form of punishment, nor should any puppy or dog be crated for a long time.

Pekingese

Courtesy of Rose Marchetti

The crate is also an ideal way to teach the dog that he can't be with you constantly, which is a good way to ward off separation anxiety. The key is to make the crate the dog's bed and the best place in the world that he can be, so the puppy only gets his best treats and a favorite toy when he's in the crate.

Introduce the crate slowly, if his breeder hasn't already done so. Be sure there's a soft, fluffy towel in there on top of newspapers until he's reliably housetrained and can have a comfy mat inside. You can feed him near the crate and toss a tiny treat in—just inside the door at first, and then further back as he gets used to going inside.

The door should be open most of the time. But on occasion, when you're in the house and moving around, shut the door, leave him in the crate, and don't let the pup out as soon as he starts to whine. This will teach him that it's normal to sometimes be with you and to sometimes be away from you.

An added bonus is that the crate is an ideal place for your dog when he rides in the car. You certainly don't want to let your dog hang his head out the window, because all sorts of flying debris can get into his eyes and ears, and he could jump or fall out, which could be fatal. You do not want the dog on your lap, where he can be a distraction. And you absolutely don't want the dog loose in the car, because if there's an accident, your dog will become a flying missile. Putting your dog's crate in the car will ensure he has a safe place, rather like having a child in a car seat. Just be sure, if you're using a lightweight crate, that you secure it with a seat belt.

If you're traveling, the best part is that the crate becomes the dog's bed in a hotel or motel room. Wouldn't you like to travel with your own bed? Not only do hoteliers appreciate seeing a crated dog and understand that you're traveling with a well-behaved canine, but for this very reason, they will occasionally make an exception if there's a No Dogs policy in place.

More Supplies

When putting together your puppy layette, have several towels ready for bath time as well as for the puppy to cuddle into in his sleeping area. Add a brush, comb, nail clipper, and tearless shampoo to your shopping list, along with a soft collar or harness and a leash. Consider buying the same type of food and water dishes the breeder has been using so the pup will find them familiar. And don't forget a soft cloth for cleaning puppy's teeth.

Add at least one first-aid kit, as well. If you're going to travel with your puppy or dog, keep one for travel and one in the house. Keep an updated photo of your dog on the travel kit in case he escapes. You'll have that for identification and can print up flyers using the current photo and an extra photocopy of his rabies vaccination certificate. Don't forget an ID tag, but do consider microchipping or tattooing; each has the advantage that they cannot be removed from your dog. Talk to your veterinarian about these options.

Keep in mind that some Toys will suffer in cold weather. Those with very little coat, such as the Italian Greyhound, smooth-coated Chihuahua, Pug, Chinese Crested, and smooth-coated Brussels Griffon, will need to wear a coat or sweater, so add one to your puppy layette or plan to buy a coat or sweater when the weather begins to change. Since small dogs lose body heat more rapidly than their larger cousins, virtually all small dogs will appreciate a nice, warm coat or sweater.

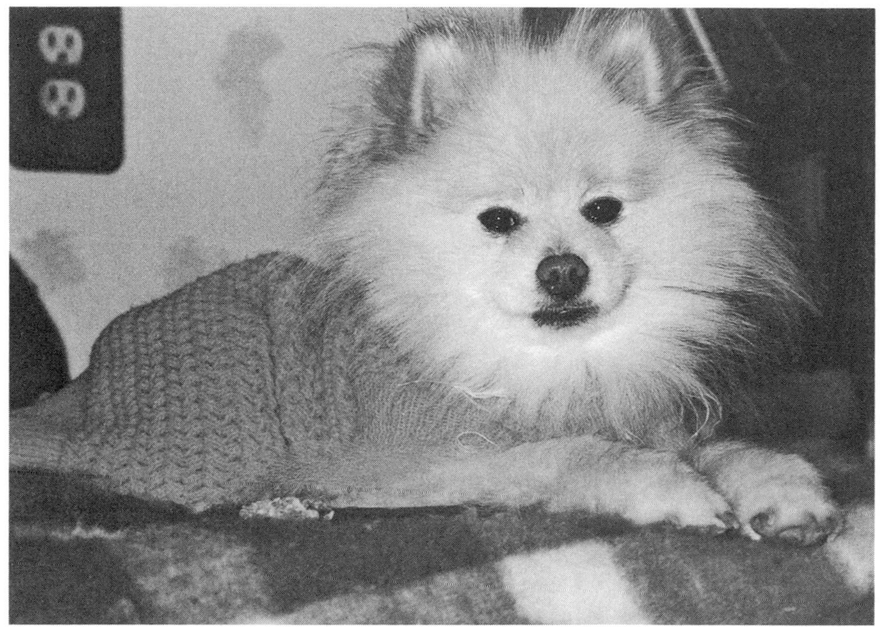

Pomeranian

Courtesy of Tracy Corso

And remember that none of these little dogs should be outside for very long in either cold or hot weather.

Getting Ready for Your Puppy

If the breeder lives nearby, you might schedule several visits so the puppy will become more familiar with you, your voice, and your touch. When it's time to go home with you, it will seem like leaving with a friend rather than a total stranger.

There are certain words the puppy will know, and the breeder should tell you what those words are. For example, some breeders will use a certain sequence of words, voice tones, or noises to call the puppies at feeding time. It will make the transition easier if the pup hears the same familiar words and voice tones so that he can make some easy associations in his new home. In fact, it will be helpful if you can observe the way the breeder uses these terms, as well as the puppy's response.

Several days before you bring your puppy home, take a blanket or towel the puppy will lie on or a soft toy he can cuddle up with to the breeder's house and have the breeder put it in the puppy's sleeping quarters. The object should pick up the scent of the puppy, as well as his mother and littermates, and, perhaps, the breeder. This way, when the puppy arrives in his new home he will have something soft to cuddle up with that smells just like his original home. Very comforting! Some breeders will send the pup home with a fake fur rug or a carpet remnant that he and his littermates have slept on. It can be used in his bedding so the pup has something he's accustomed to smelling and sleeping on.

Some breeders like to send their puppies off with other familiar items to help ease the transition. It might be a brush or the pup's favorite toy. The breeder may also ask to see the crate you've bought to make sure you have one and know how to use it properly.

The breeder should give you a packet of information along with the puppy. This will usually include health records, feeding and grooming instructions, and other information about how to care for the puppy. It often contains housetraining information. It might also include a good-size sample of the food the puppy has been eating and a bottle of the water the puppy has been drinking, even if it's just tap water.

Changes in food and water can upset any dog's digestive system. Unless you live in the same town and the breeder has been using the same kind of water that you drink, changing the water gradually is an excellent idea. As for food, if your dog's breeder has found a complete and balanced diet that their dogs do well on, then by all means use the same food, at least until the puppy has adjusted to his new family and surroundings. Later, you can slowly change to a food that you might prefer. However, if the puppy is doing well on the food there is no need to change.

Coming Home

Bringing puppy home should be a happy occasion, but don't be too boisterous because you don't want to frighten or upset him. You want to create a calm, reassuring presence. Talk to him in the car during the trip. And make sure you give him an opportunity to relieve himself before bringing him indoors, preferably in a special place that you've chosen for elimination. Many females will not eliminate in the first twenty-four hours. This is even more true of rescue dogs who are feeling insecure.

Take him to the room where he'll be spending the first week or more at home and let him explore it. The room should have been puppy-proofed before his arrival. That means no electrical cords should be exposed and there should be nothing he can get into that might cause him harm. Keep your veterinarian's phone number, as well as the emergency poison control number, near your telephone.

Confining him to one room is prudent, both because he's not housetrained and because he can get into entirely too much trouble if he has too much territory to explore all at once. If you can't do that by either closing a door or using a baby gate, then make sure he's never out of your sight. Be sure he knows there's fresh water available and let him sniff around and explore for a bit. (In fact, fresh water is important and should be available at all times.)

This is not the time to get him over-excited. Give him a toy, play with him gently, take him out to relieve himself again, and then make sure he knows where his bed or crate is and allow him to take a nap. He's bound to be tired from the excitement, not to mention the possibility of being a little confused and wondering where his mom, littermates, and breeder are. *You* know that he's home, but he's not sure yet.

Puppy's sleeping place should be set up away from drafts. In fact, it's a good idea to put the crate in your bedroom next to your bed at night so that when he cries you can reassure him that everything's just fine. This doesn't mean you should take him out of his crate and spoil him rotten! It does mean you are simply letting him hear your voice, so he knows that you are close at hand.

A young puppy probably won't be able to go through the night without relieving himself, so you'll have to get up as soon as he cries to let you know that he has to go out. He won't want to soil the place where he sleeps and you want to reinforce that idea, so this is not the time to be lazy about getting out of bed to help the puppy remain clean. You'll reap the benefits later in a housetrained dog. You'll also be helping him along if you remove all food about four hours before bedtime and let him take care of business before you crate him for the night. Be sure to leave fresh water available, though. It can be dangerous for a small dog to be without water for too many hours.

The breeder will want to hear from you within forty-eight hours to know how the puppy is doing, how you're getting along, and to answer any questions you may have. Your puppy may have cried all night the first night at home, so don't call the breeder first thing in the morning when both you and the pup are worn out. But do call later in the day, because this early communication will definitely help the transition. And responsible breeders are usually always available by telephone to answer emergency questions.

The First Check-Up

Within the first week, usually within seventy-two hours (but not the first day!), take the puppy to your veterinarian for a physical exam and to begin to establish a good rapport. The puppy should not be due for another shot when you bring him home; rather he should be in the process of building up immunities. And he should not be due for worming.

That first visit is the perfect time for your veterinarian and the puppy to get acquainted. In fact, you might want to do a "drive-by" get-acquainted stop at the veterinary hospital before that first appointment. It will be more comfortable for your puppy if he's not being poked and prodded during that first visit. You can bring along some tiny treats for the staff to give him during that first visit, to begin to establish a friendship with the staff. You'll also want to set up a schedule for any vaccinations that might still be needed, as well as a time to spay or neuter the pup if he's not a show prospect (although his breeder may have already had all of the pet-quality pups in the litter spayed and neutered before sending them off to their pet homes). This is also the time the veterinarian can show you the proper way to clean the puppy's teeth and ears, and clip his nails.

If it's a multi-vet practice, it's a good idea to let every veterinarian in the practice meet your puppy. This will give them a basic idea of what the puppy is like when he's healthy so they'll have a point of comparison for when he's sick. It's also a good idea to let the puppy become acquainted with the veterinarians and the office staff under friendly, normal circumstances so the veterinary clinic, with its strange sights and smells, won't be a place to be feared. Establishing this relationship when the puppy is well will make things easier if he becomes sick and must go there to be treated. He'll know he's in a familiar place with familiar people, which will give him some measure of comfort.

You'll want to make sure you've brought home a healthy puppy even if you have a health guarantee from the breeder. If the veterinarian finds any disease or defect that could endanger the puppy, call the breeder immediately. Your health guarantee may say that you can return the puppy for a full refund within a certain amount of time. If there's a defect the breeder wasn't aware of, he or she will need to know this so there won't be a repeat breeding of that pup's parents. Your veterinarian will also want to see that the puppy has normal responses and is not aggressive or shy.

Heartworm preventive tablets can be started between 6 and 12 weeks of age. Heartworm preventive tablets may have to be pulverized and mixed into a little bit of canned food to feed to the Toy puppy. The new preventives are so safe that even the geriatric Toys can receive them without trouble.

Easier Vaccinations

While we're on the subject of veterinary visits, routine injections should not traumatize a little dog. One veterinarian who has Toy dogs of her own says small dogs don't mind getting shots if they're held up against someone while they're being vaccinated. She'll often hold a little patient close to her and let a technician vaccinate the dog. When held this way, many Toys don't even feel the needle going in.

Toys can get especially scared sitting on the table while being vaccinated (which is one of the reasons to table train your Toy), because these dogs know exactly how small they are and feel vulnerable in some situations. Veterinarians are often advised not to allow owners to hold the dog while the vaccination is given because of liability insurance, but if the veterinarian knows the owner well, he or she may make an exception. Hold the dog very close to you and hold his head against your body so there's no worry about anyone being bitten. The metal table also feels very cold to a small dog; ask your veterinarian if you can put down a towel that you've brought along for use during the examination.

Settling In

It's important to spend time with your puppy during his first week in his new home to ensure a smooth transition. Exercise is important, but make sure you're also having fun and building a bond of trust. Play games together, rather then sending your puppy off to run around on his own. Puppies love to run after toys and bring them back to be thrown again and again. You can eventually channel this game into having the puppy bring you something you really want, such as your keys or an item you've dropped on the floor. Use the objects around your home to set up a safe, puppy-sized agility course so your pup can exercise his body and his mind. Small dogs can be taught a multitude of tasks, and now is the time to begin to lay the groundwork by establishing communication. The more the puppy understands and focuses on you, the easier it will be to train him later.

Put a leash on the puppy whenever you take him out. This is absolutely necessary for his safety. And be careful of large dogs and small children, because both can do damage when unsupervised. Although many small dogs live happily and safely with large dogs, accidental death can happen even with an adult Toy if the little dog and the big dog are, for example, racing to the front door when they hear the doorbell ring. In their haste, the Toy can be accidentally slammed into the wall or trampled underfoot. These small dogs can also be accidentally injured or killed by children or adults who might drop them, fall on them, or, in the case of people who sleep with their dogs, roll over and smother them.

If you have purchased or adopted a purebred dog, consider joining a breed club. It doesn't matter if you don't show your dog. What does matter is that you love your dog and want to learn more about him. A club is the place to get more information about your breed and how to care for your special dog. Continuing education is very important.

Keep Things Normal

Your pup should be exposed to all of the normal day-to-day noises, such as television sets blaring, radios playing, the telephone ringing, and so on. Toy dogs are still dogs, and while they require some extra care, you don't want to turn your Toy puppy into a totally dependent, quivering little wreck.

Watch out for poorly trained dogs, poorly trained people, and everyday objects that can become hazards to little guys. Be aware of your surroundings, but allow your Toy to be a dog!

The Newest Pet

What if this isn't your first dog but a new addition to the family? There are ways to introduce your new puppy to the rest of the canine household with as little trauma as possible for everyone involved. You want puppy to be accepted as a new family member, not an interloper, or else you're going to be living with a canine version of sibling rivalry.

Don't bring the puppy inside to invade your other dog's turf until they have been introduced on neutral ground. This is best accomplished outside the house as soon as you come home with the newcomer. Make sure the introductions are one-to-one, no matter how many other dogs you already have in your household. Save the more rambunctious dogs for later introductions to ease the newcomer into the process of meeting the family.

Just as you would give lots of attention to your first-born when bringing home a new baby, be sure to lavishly praise your other dogs when in the presence of the puppy. Pat the dog; pat the puppy. Not only will you be giving verbal reinforcement, but you'll be transferring the scent of your older dog to your puppy and vice versa.

After meeting outside, let your older dogs watch the puppy enter the house. Allow the older dogs to feel as if they're inviting the new puppy into their home in this manner. Be careful to ensure that the puppy has freedom of movement but is carefully monitored to prevent a jealous reaction. And do remember to remain perfectly calm throughout this entire process. If you already have dogs at home, you know how sensitive they are to your feelings. You don't want to transfer any of your anxiety to any of the dogs involved, and you certainly don't want to clutch the puppy to you or he will get the idea that there is some danger involved and will be forever fearful of the older, larger dogs.

Make sure you control all the sniffing that's taking place. When the older dogs show a caring, gentle reaction to the puppy, praise them lavishly for their good behavior. Don't let anyone feel left out. You want to create one big, happy canine family.

Whatever you do, remember that the pup must have all four feet on the ground. Older, larger dogs can be quite gentle with a tiny puppy, but the pup does need to learn to get out from underfoot of the larger dogs, who may not be able to see the little one in time to avoid stepping on him. So do let them spend time together, as long as it's under your supervision. If all the dogs are well behaved and responsive, there will be few problems.

Part II

Living in the Real World

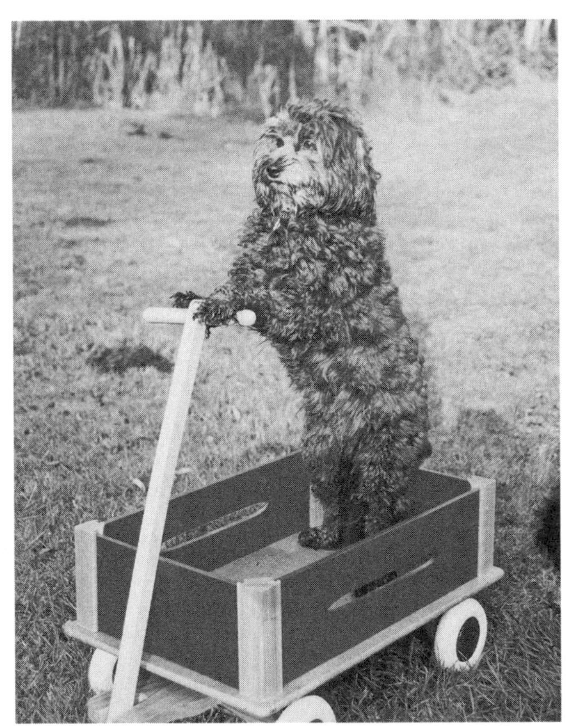

Mixed breed

Courtesy of Cheryl S. Smith

Chapter 4

Housetraining

If you're wondering why there's a whole chapter devoted to this problem, you've probably never had a small dog! Housetraining is thought to be the biggest behavior problem in small dogs both in the United States and the United Kingdom. I suspect it's the same wherever small dogs dwell. Toy dogs have the reputation of being either difficult or impossible to housetrain.

Toys *can* be housetrained. They're not stupid, but housetraining requires an owner who is both patient and consistent—just as it does with a larger dog. The truth is that housetraining any dog requires some effort.

Special Problems

Housetraining is a particular problem with small dogs, for several reasons. First of all, because they're smaller, they can get away with accidents more easily. Many Toy owners simply don't bother with housetraining, because what a little dog leaves behind is small and fairly easy to clean up. The problem, of course, is that if the puppy has an accident in the house and then continues to have more such accidents, she's actually learned that she can eliminate there and that it's acceptable to you. After all, it works and it's comfortable, because she doesn't have to go outside and get cold or get her feet wet. Why would she ever want to change her behavior?

Some owners seem to expect less of their small dogs, as well. A little dog is more like a small child, and people don't expect their Toy to be able to control herself. People tend to anthropomorphize their pets, especially small dogs, expecting childlike behavior from the little dogs and more adult behavior from larger dogs.

For many little dogs, housetraining problems start when they urinate when you are out of the house. Little dogs tend to be carried around, and they often sleep in the bed with their owner. This can create acute anxiety when you are away. Separation anxiety can trigger anxious urination, and you return to find a wet spot on the floor or carpet. Is the dog being bad? Is she breaking housetraining? Well, according to Dr. Peter Neville in Britain, some breeds of dogs, Terriers for example, may be expressing their anxiety by trying to surround themselves with their own smell. The urination may be an effort to make the home environment more comfortable and reassuring, which means this behavior is somewhat like inappropriate urination in cats.

In other words, one of the habits of nervous little dogs is anxious urination. This is one more reason to raise the Toy to be a normal, well-adjusted dog. Creating an overly dependent pet will only lead to separation anxiety and a host of other problems in a dog who clings to you as if attached with Velcro.

Outdoor Perils

It's much easier to housetrain in the spring or summer. Housetraining in the winter takes about twice as long because of the weather. You also must remember that small dogs lose body heat faster in the cold weather, so it's more unpleasant for them to go outside. Nearly all Toys will require a sweater or coat in the winter. This means you'll be faced with the canine equivalent of putting a child into a snowsuit before you can take her outdoors, which will be more frequently while housetraining, of course.

It's important to be sympathetic, especially in cold weather, but the answer is a quick walk in a warm doggy sweater. These little dogs are also going to be more uncomfortable in tall grass because, relatively speaking, it's like asking them to eliminate in a jungle. Keeping walks as comfortable as possible will go a long way toward facilitating housetraining.

Little dogs outside also feel a psychological threat, especially the females, who need to feel they're not going to be pounced upon or disturbed while they squat to eliminate, which is a vulnerable position. If there are big dog odors about, or lots of male dog odors, it can be disconcerting, especially for a shy female. These dogs will definitely benefit from having a special, protected area they can go to that a lot of other dogs don't visit.

Because Toys are so small, many things can scare them. In order to get a pup's-eye view, one behaviorist suggests getting down on your hands and knees with your chin on the pavement to see what the world looks like from the dog's perspective. Watch somebody's foot coming up, or a car door opening (which will look as if it's going to take off your head). Then see what you can do to make things more comfortable outside for your small dog.

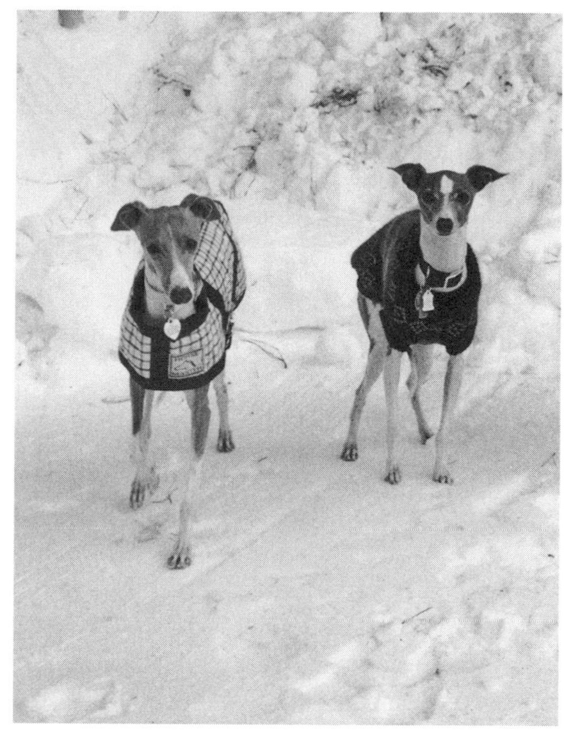

Italian Greyhounds

Courtesy of Patricia Campbell

Questions of Breeding

Some breeds are harder to housetrain than others, and part of the problem may be attributed to breeding. When a dog does a lot of winning in the show ring, that dog will usually be in great demand for breeding. But show dogs are selected mainly for their physical attributes rather than their behavior, and housetraining is not a requirement in the show ring. That doesn't mean a puppy from a long line of dogs who aren't housetrained will never get the hang of it; it just means you'll have to work harder to teach her what to do.

It is also thought that dogs of the Bichon family—which include the Bichon Frise, Maltese, Bolognese, Coton de Tulear, and Havanese—may be nearly impossible to reliably housetrain.

Unfortunately, so far, there have been no studies to prove or disprove this theory. It certainly seems that way from the anecdotal evidence.

How long it will take to housetrain your puppy will depend both on how consistent you are and on the individual puppy. There are a lot of variables, including the fact that some breeds do take a little bit longer. It's not a measure of intelligence, but more likely an indication of behavioral tendencies.

A Head Start

The transition to the new home and the housetraining process will be easier if the puppy has had a head start. If the breeder began the housetraining process at 3 weeks, it should move along rather smoothly. The key is for the breeder to set up the puppies' sleeping quarters in two areas so that they can move away from their bed and over to the elimination area, do what they have to do, and then return to their clean bed.

Once the puppies are up on their legs, the breeder should take them out and walk them or put them in an ex-pen to relieve themselves after they've eaten. The area should be cleaned immediately so the pups aren't spending any time surrounded by their waste matter or playing in or with it.

If the puppies have only received paper training, housetraining will be more difficult. It's hard to ask a new owner to suddenly remove the paper when that's all the puppy has known. Because these dogs are quite small, some people who live in apartments prefer to simply leave it at paper training or train the Toy to eliminate in a litterbox. This solution can be practical, although it should be noted that Toys enjoy and need exercise every bit as much as their larger counterparts. Still, they can get their exercise in a smaller space. If you're a couch potato, or suddenly snowbound, you can simply throw a dog toy down a long hall several times, and your puppy is going to get a workout running after it.

Some breeders today are using wee wee pads as the designated elimination place. This can become a problem when the breeder hasn't introduced another substrate and the puppy mistakes an area rug in her new home for a form of wee wee pad.

Metabolism and Control

The method for housetraining small dogs is the same as it is for larger dogs, but behaviorists do have conflicting ideas. One group says little dogs can, physiologically, wait to eliminate just as long as large dogs, but people tend to give them more leeway because they're babied more than large dogs. Another group says because small dogs have a higher metabolism they really do have to go more often. So if you can get away with taking a 10-week-old German Shepherd puppy out every hour, you might have to take your little one out every half hour. And while metabolic rate increases as a dog gets smaller, bladder size decreases, and that interaction leads to very frequent urination.

Do remember that the older the puppy is when you bring her home, the more control she will begin to have over her bodily functions. But never ask a dog—any dog—to do something she's not physically capable of. And don't forget that females are likely to avoid urinating for a day or two, especially rescues who may be feeling especially insecure.

Here We Go

An ideal time to housetrain is when you have a few days off and can really work on it. If you can't take that much time, work with your scheduling limitations, do the best you can, and be understanding with your dog.

Take the pup out as soon as she wakes up, whether she's been napping or sleeping through the night. Take her out any time she's had any food or water. Merely chewing on a rawhide or toy also counts here, because the chewing stimulates her gastrointestinal tract. What you consider a small amount of food and water is a full-size meal for such a little dog.

If she has been playing with a toy or person, or if she has been massaged at all, take her out immediately afterward or as soon as she slows down. The physical stimulation will also stimulate her need to go.

Teach your puppy to associate a specific word or phrase, such as "empty" or "go potty," with eliminating. Use the designated word or phrase as soon as she squats, even if she only squatted because her feet hit the ground and she has no muscle control. Then praise her like the brilliant pup she is as soon as she eliminates. Eventually, she'll learn that the word or phrase means she should eliminate. Remember to bring along a high-value treat that she only gets at that time. She'll learn to hurry up and do her business—very handy for both of you on cold, rainy nights!

Between 8 and 12 weeks of age, the average-size pup needs to go out just about every hour. A Toy puppy with a higher metabolic rate will need to go more frequently. If the pup is urinating six times an hour (which isn't unusual for an 8- to 10-week-old Toy), you've got to accommodate that schedule because she doesn't have the neuromuscular control yet to go less frequently.

If you don't want to take that many walks, then use a crate for training. In any case, the crate is absolutely the best housetraining tool, provided it's used properly and is not abused. It's a terrific way to set limits and better monitor what your puppy is doing. If you give your pup free run of the house, you'll never know, when you come home, what she has done and where!

Establish a Schedule

Crate training is humane and works well only if you first establish a schedule for your dog. Start the first week she's home by keeping a log of when she actually eliminates. Adjust the schedule as the puppy gets older. If you watch her behavior, you'll begin to see when she needs to go. It's extremely important that the puppy be taken outside when she needs to go, but not when she doesn't need to eliminate, because that can confuse her.

You can help make your puppy's output schedule more regular if you have a regular schedule of intake and of exercise. Feed the puppy at the same times each day, and pick the dish up in fifteen minutes whether the puppy has finished or not (more about feeding in chapter 7). The bonus is that this will help prevent the puppy from becoming a picky eater and will control her weight.

If your puppy is 4 months old and you're feeding her three times a day, she may defecate two or three times a day, depending on the individual puppy. Take notes to get a pattern of when your puppy needs to eliminate, relative to when she ate. Young dogs have an especially strong gastro-colic reflex that stimulates the colon to evacuate soon after the stomach is stimulated by eating, and you may find that she's ready to go half an hour after a meal. If so, you want to be sure to have her outside in her special elimination area at that time.

The same is true with urination. Don't take the puppy out every hour to see what happens. Instead, time the visits, taking her out just in advance of when she needs to urinate so that you're not wasting a lot of time and confusing her about what she's doing out there.

Be There to Praise

Always go out with the puppy so you know what's going on and can reward her for doing the right thing in the right place. The reward should be praise and a delicious food treat so that she understands exactly what you want her to do. It will be best if that treat is one that she gets at no other time, something really special. Emptying the bladder and bowels is a self-rewarding behavior—you're not rewarding that—but you are rewarding her choice of location, so by giving her a treat you're making an association between eliminating in the proper place and having good things happen. You can use a clicker in addition to praise, to mark the behavior of eliminating in the right place. We'll talk more about clicker training later. Even when she's an adult, you should go out with your dog and never leave her alone in the yard, even if your yard is safely fenced. Other animals can get into your fenced yard and injure or kill your little dog. And birds of prey can easily fly down and carry your little one away.

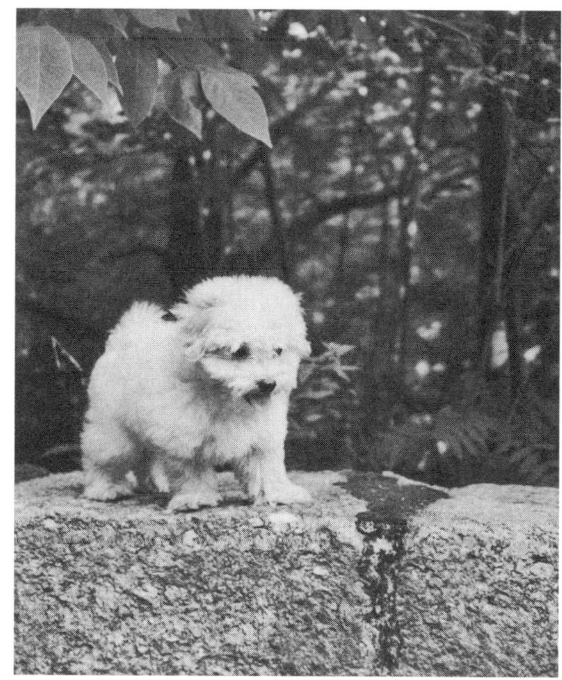

Havanese

Courtesy of Susan Bulanda

If she likes being outside, don't rush her inside immediately after she eliminates. That will only encourage her to wait and wait before she goes. Allow her some time to play, so that going out is a fun experience.

If she's afraid to go out, see what you can do to help her enjoy it. Teaching her to romp in an open space where she can eliminate and there are no threats will make all the difference.

No Punishment

Do not punish the puppy for any mistakes! Research has shown that dogs remember what they've done for about five seconds (no exaggeration!). After that, a correction does absolutely no good. Instead, your puppy will become frightened of you, especially when you walk into the house, say, "Oh, no!" and then call her over. That becomes her cue to run under the couch, not because she has any idea that she's eliminated inappropriately, but simply because she knows you're angry. This is a prime example of yelling at your puppy in a foreign language—a useless exercise for you, and a confusing and upsetting one for your puppy. It's up to you to teach her what you want by showing her, and then praising her lavishly when she does it.

If you do catch her eliminating in the wrong place, say, "Uh!" and move her immediately to the right place. Praise her enthusiastically when she goes there to help her make the right association. And remember to use an odor neutralizer on the spot where she made the mistake, so she won't return to it.

It's far better if you're watchful and consistent and don't give her the opportunity to make a mistake. The housetraining experience should be completely positive for the pup. If she has already eliminated in the wrong place, don't say anything. Just remove it and clean the spot with an odor neutralizer.

A Clean Crate

When the puppy isn't being supervised, she should be in her crate. The crate should be comfortable and as large as possible, but not so large that she has enough room to walk away from her bedding, eliminate in another part of the crate, and return to a clean bed. The general rule is to buy a crate the puppy will be able to stand up and turn around in when she's fully grown. Toys usually need the smallest, or next to smallest, size.

Dogs naturally do not want to soil their sleeping areas, so simply being crated will discourage accidents. However, do not use the crate as a substitute for following the elimination schedule you've worked out. That would be unfair. And if your pup does soil her crate, clean it immediately and thoroughly. Any lingering odor will encourage her to eliminate there again, and it's cruel to leave any animal sitting in her own waste. It's also important to remember that a crate should be the best place a puppy can be, a safe haven. It is not a punishment, so don't overuse it.

Paper Training

If you're gone a long time, you can't expect a very young puppy to hold both her urine and feces for eight to ten hours. There's nothing wrong with paper training if you prefer to do that, or if that's the only practical choice. Get a large wire crate or an exercise pen big enough for a large dog, so the puppy has a comfortable sleeping place far from the papers. Put a cardboard or plywood temporary partition in the crate or pen, or an appropriate size cardboard box can be used to block off the area where the puppy is eliminating. Begin by putting paper in a large area of the pen and then gradually making the paper area smaller. The paper can eventually be moved farther and farther away to the spot you prefer.

An excellent choice is to set up a separate room for the puppy, blocked off by a baby gate so she doesn't feel totally isolated. Set up the crate in one part of the room, making it the most inviting sleeping place with fluffy towels (you can put papers under that in case puppy has an accident), and one or two safe, cuddly toys. Leave the crate door open so puppy can come and go. Set up a separate potty area in the room using either papers or a litterbox. Add a few interesting and safe toys, and be sure to leave either the radio or television on while you're away so your puppy can hear soothing music and the sound of human voices. If you're at work all day, try to get home at lunchtime to spend a little time with your new family member.

Litterbox Training

Litterbox training is a viable alternative for apartment dwellers or people who do not have the physical ability to regularly walk their dog. There are now litterboxes available that are made specifically for dogs. And there is special doggy litter (made from paper). You can also line the box with newspapers or put down wee wee pads and train the way you would housetrain outdoors. Simply take the pup to the litterbox instead of outside.

Of course, this is more practical for females, who will always squat to eliminate. If you're training a male to use the litterbox, have something in there against which he can raise his leg. Keep the box away from any surface you don't want accidentally sprayed. And remember that litterbox training doesn't eliminate the need for outdoor socialization.

Chapter 5

Basic House Manners

Now that the newcomer is settling in, it's time to teach him house manners to ensure that your cute little puppy will grow into a dog you can live with—one who's fun to be around. Living with your Toy will be much easier if you remember during the first year to treat him, at least in some ways, as if he was a larger dog, because he *is* a dog and must be allowed to develop as one.

Spoiling your cute little dog now will result in just the monstrous, yappy, snappish, aggressive little terror or the timid, shaking little wimp you're trying to avoid. Neither extreme will make for a pleasant dog-owning experience. This isn't to say that you can't or shouldn't love your Toy. Far from it. Just use some common sense. And be sure that all family members are participating and that everyone is consistent in their training.

Teething

Toy puppies may be tiny, and they may not be able to chew their way through sheet rock, but they can gnaw at irreplaceable furniture and moldings with the best of them. Be sure to puppy-proof your home so the curious—and mischievous—newcomer won't get into serious trouble. Be sure wires are taped to walls, because your puppy could electrocute himself chewing through electrical cords. Don't keep poisonous plants and don't let any plant hang down to a level where your puppy could reach it. Patrol the floor and pick up any dropped pens, pencils, rubber bands, paper clips, string, and children's small toys that could be easily swallowed.

When puppies teethe, they may be mouthy—going through an oral stage during which they chew on everything in sight. Whether the chewing comes from trying to cut adult teeth or is just a doggy behavior isn't really known—perhaps it's a little of each. Teething may not be as painful for a dog as it is for human children. It's hard to tell, because dogs are so stoic that they don't show much pain. Veterinary dentists have seen dogs with broken teeth with the nerves exposed, yet you would never know it from the dog's demeanor. So something as mild as cutting a tooth may not have that much effect on the dog's behavior. And yet, breeders whose dogs' ears are supposed to stand up will report that the ears flop over during the teething stage, and they attribute this to mouth pain.

When children are teething, they want something in their mouth. That may be because the teething process also itches and causes irritation. Chewing is also probably a natural way to help the tooth erupt by stimulating the area under the gum line.

Babies cry when they're teething, but generally if they're given something to chew on they'll stop crying, especially if it's something cold. That's why manufacturers have developed teething toys that can be put in the freezer. Although these toys are not appropriate for puppies, there is an oral cleansing gel you can get from your veterinarian that's usually applied topically to control bacteria and serve as a healing agent. One veterinary dental consultant suggests using a highly concentrated amount of unflavored gelatin and incorporating some of the oral cleansing gel, then freezing the mixture. Don't let it get as hard as ice, because puppy could break his teeth on it. But a cold, firm gelatin will provide something soothing to chew on that will also treat the gingivitis that develops around all the teeth when they begin to erupt. (This gingivitis is also one cause of "puppy breath," because the capillaries under the gums rupture as the teeth erupt, leaving some blood in the mouth.)

Since the puppy will be chewing, make sure things you value, such as shoes, books, and clothing, aren't in harm's way. Don't give the pup an old shoe to chew on thinking he'll destroy that one and leave your expensive Italian loafers alone. Puppies aren't that discriminating. A shoe is a shoe, and it matters not how much you paid for it when puppy is after some chewing satisfaction.

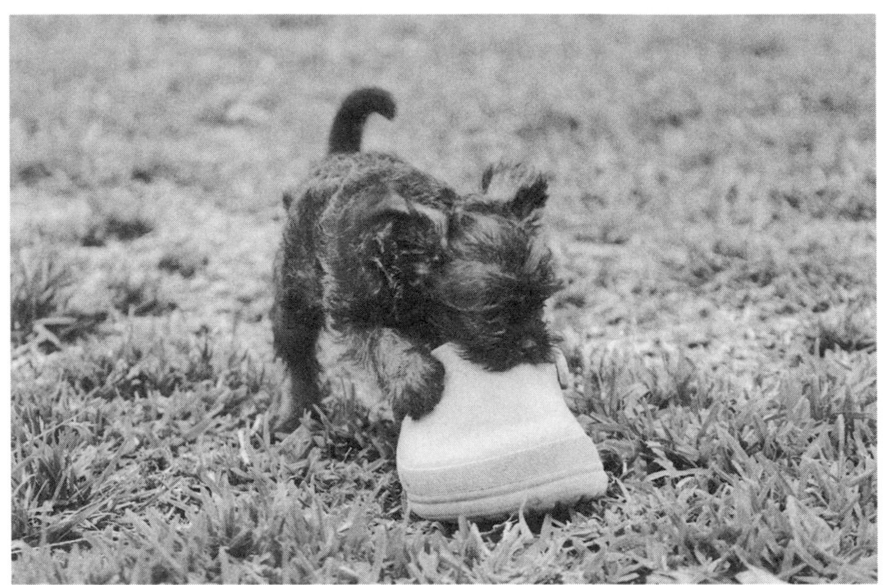

Affenpinscher

Photo by © Sean Downey, courtesy of Mary Downey

Crate the pup when you're out of the house or confine him in a safe area because, for most puppies, furniture is a prime target for chewing. Your subsequent frustration and possible anger at finding your furniture destroyed does neither one of you any good. If you catch your pup chewing something inappropriate, say "uh!" quickly and then immediately hand him an appropriate toy and praise him when he chews it. He'll get the idea. And, as with housetraining, it does no good to correct after the fact. Never yell at your puppy or dog.

If he tries to chew your finger, yelp like a puppy and give him an appropriate chew toy. Praise him lavishly when he begins to chew it.

You may opt to use one of the bitter-tasting liquids available commercially on your furniture so your puppy won't chew it. (These liquids are also handy to put on a bandage after a veterinary procedure to keep dogs from chewing the bandage.)

Appropriate Chew Toys

When his permanent teeth are beginning to erupt, provide your puppy with an appropriate chew toy, something that's soft and that's not going to be swallowed and cause intestinal blockages. Some people choose an assortment of toys of all textures. Sometimes your pup will want to chew something hard; other times he'll want something soft. He should have the option of choosing something that will satisfy those needs. In fact, dogs need to chew throughout their lives. The action helps keep their gums healthy and their teeth clean. They also derive some pleasure from chewing that we can only guess at.

Pomeranian

Courtesy of Tracy Corso

There's a wide range of chew toys on the market. Your first consideration in selecting a toy is to make sure it is the right size for your little one. Then, look at the materials.

There are hard rubber toys you can put something inside, perhaps flavored canine toothpaste or a little treat, and let the pup lick it out. This serves to keep him quiet, gives him something to do during the initial phases of separation anxiety, and is something to play with. If your house is carpeted or you can't close the puppy off in one room, crate him while he's playing with this toy so he won't make a mess. The crate will give the pup a feeling of comfort and security, as long as it's not overused.

Another toy, which comes in various sizes, has three knobs on it so there's no stick in the middle that puppies never get to, as there is with a bone-shaped toy. The knobs have little projections on them that scrub the teeth without breaking them and give the pup some chewing exercise.

Do choose carefully, because some of the products on the market are too hard, especially for little dogs. Veterinary dentists see broken teeth and sliced gums in dogs who chew on processed cow hooves, which are sawed, have sharp edges, and cause real problems. Processed pigs' ears usually soften up pretty quickly, but they make a mess on your carpet. You probably won't see a tooth broken from a sow's ear, but teeth do break on processed animal bones and a lot of the very hard chew items that are on the market.

According to a dental consultant, letting your pup play with toys that look like stringy dental floss is akin to letting him chew on a rag, which means these toys will be loaded with bacteria when they get dirty. But if the toy is clean, there's no real problem using it for a game of fetch because it is soft. And these toys will occasionally catch a loose tooth and pull it out, which is good. Be aware, however, that if the dog chews off some of the string and swallows it, the string can form a ball in the gut and your puppy may need surgery to remove it. If you choose a toy like this, consider it an interactive toy; in other words, watch the dog while he's playing with it and put it away when he isn't or when you can't supervise him.

If you have been using any good-quality beef chew with your dogs—a flat strip or high-quality rawhide chew, not a twisted chew or a novelty toy—and you're happy with it, stick with it. These flat chews have been proven to clean the teeth in the upper cheek and a little bit of the canines. They primarily provide very good chewing exercise on the back teeth and help remove some of the calculus. The heaviest calculus is deposited over the upper-cheek teeth area, and that's where dogs will chew the most, although you will see puppies and dogs take the strips between their front paws and work the incisor teeth, too.

In the Toy breeds the incisors are extremely brittle, especially in the brachycephalic breeds (those with flattened faces, such as Pugs and Pekingese). That's why these chews, too, should only be given under supervision. Another reason for caution is that owners have seen their dogs swallow a half-chewed rawhide that then got stuck crosswise in the throat. If your dog starts gagging when chewing on a rawhide chew, quickly look down his throat; you may have to reach down with two fingers to retrieve it.

One option for small dog owners who use rawhide strips is to buy the large strips that can't be swallowed whole. However, as the strips soften, dogs can bite off and swallow large pieces. It's best for these toys to be used only under supervision.

Attitude

Many Toy dogs don't know who's in charge; or, they simply know *they're* in charge. This is especially true of dogs who never receive any training. Whether or not this is a problem depends on you. Some people are not bothered that their dog runs the household. They call it spoiling their dog, but a better description would be "failing to set limits." And without limits, life for a little dog can become problematic or even dangerous.

Dogs have wonderful abilities, senses, and ways of communicating, but they must learn the limits of living in human society without pretending that they're little people who can do as they please. Dogs, like children, feel more secure and better understand how they fit into the world around them when limits are set on their behavior. The dog shouldn't bark excessively when people come to the door, run all around the house, jump up, or nip at people, and you shouldn't simply dismiss this with an offhand excuse that the dog doesn't like strangers. That's completely unacceptable.

Aggressiveness toward strangers is fairly common in Toys. Because small dogs are less dangerous, people will often put up with behavior they wouldn't dream of accepting in a larger dog. But all dogs are much more enjoyable companions when they are well mannered. A Toy dog with good manners is an ideal companion and can go everywhere. With good manners, your dog will be welcomed everywhere.

Introducing Obedience Lessons

Obedience is the ideal way to teach every dog manners and prevent or repair problems. We'll talk more about training in the next chapter, but do remember that obedience commands are introduced sooner than you might think. Like virtually everything else, it begins with the breeder and must be continued by the new owner—you. When a pup is headed for trouble, the first thing he should hear is "uh!" to interrupt what he has been doing. He must learn to stop whatever naughty thing he's in the middle of. And the interrupter should gain his attention. Always remember to praise him when he does the right thing.

Your puppy will need to learn four or five obedience exercises for his safety. Learning Wait will keep him from jumping out of the car or off the grooming table. Sit, Stay, and Come are the other important commands. Leave It and Out are also handy for curious—and mouthy—puppies. He should begin to become familiar with these words when he's 4 or 5 weeks old. He won't understand them right away, but eventually he'll begin to recognize the words and make the proper associations. This lays the groundwork for what is to come.

If you've never trained a dog before, it's wise to buy a good training book. The bookstores are full of them, so choose carefully. Look for the gentlest training method you can find—one that does not advocate force. It also helps if the author has owned small dogs. The book should preferably be a good one on clicker training, such as *Clicker Training for Dogs* by Karen Pryor or *Quick Clicks* by Mandy Book and Cheryl S. Smith.

Even better is a training class, where your dog will have the opportunity to socialize with other dogs. Definitely ask the instructor if he or she has worked with Toys in the past. See if they can set up special classes just for small dogs, so your tiny puppy does not have to take classes with very large dogs who are also untrained.

The puppy should also be taught to lie on his side at a young age. This is especially valuable for Toys with lots of coat, who will need to lie still for grooming.

Teach him to associate a word or phrase with being picked up so he won't be startled if you come up behind him, or even in front of him, and want to hold him. I've used this method for years, and the dog learns to happily anticipate being picked up. My little Yorkie would stop on a dime if he heard his special phrase for being picked up.

Leash Training

One problem with small dogs is that many people pick them up all the time and won't put a leash on them until they're 6 or 8 months old; that's how they end up with a flailing, screaming creature on his back having the canine version of a temper tantrum. The puppy should begin to be accustomed to a leash as soon as he can walk, starting with a harness, which is ideal for a small dog, or a flat, wide collar for comfort, a Martingale for little Italian Greyhounds whose needle nose will allow them to easily slip a regular collar, or a light nylon show lead (show leads are leash and slip collar all in one).

While the breeder is carefully watching the puppies to ensure that no harm comes to them, each pup can wear a show lead while playing on the floor with his littermates. They'll tug on each other's leads during the play session. The breeder should make a game of walking the dog on a leash while playing with each puppy when they're 6 or 7 weeks old, so they'll get used to the pulling sensation. Leashes of any kind should never be left on unsupervised dogs. The risk of injury is simply too great. When a dog is walking properly on a leash, the leash is loose so there is no pulling sensation.

The reason a harness is preferred is because nearly all Toy dogs have, or are predisposed to, a collapsing trachea. Putting pressure on that area can trigger an episode or trigger the condition itself in a predisposed dog. It can start the dog on a slippery slope. Never put a choke or prong collar on a small dog. It is not needed even for training a large dog, now that there are kinder, gentler methods, so why would you ever want to do anything so aversive and potentially physically damaging to a small dog? Nor is there any need for any sort of electronic collar or device.

Some Toys, Pekingese for example, are very stubborn, and if they decide they don't want to walk on a leash, it doesn't matter what you want—they'll simply dig in and refuse to budge. That's why it's imperative to make walking on a leash an enjoyable experience for the puppy. It doesn't matter if the pup is destined to be a show dog or a couch potato, every dog has to walk somewhere. Your dog should learn very early on to walk on a loose leash.

Click It!

Operant conditioning is the scientific basis for a type of training known as clicker training. Operant conditioning means that the one being trained (in this case, the dog) is "operating" the training process—making things happen. In other words, the dog thinks he is in control of the training. Of course you are, but you each get what you want, and the clicker breaks through the language barrier.

The clicker itself is a small object that makes a clicking sound when pressed. The purpose of the clicker is to associate a specific sound with the correct response from the dog. A clicker is far more consistent and distinctive in tone than your voice saying "good!" Some people will use their tongue to make a clicking sound. This may be okay but humans being human, the tone might vary.

The concept of clicker training is an interesting one. The dog is working out the puzzle of how to make you click the little noisemaker that signals his correct actions and lets him know that a treat of some sort is on the way. He thinks he's training you, but the truth is that you are doing the training and, in the end, both you and your dog are pleased. Better yet, it's easy to do, and the results can be quite satisfying.

If your little dog is sound sensitive, you can wrap tape around the clicker or put it in your pocket when you click to muffle the sound. You can also use any number of things in place of a real clicker, including a barrette, a retractable pen, or the top of a jar of baby food. With sound-sensitive dogs in mind, there are now clickers on the market that make a softer sound or a chirp. There are also finger clickers that look like a little frog. There are some that are on a coil that enable you to wear them like a bracelet, so the clicker is always handy. You'll be able to find one that suits you and your little dog.

Some dogs work for toys or pats, but most like treats. The treats can be either pieces of the dog's regular kibble or some safe food item cut in teeny pieces. Have the treats ready before you start. You can cut chicken, beef, or cheese into very tiny pieces. The idea here is to offer a treat as a reward for a correct action, not to overfeed the dog. And remember to count the treats in with your dog's ration of food for the day. You don't want your dog or puppy to become overweight.

Training can start at any time in the dog's life, so don't be afraid to do this with your older dog—who will enjoy the training process every bit as much as a younger dog. Clicker training is also a great way to help condition your dog or puppy to having his nails trimmed. It's a necessary event, but some dogs view someone cutting their nails as the human being dominant, so you want to make the experience as pleasant and non-threatening as possible.

Clicker training sessions should be short—just a few minutes at most, a couple of times a day. I always begin clicker training sessions with the words, "Do you want to play the game?" This sort of training is fun, not a chore, and you want to convey that to your dog. You will likely want to get down on the floor with your little one in the beginning, if that's possible. If not, then you're going to be doing a lot of bending at first. Alternately, you can put the puppy on a wide bench or table for training, but be very careful not to let the puppy fall. Keep the treats out of the pup's way so you can reach them but he can't.

The first behavior you teach your dog will be the behavior he will always rely upon when he's not sure what's expected of him. This is known as the default behavior. If you have a show prospect, and you want him to stand in the show ring, the first thing you will want to teach is Stand. If you have a dog who is your companion but will not be in the conformation ring, then you have choices. You can teach your dog Sit or Down, so he will either sit by your side or lie down when he is not sure what else to do. Or you can teach him to "settle," that is, to go to his designated mat on the floor. Traditionally, Down has been difficult to teach, but clicker training seems to make it pretty simple.

Getting Started

The first thing you need to do is teach your dog that the clicker means a treat is coming. If you do your training sessions right before a meal, he'll be hungry and interested. Start by clicking your clicker and immediately giving your dog a treat. Do this six or seven times, and he will associate the click with the treat. This is called loading or charging the clicker. You don't have to say anything. In fact, it's probably best if you don't. Your dog will get it.

Now you're ready to teach the default behavior. Sit is very easy. All puppies and dogs sit down on their own. Wait for your dog to sit, and as soon as his little rear end hits the floor, click and treat. Then you can say an enthusiastic "good!" When he has done this six or seven times you can begin to say "sit" as the dog sits, so he will learn to associate the word with the action.

You will probably notice that he is beginning to sit a little straighter or closer to you. He will, in a sense, be saying "Hey, you liked that behavior so how about this one?!" End your session by asking him to do something he knows how to do, and then give him several small treats at once, which is called a jackpot. Let him see you putting everything away, so he knows the game is over for now. Don't flood him—make sessions short and fun.

If you are trying to teach a behavior your dog just doesn't do on his own, you can use a treat to lure him into position. For Sit, you hold the treat up close to his nose and then bring it slowly back between his ears. As his head comes up his rear end naturally goes down into a Sit. Click and give him the treat. You can do this when you first clicker train the Sit, but quickly phase out the lure as soon as you see the dog is getting the idea.

You can begin to train your puppy to come to you by using the clicker. Always call your dog to you for good things. Never call him to yell at him or to bring him inside or to end a game, or he will soon stop responding to your calls. To train him to come, gather your family members or some friends in one room. Give each a clicker and some treats. Take turns calling the puppy by his name, followed by "come!" He'll soon be coming happily. Keep this session short, too. You can always repeat it in a few hours.

A couple of short training sessions each day should have you well on the road to a well-behaved, happy canine companion.

You can use clicker training to teach your dog all the behaviors he will need for everyday living, as well as fun tricks. The experience should be enjoyable for both of you. This sort of training will also strengthen your bond. Be sure to do your training in different rooms so he doesn't think these things are expected only in one place. And keep family members involved in the training.

Saving Your Back

It can be hard on your back to keep leaning over to give your little dog a treat or show him what you want him to do. A target stick can be extremely helpful, although it may be awkward to first to handle both the stick and the clicker. You teach your dog to touch his nose to the end of the stick, click and treat. He will soon learn to follow the stick. Unfortunately, there are no extra-long target sticks available for training small dogs. You can use a dowel cut to size. You can also get a Click Stick from Legacy Canine (www.legacycanine.com). The folding target stick has a clicker attached to it, making it easy for even the least coordinated person to use both target stick and clicker.

When you're giving your dog a treat, if you want to avoid bending, you can use a dowel, attach something like a spoon to the end of it, and put a treat that can be licked off on the spoon.

The Dog's Point of View

Many trainers insist that you ask for eye contact from your dog when you begin training. Clearly, these people have not carefully considered the vantage point of the small dog. If the dog has to keep looking up at you, it's going to be painful for him. To understand this, sit at the feet of someone who is standing and then look up. If the dog is in Heel position right next to you, it becomes even more painful. A better option is to teach your dog to take his cue from somewhere in the vicinity of your calf.

Another consideration while training is to avoid the wrap-around heeling that is so popular in some countries, in which the dog is wrapped around your leg and looking up at you. How can your dog possibly see where he's going if he's wrapped around your leg?

An Introduction to Aggression

A dog's temperament should always be matched to his owner's. If the dog has a strong will and is assertive, he shouldn't be matched with an owner who is either unwilling or unable to be the dog's guide through life, because soon the canine will be running the house.

Because Toys are small, they're often given access to places where big dogs aren't permitted, so they tend to be allowed onto furniture and beds, and they're often carried. With some of these little dogs, this freedom of access can lead to various forms of aggression, such as dominance aggression where the dog will guard a chair and not allow you to sit there.

As with all dogs, aggression can also be caused by a number of other problems. These range from maternal aggression, which may be appropriate because a bitch is protecting her young, to dominance aggression and territorial aggression.

It is a mistake to ignore aggression in a small dog. First of all, a little dog can still bite. But beyond that, an aggressive dog cannot be trusted and is not a good companion. Aggression is a problem, and both you and the dog will feel better when it is dealt with. A dog who is displaying truly aggressive tendencies should not be bred. It is important to breed for temperament as well as conformation.

You Always Hurt the One You Love

Dominance aggression is typically directed toward the owner or other persons in the household. It may be directed only at certain individuals, and it's common for one or two people to be particular targets. In general, this type of aggression occurs in specific situations, although not consistently—the dog may be very sweet most of the time, but every once in a while when someone tries to move him from his favorite resting place, approach him while he's eating, pet him in certain areas, or groom him, he suddenly becomes a mouthful of teeth with a dog attached.

In fact, dominance aggression associated with grooming is fairly common in long-coated breeds that require long and frequent grooming sessions. A little battle over whether the dog should be groomed often ensues. It can become a really serious problem, and changing the behavior may have to start with giving the dog a very short haircut. The hair will grow back, and you won't have the immediate struggle.

Work on getting his behavior under control as the coat grows in. While the coat is short, begin with very light, short grooming sessions and reward the dog for good behavior. Talk to the dog throughout the session and have a little playtime afterward.

Remember, too, that grooming a long-coated dog is a lot of work, and you have to keep up with it regularly so that it's not such a terrible experience for the dog. Since detangling can hurt, obviously it's better if you don't let the coat reach that stage. Even if your dog sees a professional groomer, he still needs daily brushing and combing to keep his coat healthy and tangle-free.

The typical dominant-aggressive dog is young and male. The behavior surfaces as the dog approaches social maturity, which is between 1 and 2 years of age, whether he's neutered or not, as he is putting aside puppy-type behaviors and adopting adult behavior patterns. And it tends to escalate over time, partly because the owner tends to reinforce the behavior: The owner steps back when the dog growls, and the dog learns that growling gets him what he wants.

Both nature and nurture are at work here. There is almost certainly a genetic component to behavior in dogs. We know this because certain breeds, and certain lines within a breed, have a greater tendency to be aggressive. However, while you cannot overcome nature, how you nurture will make a huge difference. Setting limits is very helpful.

Interestingly, there's no evidence that the most common interactions with owners—letting the dog sit in your lap or sleep on your bed, giving special treats, or carrying the dog—cause dominance aggression. In fact, one study showed these things *don't* cause it.

However, if you begin to see a dominance aggression problem, you'll need to change the way you interact with your dog. For example, if your dog snaps at you as you try to move him off your bed, he's no longer allowed to sleep on your bed. It's important for your dog to understand that you are the one in charge of the household, not he, and changing your behavior will teach him that he only gets to enjoy the rewards and benefits of living in your household if he behaves in an acceptable way.

Physical punishment is not needed, but temporarily withdrawing some of the things the dog enjoys is. This might include being talked to, petting, treats, and so on. Since dogs have a short memory, do this for short periods. He'll get the message. The dog should sit and stay quietly and acquiesce to your control. You teach this behavior gradually by showing the dog what the rules are. It works best if everyone in the household is consistent, using the same techniques to accomplish the goal.

This Place Isn't Big Enough for Both of Us!

Every dog has the instinct to protect his territory and, within limits, most owners want a dog who is vigilant and alerts them when people arrive. This takes advantage of the dog's ability to hear and smell so much better than we can. However, when this natural instinct is constantly reinforced with no limits, it can lead to territorial aggression. The dog becomes a crazy little barking, snapping, furry, whirling dervish who is out of control any time someone comes to the door.

You need to watch carefully to make sure you don't inadvertently reinforce the dog's behavior. It's fine to have a little barking to alert you to a stranger, but teach the dog to be quiet on command so that he understands you are the gatekeeper, not him.

This can be especially difficult, because in many cases territorial aggression is self-rewarding. When a delivery person comes to the door and the dog barks, the interloper leaves. The dog believes he has successfully chased that person from his territory and he has now learned that he can make a stranger go away.

There's no reason why your Toy dog can't learn the same limits a big dog learns—you just have to clearly communicate your expectations. You can ask the delivery person to step inside the house for a moment and give the dog a treat. Most of these people are happy to help out, because it makes their work much easier if they have a good rapport with the dogs on their route. Have the dog sit and be quiet for the treat. The command can come from you, but the reward should come from the stranger. Praise the dog when he takes his treat.

When ordering pet supplies from a mail-order company, you can occasionally order a toy, making sure the pup sees you take the box from the delivery person. Then let him watch you open it and make sure he sees you take out the toy before you give it to him.

It is also helpful to simply acknowledge the dog's announcement with a simple "thank you." Dogs usually understand that you've gotten the message.

Territorial aggression can extend to objects, as well. Little dogs are particularly good at keeping things once they've got them. If they've stolen something, they can easily take it under a piece of furniture out of your reach. Terriers, which were originally bred to run into underground burrows chasing small vermin, particularly have an underground fighting mentality that makes them very stubborn. The fact that these dogs can be very loving outside doesn't mean they can't be little tyrants inside. While you can admire their bravado, there should be a balance. You don't want to allow your dog to become either an autocrat or a timid little creature.

The Battle for Top Dog

When dogs live together in the wild, they form a pack. Every pack has its hierarchy, and every hierarchy has one dog at the top, which animal behaviorists call the alpha dog. When domestic dogs live together in the same household, they also establish a hierarchy. This is usually done with a lot of body language and a minimum of fuss. Usually, but not always.

Dog aggression is about social status. It can be a particular problem with small dogs, simply because Toy dog owners are more likely to keep several dogs. After all, two Shih Tzu still take up less space than one St. Bernard.

There's a lot of conventional "wisdom" about what combinations of dogs work best. Most of it is not very wise. Some people think it's a good idea to buy two brothers from the same litter. While every litter does work out its own natural hierarchy, two adult, intact male dogs can become very aggressive, even if they're brothers. Neutering a dog—male or female—tends to reduce aggressive behavior, but not entirely and not in all dogs.

Littermates can also be a problem because when the status of the two dogs is very close and there is no clearly dominant dog, they will be constantly fighting for the top spot. For example, when one dog is sitting on the owner's lap, the other might stand by jealously and attack him when he gets down. Or if one dog is on the bed, he'll try to keep the other dog off. Without a clear hierarchy, neither dog knows when to back down.

Others suggest combining a male and a female. If you plan to neuter your dogs at an early age, this can be a good idea. But if either one of them remains intact, or if they are neutered after they have developed their sexual characteristics, Mother Nature can take over in ways you never intended.

About the best of the conventional wisdom is that the dogs should be well spaced in age. That means bringing a puppy home to live with your adult dog.

No matter what the combination, you have to walk a fine line between letting the dogs sort out their status on their own and making sure no one gets hurt. Be careful not to show favoritism or enhance the dominant status of the top dog by allowing him special privileges. On the other hand, it's important not to give extra attention to the underdog, although, human nature being what it is, this is very tempting. But when you try to change the hierarchy the dogs have worked out for themselves by boosting the underdog, it will just create more tension between the dogs, because the top will feel obliged to remind his underling who's boss time and again.

Remember, your dogs will use your status to enhance their own. When a dog is on your lap or sitting next to you on the couch, he's claiming a privileged position.

If the dogs are well spaced in age and know their place, you tend to get much less aggression, because one dog knows he's boss of the pair, and the other dog knows he's not. But sooner or later the dogs will disagree about something, especially the feisty little Terriers and Spaniels. And most dogs will occasionally grumble with one another as they test the limits of their status. It's important for you to understand canine social behavior so you will know what is a problem and what isn't. A consultation with a professional trainer or a behaviorist may be in order.

Professional Help

For all these types of aggression, it is wise to get a referral from your veterinarian to a behavior consultant or a veterinary behaviorist. These are very complex problems and they require professional solutions. You can also search for a local practitioner at the web site of the International Association of Animal Behavior Consultants (www.iaabc.org).

You can also ask your veterinarian for a referral to a reputable dog trainer, because trainers aren't licensed and you want someone who uses gentle methods. A professional will set up an entire program for you and will work with you to treat your dog's problem.

Don't wait until you're at the end of your rope. Usually, by the time the behaviorist sees the dog, the problem has been going on longer than it would in a bigger dog. Perhaps you think a small dog can't hurt anyone if he bites, but a dog who is up near your face can, indeed, do damage. The sooner you begin to work on the problem, the sooner it will be resolved.

Little Dog, Big Dog

Little dogs often think they're big dogs. Breeders call it attitude. But is this a problem? Yes! A Chihuahua who sees himself as alpha will attempt to attack a Great Dane, which isn't exactly prudent; the Dane may decide to retaliate. Because of his diminutive size, the Toy cannot defend himself from most of the situations he will meet in life. If your little dog is inappropriately aggressive and you're holding him, you've already elevated his status. You've also set the dog up in a position where he doesn't have any choice but to attack whoever is coming at him in order to defend that status.

Most dogs go through a period of social readjustment when they reach maturity at 18 to 24 months of age. Toys actually mature socially a little earlier than the larger breeds, so you'll see a Toy dog start to challenge the status of other dogs at a younger age than you would see the same behavior in a larger dog. While you'd probably like to protect your dog from these challenges, the truth is that all dogs who live together, play together, or simply meet in the street establish a hierarchy, and there's nothing you can do to change that. Remember, too, that your attention conveys status and size has nothing to do with it. So if your small dog is behaving and challenging other dogs inappropriately and you always protect him, you are artificially conferring status on the dog—even if your only intent is to protect your little dog from a bigger one.

Mixed breed dogs

Courtesy of Cheryl S. Smith

Toys will also be aggressive toward large dogs out of fear. Your little guy may just want to announce that he's there and doesn't want to be looked upon as prey.

Whatever the cause, the safest thing to do is use your common sense and keep small dogs out of harm's way. When a dog owner thinks it's amusing to see a little dog with a macho attitude, the dog reads the amusement as reinforcement. But you don't want to reinforce a behavior that could get your dog injured or killed. Big dog–little dog problems are some of the most common, and the most lethal, in the United States. You want your small dog to act like a dog, but don't be foolish about it.

Of necessity, to keep them safe from traffic and from getting lost, dogs are kept on leashes that are short enough to keep them under reasonable control. But the leash artificially raises their level of confidence about the appropriateness of their behaviors. Never think because your dog is on a leash and because all the other dogs you see are also leashed, that your dog is safe. It is your responsibility to be as aware as possible when you are around other dogs. It can't be stressed enough that while Toys can get along extremely well with large dogs, they can also be killed by them, especially those with whom they haven't developed a relationship.

People forget that adult dogs will physically *correct* smaller dogs. Their corrections are firm enough to get the point across and gentle enough to do no harm. There are some larger dogs who will gently correct the small ones when they become too aggressive and will stop puppies from hurting each other in a group situation. If you can find a bigger dog who acts appropriately with small dogs, this could work wonderfully in socializing your small dog with larger ones.

Dog Show Safety

There is the story of two Borzoi at a dog show who suddenly drew up, on the alert, seeing what none of the humans could see: two Chihuahuas being walked by a woman across the show grounds. The Borzoi snapped their leashes and took off with typical sighthound speed. Without breaking stride, each Borzoi grabbed a Chihuahua. The little dogs were killed.

These incidents are not very common, but it's better to be safe than sorry. Small dogs have been killed or injured at dog shows. This happens because dogs can't help being dogs. Sighthounds, for instance, were bred to hunt small animals on the move. It's not cruelty, it's genetics.

If you're going to show your Toy, bring him to the ring in his crate if you can. The problem is that some dog clubs won't allow crates near the rings because they can block the aisles. If you're showing several dogs, it's virtually impossible to stand at ringside holding all of them; you'll have to put them down at some point just to comb or brush them before entering the ring. It can also be difficult to line up several other people to hold your dogs at ringside.

Toy exhibitors have made several suggestions to alleviate the problem. One is to set up a holding area for exhibitors and their small dogs who are going into the ring next, to keep the dogs out of the busy aisles where they could accidentally be stepped on. A holding area wouldn't be foolproof, but it would help.

In the past, the Toys have been put at one end of the show grounds and the large dogs at the other end. Show superintendents could, conceivably, still do this. The club giving the show simply needs to ask.

In the Obedience rings, handlers are required to enter with their dog on leash, on the ground. But the aisles are often very crowded. And sometimes someone is waiting their turn to go into the Obedience ring with a large dog who just can't help noticing a little dog who looks a lot like a prey animal. It would make perfect sense to change the rules in Obedience to allow handlers with small dogs to carry them two or three feet into the Obedience ring and then set them down. They should also be able to pick the dogs up just inside the ring gate when they're leaving and carry them out. While not foolproof, this would give an extra measure of security.

One would hope dogs who aren't dog-friendly wouldn't be brought to shows. But that's not always the case. Dog owners and handlers should have their dogs under control at all times, but you can't always depend on someone else to do what they should. Show leads are also very light, and it's hard to control a big dog on a light lead. It has been suggested that the larger breeds wear a leather buckle collar along with the show lead when walking to and from the ring, giving the handler more control, but so far this is just a suggestion and not a rule. Many big dogs are also on retractable leads, and the owner or handler isn't always paying attention when the dog wanders out.

When owners of large dogs complain that Toy dog owners should be holding their dogs to prevent injury, they forget how many owners have been injured doing just that. Some injuries have required multiple stitches to close the wound. Another problem is that large dogs walking past Toys on a grooming table might see them as an elevated snack. These things can happen anywhere and at any time. Ideally, owners of both size dogs should be in control of their dogs, but always expect the unexpected.

The American Kennel Club (AKC) has taken a step in the right direction. If a superintendent or show committee member sees one dog being aggressive toward another dog, in or out of the ring (and it could be the little dog who's behaving badly), the owner or handler who fails to control their dog can be brought before a show committee, a hearing held, and recommendations for sanctions made to the AKC. We're not talking about Terriers that naturally face off, but about a threat to safety where, for example, a large dog lunges for a small dog or a small dog is goading a large one. It's up to the show committee to determine which owner or handler has failed to control their dog, and that person can be brought up for disciplinary action by the AKC. Penalties can include suspension from all AKC activities for up to one year and/or fines of up to $500. Although this rule won't make dog shows completely safe, it's a start.

Fear Not

Small dogs are often fearful. They can be high-strung, fidgety, and nervous. Some Toys are afraid of things and of people—add something new to their environment or bring them someplace unfamiliar and they shake.

In reality, they have a lot to be fearful of. Everything in the world is giant to them. Even the simple gesture of patting can look different from a Toy dog's perspective, when a hand as big as his whole body is coming down on him. Far better to bring your hand around front where he can see it and gently stroke him under his chin, then reach around and rub gently behind his ears. Of course, with coated breeds, be careful not to tangle the coat. Many little dogs do enjoy being patted on the head, but make sure the introduction is a gentle one.

Toys can become fearful of painful situations very quickly, because a little bit of force can quickly become too much for a tiny dog. When you're choosing a veterinarian, think about going to a feline practitioner who is used to working with small animals; they might handle your dog with more sensitivity than a veterinarian who is used to working with larger dogs. The veterinarian needs to moderate their touch to suit your tiny dog and, ideally, the veterinarian should move slowly while examining the dog. It requires patience to have a little patient.

Toys can also become fearful when you try to medicate them. Even putting eye drops into the eye can create fear aggression if the dog perceives the bottle as being very large. And if they've had scary experiences with medicine when they were young, when they're older it will be even more difficult if they're fussy.

Anxious dogs are not healthy dogs. Most people don't realize that the first signs of anxiety in little dogs can be chewing around the base of their nails or sucking, licking, or plucking at their fur, especially on their feet. The subsequent lesions aren't very big, so watch for subtle signs.

Dogs will also lick their feet a lot in the winter, because salt and sand on the road irritates them. (Wash it off immediately, because road salt is toxic.) And allergies always show up in the skin of animals, particularly their feet. But if the problem isn't seasonal, it's probably a symptom of stress. Look at your dog's environment. Look at the messages you're giving him and at what you're asking him to do.

Try to keep this in mind as your dog deals with potentially fearful situations early in life, because it's also possible you are reinforcing and even encouraging these fearful reactions. If you were out with a 6-month-old Rottweiler and a passing bus startled him, you couldn't pick him up and reassure him. But you can pick up a Toy and say, "Oh, baby, it's okay!" The hug is a reward for showing fear, and the dog's anxiety just grows.

It's hard to say how much of the pup's ability to learn in potentially scary situations requires that he be able to make mistakes. If you see something coming that might startle your puppy and you tense up in anticipation of his reaction, he will pick up on your anxiety. Dogs are masters at reading body language, and they take their cues from you. If you seem tense, they will feel tense and anxious, too. People sometimes intervene a little too early in the social interactions of Toy dogs. This is partly because they fear for their dog's safety. But that fear gets telegraphed to the dog, and if you pick him up he'll be better able to observe your fearful body language. You really have to watch yourself on this one.

Chapter 6

The Rewards of Training

Every dog needs to be socialized to help her become a happy, well-adjusted companion who can be taken anywhere and will be comfortable in a variety of places and situations. Socialization means introducing the puppy to a wide variety of people and activities, so she begins to feel at home in an average household. Just don't flood her with too many experiences at once. Pace yourself—and your dog.

Dog behaviorists believe the first 12 weeks of a puppy's life is a crucial socialization period and that she needs to be exposed to as many positive experiences as possible. This is the breeder's job, as we discussed in chapter 2. But socialization doesn't end there.

Portable Pups

After the puppy has moved to her new home, it's up to you to continue the socialization process. Happily, socializing Toys can often be done more easily than with larger dogs, because these people-oriented dogs are so portable.

One of the most obvious places to take your puppy is shopping malls. If you live in the city, a walk down the block will expose the pup to all sorts of sights, sounds, and smells, along with a wide variety of people. Take her to the park or to visit friends in the country so

Schipperke

Courtesy of Judith Swan

she'll be exposed to grass, birds, trees, and so on. If you live in the country or the suburbs, plan to go to the city so the pup will get used to things such as buses and car horns.

It's important that these experiences be positive. That means everyone who meets your puppy must be reminded that small dog are always looking up at people and have a different perspective. They're also very much underfoot, and you must be aware of this, too, so you won't accidentally do any damage. It's never nice when you step on a puppy's foot, but a Toy puppy can be even more fragile. So make sure everyone exercises some caution and watches where they tread.

If you don't have children but want to carefully expose your pup to kids, take her to a park to watch the children play baseball or soccer—from a safe distance, of course, because you don't want the puppy getting injured by a flying ball or bat. An ice cream stand is another good place to encounter children. Just be sure the kids are gentle and approach the puppy carefully while you supervise the meeting.

The puppy should become accustomed to riding in the car in her crate and trips should be happy adventures, not just treks to the veterinarian or the groomer. If you only take your dog to visit those places, she'll soon associate riding in the car with being poked, prodded, bathed, and vaccinated.

When you walk your puppy, you'll notice her looking at everything; that new little life is investigating all sorts of new sights, sounds, and smells, and then looking back at you to check your reaction. If something startles the puppy, the last thing you want to do is overreact by telling her that you'll protect her or cooing, "Everything's okay." You'll only confirm in her mind that whatever startled her is dangerous and should be feared. Although you think you're reassuring the puppy, in fact you're creating the exact opposite response! If the puppy is startled and you don't react at all but just keep walking as if it were something natural, she will simply go on without fuss.

One of the nice bonuses of having a small dog is that she can usually ride in the airplane cabin with you when you fly, instead of with the luggage. Get your puppy accustomed to riding in a soft-sided carry bag and you can take her almost anywhere. The carrier must fit under the seat of the plane, and you want one that conforms to the shape under the seat but won't collapse on the dog.

Introduce the carrier at home. If she's used to a crate, this should be fairly easy. Put a toy and a small treat in the carrier. Keep the carrier near your feet so she'll get used to the fact that your feet will be near her when she's traveling. Your next step will be to close the carrier for a few minutes with the dog inside so she'll become accustomed to being in the carrier with no exit for a period of time. Some carriers have a zippered opening at the top that's big enough to fit your hand through so you can pat your dog during the flight, which can be reassuring. More than likely, however, your little companion will spend her flight time napping.

Whenever you travel be sure to take along a first-aid kit and tape a current picture of your dog to the top of the carrier. In case she gets away from you, you'll be able to use the photo to make up flyers. And don't forget to have her microchipped and/or tattooed for identification. And, of course, she should be wearing a tag.

Before you leave for a trip, try to get the name of a veterinarian in the area where you're heading. Hopefully, you'll never need that person, but in case there's an emergency, it's just as well to be prepared. Your veterinarian may be able to suggest a colleague in that area, or perhaps someone you know who lives there can make a referral. You will need to get a health certificate from your veterinarian within ten days before your trip.

Another Country Heard From

It is up to you to make sure your dog minds her manners so she will be accepted wherever she goes. One thing visitors from the United States often comment on after visiting the United Kingdom is how wonderful it is to see well-behaved dogs everywhere with their owners. This deserves a closer look.

Interestingly, an increasing number of people in the United Kingdom keep smaller dogs. The small dogs that are rising most in popularity right now are Yorkshire Terriers, Lhasa Apsos, and Shih Tzu. Both the United States and the United Kingdom have seen a lot of urbanization, and it's less convenient to keep a large dog in the city. Most people want dogs simply for their companionship, and it's easier in a smaller living space to have a smaller pet. That's why the number of pet cats is going up in Britain, as well.

Looking at the British, who are dyed-in-the-wool dog lovers, the question is: What is it that makes these dogs so comfortable and well-mannered in public places? Are British dog owners raising their pups any differently or socializing them differently?

The answer is that the dogs are extremely well socialized and trained right from the start, going to obedience class after they've received their vaccinations. Virtually everyone in the

United Kingdom trains their dog, no matter what the dog's size. The dogs are therefore under better control and create fewer problems. This makes close encounters of the canine kind far more enjoyable, both for the dogs and the people involved.

Conventional British wisdom is that dogs should be taken to the park twice a day. Since almost everyone does this, their dogs are always socializing with lots of other dogs. Conventional wisdom also says dogs should be taken to obedience school, along with their owners. The result is that everyone expects all dogs to be well socialized and have good manners, and so dogs are permitted almost everywhere. British people, therefore, encounter dogs frequently, whether they own one or not, and the society as a whole tends to be very dog tolerant.

We can learn a lot from our friends across the pond.

Silky Terriers

Courtesy of Linda Hart

The Value of Training

It doesn't matter that you can pick your dog up to get her out of harm's way; for safety's sake the dog should respond to basic commands. These little dogs have been known to slip their collars and take off, bolt out the door, jump down from people's arms, and even escape from crates and carriers. You can prevent disaster if your dog is trained to respond to Sit, Stay, or Come. As an added precaution for Italian Greyhounds, who can use that little needle nose to slip through virtually any collar, consider using a Martingale collar, which will tighten a limited amount but will not choke the dog.

Toy dog owners will often become overprotective when opening the door to the house. Some owners, even though their dogs are trained to Stay, will either put the dog in another room or will hold the dog in their arms before opening the door because some of the more curious and active Toys will, on rare occasion, take it into their head to bolt out the door and under the wheels of a car or truck. A six-foot fence is seldom an obstacle to a determined little dog who aims to get to the other side. Keeping in mind that a dead dog is not a fun companion—always exercise caution.

Training will resolve many common problems, such as digging, jumping up on people, and excessive barking. All dogs seem to love digging. To resolve this problem, you might want to choose a DDA—designated digging area—in your yard where your dog is allowed to dig. To train her to use the appointed area, bury a toy in that spot and let her dig it up.

Although you may not think jumping up is a problem in a such a small dog, in fact, it is an unacceptable behavior that can generalize to other behaviors that do matter to you. Small dogs should not be allowed to jump up on people any more than large dogs should.

Teaching your little dog Leave It can be very handy when she picks up something dangerous while you're out on a walk. And speaking of that walk, your little dog should learn to walk on a loose leash. There shouldn't be any pulling.

Far too many dogs are put to death in the United States because of behavior problems. Raising a well-adjusted, well-behaved dog is the best way to avoid that.

Obedience training also establishes a set of rules that help your dog live more comfortably in society. Your dog will feel more secure knowing that you're the one to whom she can turn to keep her safe and provide everything she needs in life, including instruction on proper comportment in order to be a good little citizen. Training gives the dog another place to focus her attention. The overconfident dog is brought under your control, and the shy dog can gain some much-needed self-confidence when her energies are properly channeled and she learns what she can accomplish. And as you work together, training deepens the bond between you.

Obedience training is invaluable for older dogs as well. It will give the dog a sense of security and purpose. An added bonus is that it will make the dog easier for your veterinarian to examine and treat. You can also enjoy more activities with your dog when she is obedience trained.

Reinforcing the training the breeder has started should begin on your puppy's first day at home. Ask the breeder what obedience exercises and concepts the dog knows and review them with your pup every day.

In a Class by Themselves

Formal training should begin as soon as your puppy has adjusted to being in her new home. The old idea was to wait until a pup was 6 months old to begin training, but current thinking is that it's easier to shape the dog's behavior and responses to her environment if you start early. If you wait, you're going to have an unruly adolescent dog, and the training experience will be more difficult.

Puppy kindergarten—classes in socialization and a few basic commands—is a good place to start. The young puppy isn't expected to concentrate, but you can establish the idea of learning certain exercises in the pup's mind. However, puppy kindergarten can be a scary place for a tiny dog stuck in a class full of big, rambunctious puppies, especially because most classes are not segregated by size.

Under carefully controlled circumstances, however, in a class run by a professional, puppy kindergarten should be a place for your Toy to safely meet other dogs of all shapes and sizes, preferably in her own age range. But do remember that puppies are basically untrained, and anything can happen.

The obedience instructor you choose should have experience with small dogs and should like them. Ask around among other dog owners, veterinarians, and groomers to find someone in your area who fits these criteria. An inexperienced trainer could inadvertently put your dog into a dangerous situation with a large dog, so choose carefully. Your puppy shouldn't be afraid to be in obedience class. She'll learn better and faster if she feels good about herself and the experience. You can also locate trainers in your area through the Association of Pet Dog Trainers (www.apdt.com), and you can find clicker trainers by going to the trainer locator at www.clickertraining.com. Be sure to observe a class before signing up. And leave your puppy at home when you visit the class.

The British view (which may be why their dogs are so comfortable in all circumstances) is that it's important for companion dogs to encounter every breed imaginable, because they'll be meeting big dogs and small, hairy and smooth-coated, when they're out and about with their owners.

Look for someone who uses positive training methods. You don't want your pup, or even an adult dog, in a class where a choke collar is used, even if it's called a training collar. Nor should you put a prong collar on your pup. Any dog of any size can be trained using a buckle collar or a halter, and it's especially important for a small dog whose trachea is at risk. Using a choke chain on a dog with a collapsing trachea is definitely not a good idea!

Play groups can also be fun for dogs, and they help in socialization and building confidence. Often they are formed in association with training classes. You may want to look for a play group that is geared only to small dogs. If there isn't one in your area, you could request one. According to some animal behaviorists in the United States, small, frightened Toy puppies shouldn't be forced to play with large dogs. The tiny puppy could be injured by a larger breed puppy during the roughhousing of playtime.

It would be helpful if more training classes and play groups sorted their puppies by size. The little dogs could start in a class or play group of other small dogs and then gradually be introduced to bigger puppies and more energetic classes. The slower introduction would make things easier for both the little pup and her owner. And there should be places in the room where every dog can go to feel safe when she wants to get away from the other pups for a while.

Canine Good Citizen

Every dog owner should participate in the AKC's Canine Good Citizen (CGC) program. Who could possibly disagree with a program that emphasizes responsible dog ownership for owners, along with good manners at home and in the community for dogs? This certification program is open to all dogs, mixed breed as well as purebred.

The CGC test measures a dog's social skills and public manners. The test has ten steps and there are no scores—dogs simply pass or fail. A dog needs to pass the entire test only once to receive a CGC certificate, and you can take the test as many times as you need to pass (although you can't try more than once on the same day). Unlike an Obedience trial, where the rules are very specific for each skill, in a CGC test, neither dog nor owner has to perform with precision. The dog is always on a leash, and you can talk to the dog throughout the test but cannot offer the dog food. The examiner is a person with dog knowledge and experience, such as a dog club member, private trainer, groomer, veterinarian, or veterinary technician.

The tests are what you'd expect of a well-behaved dog: accepting a friendly stranger; sitting politely for petting; appearance and grooming; going out for a walk (walking on a loose leash); walking through a crowd; Sit and Down on command and staying in place; settling down after praise and interaction; reacting to another dog (the dogs should show no more than a casual interest in each other); reacting to distractions such as someone using a wheelchair or walker, or a jogger running in front of the dog; and supervised separation to demon-

Mixed breed *(Courtesy of Elizabeth Currin)*

Affenpinscher *(Courtesy of Nancy Baybutt)*

Affenpinscher *(Courtesy of Barry Kurth)*

Yorkshire Terriers *(Courtesy of Linda Grimm)*

Mixed breed *(Courtesy of Judith Lynn Laffoon)*

Italian Greyhound *(Courtesy of Judith Hamilton Jerome)*

Pug *(Courtesy of Stephanie Alford)*

Cavalier King Charles Spaniels *(Courtesy of Bressler West©)*

Lhasa Apso *(Courtesy of Fran Strayer)*

Pekingese *(Courtesy of Rose Marchetti)*

strate that the dog can be left with a trusted person, if necessary, and will maintain her training and good manners.

Any dog who eliminates during the test must be failed. The only exception to this rule is during supervised separation, when that test is held outdoors. Grounds for dismissal would be growling, snapping, biting, attacking, or attempting to attack another dog or a person.

The Canine Good Citizen test is sponsored by local groups such as dog clubs, community colleges, private training schools, and service organizations. In 1991, Florida became the first state to pass a resolution supporting the program. Many other states have followed.

Obedience and Other Sports

Toy dogs often do very well in competitive Obedience and prove that they're more than little lapdogs. Some breeds, such as Papillons, Toy Poodles, Pomeranians, and Yorkshire Terriers, excel at it. One veterinarian who competes with her Toys says training a Papillon is almost like training a Border Collie.

Toys competing in Obedience will have to learn to deal with large dogs, so you'll want the introductions to come early in training classes under controlled circumstances.

Little dogs are more aware of noise, which is good, because that extra awareness can keep them from being stepped on or crushed. But it can make Obedience competition a little challenging. The dogs are asked to watch you all the time for signals, but if a Toy hears a noise outside the ring—someone collapsing a crate, for example—she must be able to look to reassure herself that it's not something about to swoop down on top of her. Toys can be taught, however, that it's fine to look away to make sure everything's okay, as long as they look right back at you.

The American Kennel Club sanctions Obedience trials and offers titles to successful competitors. Other clubs and registries, such as the United Kennel Club (UKC), also offer Obedience competition with the opportunity to earn titles. For brevity's sake, we'll talk just about AKC events, since the AKC is the largest registry and sanctions the most competitions in the United States. In any case, every Obedience trial has the same goal: owners and their well-trained dogs bonding and having fun together.

Competition in the Obedience ring is divided into three classes, each more difficult than the previous one and each offering an Obedience title. To receive a title, a dog must earn

three "legs" in competition. To achieve a leg, a dog must score at least 170 points out of a possible 200 and get more than half the points available for each exercise.

Each class requires the dog to have different skills. In the Novice class a dog must heel on leash, stand to be examined by a judge, heel off leash, recall (Come), and do a group long Sit and long Down. The successful dog earns a Companion Dog (CD) title.

In the Open class a dog must heel off leash, drop on recall, retrieve on a flat surface, retrieve over the high jump, and do the broad jump, long Sit, and long Down, all for a Companion Dog Excellent (CDX) title.

In the Utility class a dog must perform exercises with only hand signals for guidance, pass two scent discrimination tests, perform a directed retrieve and directed jumping, and stand for a group examination. This earns the Utility Dog (UD) title.

There are also two more titles. Utility Dog Excellent (UDX) is earned by qualifying in both the Utility and Open classes at several shows. Obedience Trial Champion (OTCh) is earned by placing first or second in the Utility and Open classes at many, many Obedience trials.

If your dog has a nose for it, she might even go on to earn Tracking titles. This outdoor sport further develops the dog's ability to recognize and follow human scent. Not every AKC club sponsors Tracking events, but a little networking will help you find people in the sport.

Any purebred dog over the age of 6 months and registered with the AKC, as well as dogs with an Indefinite Listing Privilege (ILP) number (breeds in the Miscellaneous Class or purebred dogs without registered parents who nevertheless meet certain criteria) can be entered in Obedience or Tracking events. Anyone can handle their dog in these events, including people of any age as well as those with disabilities.

There are opportunities to practice Obedience at fun matches, where your dog will receive no points toward a title but you will both gain valuable experience. Because no points are awarded, fun matches are also usually open to mixed breeds and unregistered purebreds.

AKC-sanctioned matches are informal events that are sanctioned by the American Kennel Club where the results do not count toward any AKC title. Usually they include Obedience and breed judging. Clubs will accept entries from both members and nonmembers, and these matches are conducted in accordance with AKC rules to give everyone involved experience toward licensed events.

These are also fun events to watch, especially if you have never attended a dog show before. You might not understand the nuances of conformation (breed) judging, but you'll have no trouble enjoying the performances in the Obedience ring, especially when you watch the more advanced dogs retrieving over a jump or doing scent discrimination exercises. And it might encourage you to get involved in further training your own dog.

Rally-O

Rally-O is fairly new. This fun off-shoot of Obedience is less formal than an Obedience trial. The name of this AKC-sanctioned sport reflects its origins: it stands for Rally Obedience. The ring is set up with signs that indicate what the dog is supposed to do at each place along the course, and each activity must be done within two to four feet of the sign. The course is different at each trial.

The layout of the course is posted at ringside and handlers and their dogs can walk the course before the competition begins. The nice thing is that you can encourage your dog during the trial but, of course, you cannot touch her or give leash corrections (in an Obedience trial you are not allowed to talk to your dog while executing the moves). You can, however, talk, sing, clap, whistle, etc.

There are two levels of competition. Level One is for novices, and it's done on leash. Level Two is done off-leash and is more advanced. The more advanced course includes at least one jump. There are both timed and untimed courses.

Agility

The AKC and UKC, along with several other groups, offer Agility trials, which test a dog's ability to maneuver over and through various obstacles and the human handler's ability to guide the dog along a specified route. Toys actually have an advantage here. The jumps are adjusted for the size of each dog, but the other obstacles, such as tunnels and weave poles, are not. While these obstacles can be tough for a Great Dane to maneuver, they're no problem for an agile little Toy.

The dog is trained slowly and carefully to run an Agility course. Probably the scariest thing for these little dogs is the soft tunnel, a long nylon tube, because they can get lost inside. To get them used to the idea, you can do fun things at home like playing with a sheet,

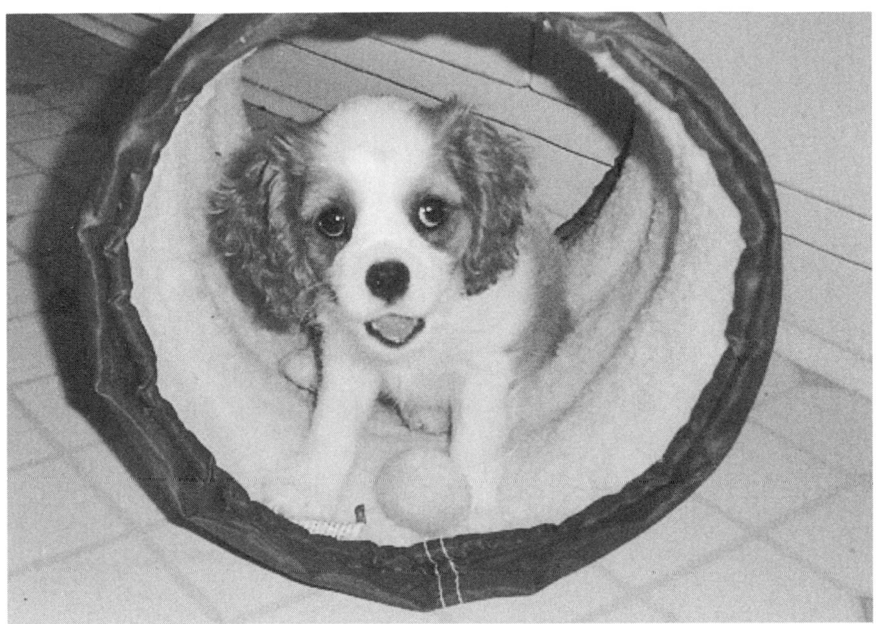

Cavalier King Charles Spaniel

Courtesy of Bressler West ©

letting the dog get under it and then popping out. These games can start when the puppy is about 8 weeks old.

Training for the high obstacles begins by doing all the work on very low obstacles for a long time so the dog gains confidence. A Toy should never be allowed to jump off the side of an obstacle, because she can get seriously hurt.

Since dogs run the Agility course off leash, you do have to be very aware of the other dogs near the Agility course. Most dogs running in Agility are very well mannered and in control, but you must always expect the unexpected.

Dogs must be at least 1 year old to participate in AKC Agility events. Sanctioned Agility trials are informal events, while a licensed Agility trial gives the dog the opportunity to earn qualifying scores toward titles. Titles earned at AKC Agility trials are Novice Agility (NA), Open Agility (OA), Agility Excellent (AX), and Master Agility Excellent (MX).

Among the Toys, Papillons, and Cavalier King Charles Spaniels have done particularly well in Agility. But all breeds compete, and there are some AX titles among Brussels Griffons, Italian Greyhounds, and other breeds you might not expect.

Flyball

Flyball, although not an AKC sport, is popular and growing. Basically, this is a canine relay race. The first dog runs down a straight course, jumping four hurdles on the way. At the end of the course, she must press a lever on a spring-loaded box, catch the tennis ball that pops up, and then return over the hurdles to the start point. As soon as the dog crosses the start-finish line, her teammate takes a turn. Two teams of four dogs each compete against each other. The team with the fastest total time wins.

Flyball is open to all dogs over the age of 1 year, including mixed breeds. Among the Toys that are potential flyball candidates are the Toy Manchester Terrier and Cavalier King Charles Spaniel. Some Toys, obviously, are just too small to catch a tennis ball!

Often a Toy is considered an advantage on a relay team, because the hurdles are set four inches below the withers (the top of the shoulder) of the smallest dog running. But eight inches is the minimum height, so make sure your little dog can clear at least that much.

Canine Freestyle

If a canine Fred Astaire or Ginger Rogers seems a little farfetched (pun intended!), think again. There's a new sport, and it's one little dogs are enjoying immensely. Canine Freestyle offers you the novel pleasure of dancing with your dog.

The sport was enjoyed in Canada—where it's called Musical Freestyle—for several years before crossing the border, and this Canadian import has definitely caught on. The first demonstrations in the United States took place in November 1993, and the first Cycle Canine Freestyle Competition was held in Eugene, Oregon, on November 15, 1996.

According to the Musical Canine Sports International Format, "A Musical Freestyle is a choreographed musical performance executed by handlers and their dogs (purebred or mixed breed)." There are no age limitations on either the dog or the handler.

The object of Freestyle is to show the dog and her handler to their best advantage in a creative and artistic manner. Freestyle should demonstrate, with appropriate music, the

grace, beauty, and intelligence of the dog working together with the handler. A Freestyle presentation should clearly show the dog's athleticism, attentiveness, pace, and flexibility working in harmony with the handler.

Among the first Toys to participate in Freestyle were a Toy Poodle, a Miniature Pinscher, a Cavalier King Charles Spaniel, and a 2.7-pound Yorkshire Terrier named Misha, who stood about seven inches high, loved to pirouette, and learned her routine in less than a day.

Freestyle is a wonderful activity for all dogs. Since Freestyle dogs must work on all sides of the owner, these dogs are better balanced than most. The World Canine Freestyle Organization has divisions for everyone from Juniors to Sassy Seniors, as well as a Handi Dandi division for handicapped dogs and/or owners. There are many rescued dogs and mixed breeds doing Freestyle. It's fun, helps dogs gain confidence, and it strengthens the bond between dog and owner.

K9 Dressage

This new sport, created by Sandra Davis (one of the world's best canine Freestylers), is derived from equine dressage, and the handlers' clothing during competition reflects this classic heritage. K9 Dressage, which has three levels, will help develop a dog who is both physically and mentally well-balanced and flexible—and it promotes the bond between dog and owner.

There are three levels of competition: Novice, Intermediate, and Advanced. Combining heeling and Freestyle moves, K9 Dressage offers something new and different for people who want to have fun with their dogs. There are sixteen standard movements; ten are basic and six are expansions of those moves. There are also specialty sequences designed by the handler at the Advanced level.

The competition occurs in a forty-by-fifty-foot gated or roped ring, and the moves are always the same for each course. Owners can talk to the dog, praise her, and use hand and arm gestures that are move obvious at the Novice level. Those gestures should fade with the move up to the higher levels. More information about this new sport can be obtained from the World Canine Freestyle Organization (www.worldcaninefreestyle.org).

Therapy Visits

When your little dog is well socialized, has been obedience trained and, hopefully, has earned her Canine Good Citizen title, consider enrolling in a therapy program in which you visit children, hospital patients, or the elderly regularly.

These programs require some training, but those who become involved say they get far more than they give during these volunteer visits. Often there are reports of elderly people who haven't spoken in years who will suddenly begin to speak when a dog is brought into the room. Just the contact with that soft little body is so meaningful for so many people of all ages who are confined to a nursing home or hospital bed. And almost no one is afraid of small dogs.

Just make sure everyone handles your dog gently. You are responsible for your small dog's safety. Not every dog is a good candidate for this work, but those who are can make a real difference for many people.

Havanese

Courtesy of Nancy Dionne

School Visits

You and your well-behaved companion may be good candidates for humane education programs in your local school. There are several formal programs, including one sponsored by the AKC and one sponsored by the Delta Society, that can be presented at your local elementary school.

When you educate a child about responsible dog ownership, you are educating more than one generation. Not only are those children learning something to pass on to their own children someday, but they will also go home and tell their parents what they have learned.

Part III

Sickness and Health

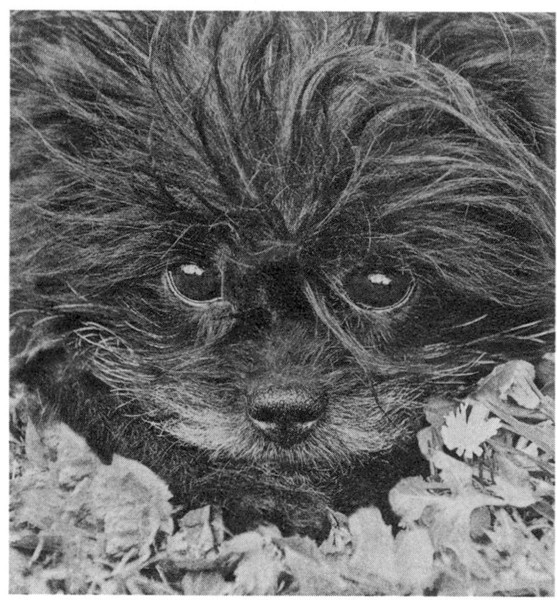

Affenpinscher

Courtesy of Stuart Cordon ©

Chapter 7

Nutrition

The smaller the animal, the higher his relative energy needs. So when it comes to nutrition, small dogs are not the same as the larger breeds. Their energy requirements are much higher per pound of body weight. Toys need more calories per pound—sometimes even two or three times more. And proper nutrition begins earlier than you may suspect: It begins in the womb.

During pregnancy, the mother should be on a pregnancy/lactation diet to meet her extra caloric needs. One veterinary nutritionist recommends cat or kitten food because it's more nutrient-dense.

The puppies need to nurse within the first few hours after they're delivered in order to get their mother's colostrum, the first milk, which is filled with maternal antibodies and gives the pups natural immunity from many diseases. Although the immunity wears off relatively soon, it is very important to protect the pups before they are old enough to be vaccinated. The new modified live vaccines are designed to protect the puppy at an earlier age and lessen the opportunity for the pup to get a disease when his immunity from the colostrum has worn off.

Toys have to be monitored very closely to make sure they're nursing and growing. The two major reasons why a Toy dog will not grow are inadequate nutrition and a congenital defect. Nutrition, we can control.

Cavalier King Charles Spaniels

Courtesy of Bressler West ©

When to Wean?

Experts disagree on the best time for weaning. The general recommendation has been to begin weaning puppies around 4 to 5 weeks of age by offering solid food in soft, small pieces that are easily digested and absorbed. Much past 4 weeks, the quality of the mother's milk starts decreasing as the nutritional requirements of the puppies are increasing.

Toy breeders have observed that their puppies are more likely to get food in their lungs if the weaning process is started too soon, leading to aspiration pneumonia. This makes sense, since these pups develop more slowly than larger breeds. One breeder begins introducing solid food on the twenty-eighth day, giving the puppies a mushy mixture to "play with" a couple of times a day for about five days to begin the weaning process. Food should be introduced

slowly, as the pups continue to nurse. Solid food is less digestible than milk, and you don't want the puppies to become malnourished during the weaning process. As fiber is added to the puppy's diet, it slows the passage of material through the gastrointestinal tract, enabling the puppy to extract the maximum nutritional benefit from his food. However, according to nutritionists, less than 5 percent fiber is about all young puppies can handle in their food.

Toy puppies appear to do best on a puppy-formula diet rather than one designed for all life stages. Nutritionists recommend a specifically formulated growth diet because it contains more calories and other nutrients in a balanced mixture.

Most dogs should be completely weaned to solid food between 6 and 8 weeks of age, but small dogs may need to be a little older than that—up to 10 weeks. This is about the time some Toys are being placed in a new home. During this critical period, the puppies must be fed a canned food growth diet made into a slurry mixture. They prefer the texture, probably just because it's more familiar. And Toy pups are so small that when given dry food, they'll keep chewing it but won't be able to take enough in to maintain their blood glucose levels. As they get older and their teeth develop, they do very well on dry food, but introduce it into their diet a little at a time.

Proper pediatric nutrition is extremely important. It is not unheard of for a puppy to be rushed to the veterinary hospital a week after he is brought home, suffering from seizures caused by low blood glucose levels. This happens when the puppy is not getting enough calories to sustain him.

Chihuahua

Courtesy of Susan Payne

Wet or Dry?

While canned food is essential for young puppies, what about adults? Some veterinarians and nutritionists believe chewing dry food is better for the teeth; because dry foods create more friction, there is less accumulation of tartar on the teeth. Other experts believe canned food, with its high water content, is better to prevent kidney

stones. And when it comes to dental health, the real question is how much the food sticks to the teeth; some dry foods are actually stickier than canned foods, and some canned foods aren't as sticky.

The custom in Europe has long been to provide a meat base with a dry food added in. The first commercial pet food available in Britain was a dry food biscuit that was mixed in with table scraps. Today the standard method of feeding in Europe is canned food with a dry mixer of some kind, or a complete dry food. The French tend to mix a lot of rice or potatoes into the canned food.

One option for dog owners in the United States is feeding three parts dry food to one part canned food. This helps make the dry food more palatable. Stay with the same company for both kinds of food so that they are nutritionally compatible.

Remember that the dry food has about three and a half times the calorie density of the canned food. That means one ounce of dry food has three and a half times more calories than one ounce of wet food. When you're mixing wet and dry food, you must adjust for this calorie difference. You could be overfeeding if you don't. If you're taking away a fraction of the dog's daily portion of canned food and adding dry, weigh the amount of canned food you're taking away, divide by three and a half, and you'll know how much dry food to add. In other words, if you take away 3.5 ounces of wet food, replace it with 1 ounce of dry food (because dry food is much more calorie-dense than wet food). If you want to mix a small amount of canned food into the dry food, multiply the weight of the dry food you are taking away by three and a half to determine how much canned food you should add.

Looking at Ingredients

There are dog foods made especially for young dogs, old dogs, pregnant and nursing dogs, and overweight dogs, and, happily, there are now dog foods formulated specifically for small dogs.

The Association of American Feed Control Officials (AAFCO), composed of a panel of veterinarians and nutritionists, has set nutritional guidelines for dog food when the dog is growing and when he's an adult. AAFCO has established minimums and maximums for some nutrients, and then assumed the optimum is somewhere in between. To choose a complete and balanced food for your dog, look for a statement on the package that says the food meets AAFCO requirements.

However, levels of specific nutrients are far from the whole story. Pet foods are formulated according to the energy density of the product, because the idea is that an animal will eat enough to meet his energy needs. In a complete and balanced diet, however, when the animal has eaten enough to meet his energy needs, he should also have met all his other nutritional needs. Nutrients also interact in a delicate balance, so these interactions, plus digestibility, availability, and palatability of the food must be considered, as well. Making a good dog food is even more difficult than choosing one!

One issue that has caused some controversy is the preservatives used in dry food. All the preservatives used in pet foods are clinically tested for safety, so the evidence against them is strictly anecdotal. Some breeders, for instance, will swear that synthetic preservatives cause their bitches to have all sorts of reproductive problems. The Food and Drug Administration has looked at these claims and can find nothing scientific to back them up. And manufacturers have been using synthetic preservatives for more than thirty years. Still, for those who prefer only natural ingredients, there are foods preserved with added vitamins C and E. These foods will say so on the label. Make sure to look at the freshness date on the package, because a food with only natural preservatives has a shorter shelf life.

There has been much talk in human nutrition about chelated minerals. A chelated mineral is one that's attached to an organic compound. Some—but certainly not all—nutritionists believe that in this form the mineral will be better absorbed into the bloodstream. We do know that the way minerals are absorbed is affected by the form in which they are consumed. And there is some evidence that the biological availability of certain minerals might be improved by giving them as an organic complex, as opposed to an inorganic molecule. This means dogs could eat less of a chelated mineral and still absorb all they need. What's not clear is how valuable that outcome really is. If you know the bioavailability of an inorganic mineral, you can still calculate how much of the mineral you must add to the dog's food to ensure he gets enough. This is simpler and less expensive than using chelated minerals, which are more complicated to manufacture.

Minerals that are more efficiently absorbed are not always a good thing, either. With iron, for instance, the body will regulate absorption as needed. In this way the body avoids both iron deficiency and iron excess—each dangerous in its own way. But if you start attaching iron to organic compounds that are being absorbed via different mechanisms, it cheats the natural regulatory system. The body might then end up with too much iron.

Finding the Right Food

Most high-quality commercial pet foods on the market today are formulated not simply to meet the minimum requirements, but to provide optimum nutrition for the vast majority of dogs. If you steer clear of the bargain brands, most commercial pet foods can be appropriate for a small dog (or a large dog, for that matter).

With that in mind, it's important to remember that no one dog food is right for every dog. If your dog doesn't seem to be getting enough energy or enough nutrition from the diet you're feeding, if he's losing weight or his coat looks dull, you might want to switch to a more nutrient-dense product. Conversely, if your dog is gaining weight on a high-calorie product, you might want to switch to a less rich food or simply cut back a little on the amount you feed him.

Breeders should send puppies to their new homes with a bag of the food they have been eating. That way the stress of a new environment is not compounded by the stress of a new diet.

However, some breeders feed their own concoctions, and they're not necessarily the best food for your pup. One veterinary nutritionist offers some breeder's recommendations that you should beware of:

- Feeding five or six different supplements (that means the basic diet isn't balanced)
- Feeding raw foods that you wouldn't eat, such as egg, meat, or liver
- Diets that are more complicated than they need to be, such as feeding one food in the morning and another at night

Usually these kinds of homemade diets are not balanced, and the breeder will not offer specific amounts of each ingredient. Consider changing the puppy over to a commercial diet that meets the AAFCO standards for a growth food.

Most puppies and dogs can tolerate having their diet changed gradually, over four days. Feed 25 percent new food and 75 percent old food on the first day, half and half on the second day, 75 percent new and 25 percent old on the third day, and all new food on the fourth.

Small dogs seem to be more sensitive to the feel of the food in their mouth than larger dogs. Obviously, the Toy puppy, with his small mouth, will need a dry food that comes in

small pieces. If the kibble is too hard, the puppy might find it somewhat hard to handle as well. Some adult small dogs can handle the larger kibble pieces, but given the choice, most Toys prefer the smaller size. It's hard to chew up something that fills your whole mouth with every bite.

Additives and Supplements

There are nutraceuticals (nutritional supplements that purport to have health benefits) added to some foods to help promote joint health or add other benefits. This is a controversial area because there is no government regulation of nutraceuticals, so clinical proof of their efficacy, and whether there is enough of a particular substance in the food to make a difference, would likely be difficult to ascertain. However, some people have reported good results with these additives.

Vitamin and mineral supplements aren't necessary if a diet is complete and balanced. They just cost more and will only unbalance the balanced diet you're already paying for when you buy pet food. A complete and balanced dog food gives a dog two to ten times the minimum daily requirement of vitamins and minerals. And overfeeding minerals or the fat-soluble vitamins can be toxic.

That said, there's probably no harm done in giving supplements, because the more dangerous nutrients in many of the supplements have been minimized so the dog won't overdose. In fact, most supplements have only a fraction of the nutrients that are in a good commercial dog food. That's why feeding a good food is really enough.

People who show their dogs are big believers in supplements, particularly oils, which they believe make a dog's coat look very glossy. The evidence for this is mostly anecdotal. Show dogs are extremely well cared for in any case, and great attention is paid to their coats. It's not clear how much benefit they derive from extra fat in their diet. The dangers of too much fat, however, have been well documented.

Raw Foods

Diets of raw food and bones have become something of a fad for pets, but these diets are not necessarily complete and balanced. Raw food fans can be fanatical in their devotion to

their diet choice for their dogs. That doesn't lessen the danger of such a diet. Bones can shatter or splinter and can cause internal damage.

Many people who feed these diets argue that our own diets are not always complete and balanced. That doesn't seem like a very good excuse for feeding an unbalanced diet to your dog. After all, we are responsible for our dogs; they don't have the opportunity to choose whether they will eat a complete and balanced diet. They eat what is put in their dish.

Also, if you are immune-compromised, you should not be handling raw food. Further, the dog eating raw food who kisses someone who is immune-compromised can pass along dangerous bacteria. Salmonella poisoning is a definite possibility.

If you are determined to feed your dog a raw diet, be certain that you do it under the supervision of a veterinarian, preferably a veterinary nutritionist. An unbalanced diet of any sort can be dangerous.

Avoiding the Finicky Eater

Although Toys have a reputation for being picky, that doesn't apply to all small dogs. There have been some real gluttons among the Toys, while others tend to be more like cats in their fussiness about food.

Finicky eaters are created, not born. Food is a social issue for humans who, unfortunately, try to make it a social issue for their dogs. Toys are very attached to their owners, some of whom treat these little dogs so much like human family members that they make too much out of mealtimes. Socialization related to dogs should involve toys, games, walks, and similar things, not food. Owners who don't allow food to become an issue for their dogs have a much easier time feeding them and can better regulate food intake.

You can avoid creating a picky eater if you begin by feeding your puppy the right way. A larger dog is usually fed one dry food, perhaps in tandem with one canned food, every day. But little dogs are usually fed a wide variety of different things. There's no reason for this. Your Toy will do fine on one food, only changing from that company's growth formula to its adult formula.

Feed a complete and balanced food developed by a reputable company. Hopefully, the breeder has been using one and has sent the puppy home with some of it. If so, stick with that food until you have a reason to change the dog's diet. For example, if the puppy isn't

gaining weight or has lost weight, it could be because he's not eating enough. Find out if he's sick before you make any changes in his diet, though. Changing the flavor within a brand of food will perk up the appetite, but it might also create a picky eater.

Some smaller dogs will develop a more selective approach to food, particularly an older Toy who has been given a reasonable amount of variety in the past. If you have acquired an older, already picky dog, try to find one or two foods the dog will eat and stick with those. But remember that if a dog doesn't eat one food and you quickly give him another, he'll rapidly become more and more fussy about what he will and won't eat.

Sometimes lack of appetite is mistakenly attributed to boredom with the same food. If a dog is eating less or seems to lack enthusiasm at mealtimes, he may simply not be hungry. The feeding guidelines on the back of the bag of food are required to be there by law, but they should only be a starting point. Food amounts can be adjusted up or down, depending on the energy requirements and activity level of each individual dog. Your dog's weight and body condition will be your best guide when making those adjustments.

A finicky dog may just want attention, in which case you could take him for a walk or play with him. Or he may not be feeling well. If he doesn't eat for one or two days, a trip to the veterinarian is in order. If all these possibilities have been eliminated, try another flavor of the same brand of dog food. Palatability probably depends on the individual dog. A commercial diet will come in a flavor your small dog will eat.

Avoid adding bits of table food to the dog's dish. Many people, breeders included, like to add a little rice, potato, vegetable, meat, or egg. All they're doing is unbalancing the dog food they've paid for, creating a potential for obesity and encouraging the dog to be picky.

Another consideration: When there's more than one dog in the house, there's a bit of competition for the food. You'll be amazed at how quickly finicky dogs will eat what's in their dish when they have some competition for it.

How Many Meals?

Puppyhood is the time to put a dog on a regular feeding schedule. All dogs appreciate consistency in their lives, and a feeding schedule will also help with housetraining.

Offer the puppy food four times a day. His full day's ration should be divided into four equal meals. Announce the meal using one word, preferably the one the breeder has been

using. Put the food down for ten minutes and then pick up the dish whether or not puppy has finished, or eaten at all. This will teach him to understand the schedule. Wait until the next scheduled mealtime to feed the puppy, as long as he doesn't become hypoglycemic. (If he does, put sugar water or Karo Syrup on his gums and feed him as soon as he revives.) Puppies tend to eat for a few minutes, then get bored or distracted. That's probably as long as they would be eating in any case, and there's no need to tempt them to eat more. At 6 months of age the puppy can be fed three times a day. Every puppy and dog should have plenty of fresh water available all day and night.

What about adult dogs? Many Toy dog breeders believe that as adults, these dogs metabolize their food more efficiently when it's divided into two meals. In a 1985 study conducted by Pierre Diamond and others at LaVal University in Quebec, Canada, the researchers fed some dogs four times a day and some dogs just once a day. They found the dogs maintained a better body weight on one meal. The act of eating stimulates the metabolism, so the animals who ate more often actually expended more calories than those who were fed once a day. However, metabolic efficiency is not the only consideration in deciding how often to feed a dog. Because Toys come in smaller packages, their stomachs are smaller and they can't handle a lot of food at one time. They therefore require small portions but more frequent feedings of nutritionally dense food.

Depending on what kind of food is consumed, a dog can completely digest his food in as few as four to six hours or as many as twelve hours or more. A moist diet, such as a good quality, highly digestible canned food, might be completely out of the system within six hours, while a dry food, even a good-quality dry food, takes longer to digest. This can be an asset or a detriment, depending on the animal. In general, the dry food actually enables the animal to more slowly absorb the nutrients and maintain a more stable plane of nutrition over a longer period of time.

As the food is digested, the animal gets a peak of calories and nutrients. The body puts some of those into storage and then, after the digestive phase is completed, the body draws on those stores; it's a cyclical arrangement. Feeding Toy dogs twice a day makes things a little easier, because they don't have to store as much to maintain their needs over a twenty-four-hour period.

Many Toy dogs are susceptible to low blood sugar, and feeding twice a day can also help in that regard. And feeding two, or even three small meals increases the digestibility of the food. Also, if your dog stops eating because he's ill, you'll know a bit sooner.

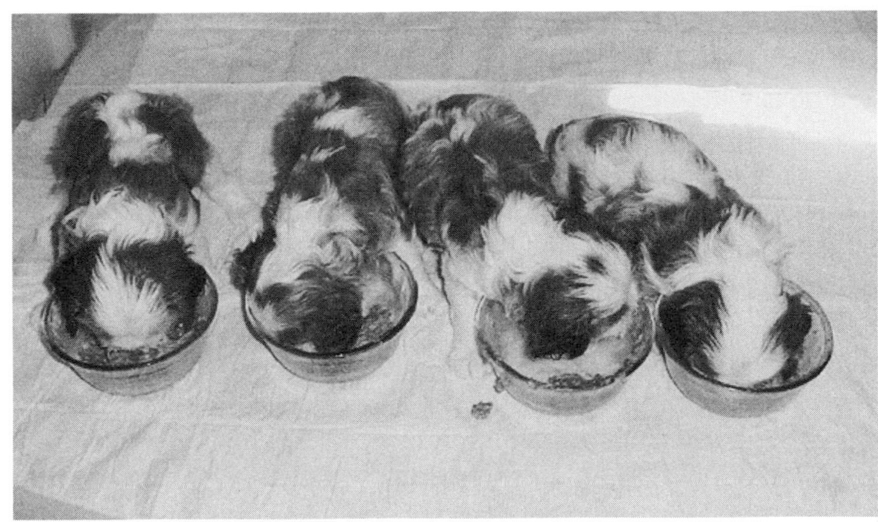

Cavalier King Charles Spaniels

Courtesy of Bressler West ©

Then there's the social factor. There's a tendency to treat Toy dogs like human babies. Owners often feed them more, especially around dinnertime when the little dog sidles up to family members and guests at the table. Feeding your dog at breakfast and dinnertime, when the family is eating, reduces the temptation to slip him treats while you are eating. The dog can have his meal and be taught to stay out of the dining room and not beg for table scraps, especially if you start when he's a puppy. If you're home for three meals a day, you can decide to divide the dog's ration into three meals.

Obesity

Americans overfeed their dogs the same way they overfeed themselves. Consequently, obesity is the number-one health problem in dogs. Many dogs get a lot of calories from foods other than their commercial dog food: They're being fed table scraps, treats, and other things they really don't need from a nutritional perspective. Some Toys, such as Yorkies, have been

seen weighing twenty pounds—when seven pounds or less is their normal weight. These dogs are being loved to death by their owners.

Part of the problem is that owners tend to feed their dogs from the table, and the food tends to be meat scraps and other items that are high in fat. Constant treats continuously pique the appetite, as well, which leads to obesity. Some people see their dog happily wolfing down his dog food and add more to the dish day after day.

Manufacturers put a lot of work into developing the feeding guidelines that appear on dog food packages, but simply following them is not enough. There is data showing that the actual number of calories it takes to maintain an individual dog can vary by up to 25 percent above or below the general calculated requirements. And because those calculations are figured across the average for all dogs of all sizes, an individual small dog may vary from the calculated need by as much as 50 percent. The point is to look at the body condition of your dog. If he's overweight, you must commit to working with your veterinarian or a veterinary nutritionist to develop a safe, healthy weight-loss program.

Treats are often a culprit in obesity. Use them sparingly. If you're training your dog using food rewards, the reward need only be a tiny morsel, and you should count it as part of your dog's daily ration of food. You can also cut up a packaged dog treat into smaller pieces. Don't forget that expecting—but not always getting—a treat is a powerful training tool, so you can let the dog see the treat but not always give it to him. If you watch show dogs in the conformation ring, you'll see their handlers get them to do all kinds of things this way.

Sometimes people use food to keep their dogs quiet. While it's true a dog can't bark when he's eating, excessive barking is more effectively dealt with using obedience training and giving the dog enough attention and exercise. Consider, too, that if you give your dog something to eat when he barks, you are rewarding him for barking and exacerbating the problem. Too much food also leads to numerous health problems.

Weather or Not

Small dogs tend to spend less time outdoors than most larger dogs do, so the question of increasing or decreasing food in hot or cold weather may not come into play for the Toy dog owner. Exercise levels don't change much from season to season for dogs who take much of their exercise indoors.

Even so, the weather does affect the way your dog metabolizes his meals. Dogs actually expend more energy in hot weather. The act of eating makes them feel hot, and it takes more energy to pant in an effort to cool down on a hot day. This can make a dog tired. If your home isn't air conditioned, it helps if the dog can be fed in a cooler environment, such as the basement, on very hot days.

Seasonal shedding will also alter the dog's nutritional requirements. Hair is synthesized from protein, so dogs who are growing in a new coat–often as the weather gets cooler–tend to need more protein in their diet. Most reputable commercial foods will have much more protein than the minimum requirements, anyway, so supplements are not needed.

The Senior Dog

The age at which a dog is considered old depends on the size of the dog. Because small dogs have a longer average life span, they're considered to be seniors much later than large dogs. Generally, small dogs are considered seniors at 12 years of age.

As with humans, a dog's sense of taste diminishes with age. The older the dog becomes, the more he may like stronger flavors–things he can really taste. The metabolism of many older dogs also changes, slowing down as they become less active.

All geriatric dogs should have plenty of fresh water available at all times and should be fed at least twice a day. Food should be left out for twenty to thirty minutes and then picked up. There's nothing wrong with feeding a geriatric dog three times a day. It's important to not overfeed an older dog, but having him on a very regular feeding program is extremely important. That way if the dog isn't eating as much or stops eating, which can be a sign of a health problem, you can recognize it sooner and get him to a veterinarian.

It's usually assumed that the heart and kidneys of most geriatric dogs will be less efficient, and they'll need a diet that's lower in fat, protein, and salt and higher in fiber. However, not all geriatric dogs fit that profile. In other words, not all senior dogs need a senior diet. Only change your dog's diet based on his actual condition, as confirmed by your veterinarian.

Sometimes a healthy geriatric dog doesn't eat enough. If that happens, he can be fed a growth diet that is more nutritionally dense to ensure that he's getting adequate nutrition.

Conversely, some dogs eat the same amount of food they've always eaten as they become less active, so they grow fatter as they age. If the problem isn't too extreme, you can try one of the low-cal foods and take your dog for a moderate daily walk, but check with your veterinarian first to make sure the dog is able to begin a mild exercise program. If the dog has become extremely obese, seek veterinary advice. Obesity is a dangerous condition, especially for older dogs.

Special Diets

Dogs fall prey to many of the physical disorders humans do, such as diabetes, kidney disease, and pancreatitis. Nutritional management is important for these conditions, and many special veterinary diets have been developed to deal with them. While these diets may not be as palatable as the typical commercial dog food because they lack fat or salt or some other flavor enhancer, they are nutritionally correct and may be vital to your dog's health.

If a dog hasn't eaten in several days, the veterinarian will probably want to replace some vitamins that can't be stored by the body. Be sure to carefully monitor the weight of your ill Toy dog, because a loss of half a pound can be 7 percent or more of a small dog's total body weight.

Another consideration with an ongoing illness, such as Addison's disease or Cushing's disease, is that food may not taste the same way to the dog as it once did. A new flavor may be enough to tempt his palate and get him eating again.

Chapter 8

The Body Eclectic

Some health problems in small dogs are genetic, some relate to their size, and some occur because little dogs tend to live longer than other breeds and geriatric problems therefore appear more frequently.

One of the challenges of veterinary medicine is that there's so much variation from patient to patient that common guidelines are not always applicable. In addition, everything must be adjusted to the Toys' smaller size. For example, they require fractional doses of medications in proportion to their body weight. And sometimes all bets are off, even with fractional doses.

Any illness must be attended to immediately, because little dogs go downhill amazingly fast. Diarrhea for two days in a Toy can be much more critical than in a larger dog, because their fluid balance is more sensitive and they can dehydrate more quickly than their larger counterparts. You must be extremely observant, watching a small dog as you would a baby.

Small dogs, for example, are particularly sensitive to high or low temperatures. All dogs should be watched in extreme temperatures. Leaving a dog in a car on a cold day can kill her just as surely as it can on a hot day.

The brachycephalic breeds (those with flat faces, such as the Pekingese, English Toy Spaniel, and Pug) will suffer terribly in the heat; they can't be taken outside for very long

periods in warm weather and are better off in an air-conditioned home. During the summer months, it's wise to touch the pavement before allowing your dog to walk on it. The general rule is that if it's too hot for your hand, it will be too hot for the pads of your dog's feet; they can burn, and tar can melt and stick to her paws. Petroleum jelly will help get the tar off her pads, but you'll also need a trip to the veterinarian. Better to prevent the problem from occurring. If your dog is hairless, she will need sunscreen. Hairless breeds will sunburn just the way you would, and it certainly must be as painful for the dog as it would be for you.

Those with very short coats, such as the Italian Greyhound and the smooth-coat Chihuahua, will suffer from the cold and must be kept warm. After walking a dog in the winter, always clean her feet with an absorbent towel to remove any salt that might have been on the ground, because it's toxic if licked off the paws. And if you've trimmed the hair off your long-haired small dog, you've taken away some of her natural protection, so you'll have to make sure she wears a snugly fitting sweater or coat in winter and is protected from the sun and heat in summer.

It's important to know that a dog's normal body temperature ranges from 99.5 to 102.5 degrees Fahrenheit, with an average temperature of 101.5 degrees. If your dog's temperature rises above 103 degrees, unless she's excited, that's considered a fever.

Many of the diseases in dogs today have a genetic component. It is the responsibility of every ethical breeder to screen their dogs for genetic defects before breeding, and the potential puppy buyer should be shown the clearance certificates. The buyer also has every right to ask for, and expect to be given, a health guarantee to a reasonable age.

Not every canine health problem is mentioned in this section—that would be a book unto itself. You will, however, find the most common or some newly emerging problems seen in small dogs. There are veterinary specialists in virtually every field, just as there are in human medicine. If your dog has a serious problem, ask your veterinarian for a referral.

Cardiology

Heart disease is more common in large dogs than in small ones. But chronic valvular heart disease and congenital heart disease do occur in Toys to a recognizable degree.

Chronic Valvular Heart Disease

Chronic valvular heart disease, also commonly called mitral valve disease, is similar, if not identical, to mitral valve prolapse in people. A chronic degenerative change causes the valve between the upper and lower chambers on the left side of the heart (the mitral valve) to fail. Other valves can fail, but mitral failure is the most common type.

The disease begins in some dogs as early as 3 to 5 years old and now has a high incidence among Cavalier King Charles Spaniels, some of whom are stricken by age two. In older dogs, the disease is first detected as a heart murmur at about 7 to 10 years.

In some dogs, mitral valve disease rarely causes a problem other than a heart murmur and worry for the owners. In others, it clearly causes more severe changes. The most common sign is a dry cough, as the body tries to rid itself of excess fluid. In severe cases, this fluid can build up in the lungs and cause labored or rapid breathing.

As they get older, affected dogs develop scar tissue around the mitral valve. This can put an extra strain on the heart, which can predispose them to heart failure. Depending upon the severity, heart failure can be gradual or fairly quick. On occasion, the supporting structures of the valves that attach to the muscle in the heart will rupture, damaged by the same degenerative changes as the valve tissue. When this happens in humans, emergency valve replacement surgery is performed to save the person's life. Artificial heart valves have been used experimentally by veterinarians as well, but their use is not common or widespread. Many dogs simply cannot be saved.

Occasionally, the left atrium (the upper chamber of the heart) wall will become altered in thickness, which can cause marked lethargy or weakness. If the dog gets a little tear in the left atrium, she can bleed into the pericardium, the sac that surrounds the heart. The pressure prevents the heart from working properly and can lead to heart failure.

Fortunately, for the majority of dogs chronic valvular heart disease is very treatable. Treatment begins with an evaluation. The heart murmur is not the best diagnostic tool; dogs can have very loud murmurs and very mild disease or very soft murmurs and very severe disease. Certain little clues tell a veterinarian that the heart may be enlarged, but X-rays or an echocardiogram are needed to determine the severity of the disease.

The majority of veterinarians have seen dogs with very mild disease remain stable for years. They usually prefer not to put such dogs on medication, because it has never been proven that starting medication the first time they hear the murmur is actually going to prolong a dog's life.

In the more advanced stages of the disease, studies have shown that some medications do prolong life. ACE inhibitors were part of a large study in which a number of veterinary cardiologists participated. One of them was Dr. Neil Harpster, director of cardiology at Angell Animal Medical Center in Boston, who was impressed by how well this drug performed, compared with the medications veterinarians had been using. ACE inhibitors, developed to treat hypertension in humans, lower blood pressure and decrease the workload on the heart. Some studies have shown the drug is helpful for human heart failure patients, and those results have now been extended to dogs.

ACE inhibitors are the first line of defense. As the disease progresses, and if some degree of heart failure has occurred, the majority of dogs will also be on furosemide, a diuretic. Harpster also puts the majority of dogs with heart failure on digitalis, or digoxin, which tends to strengthen the heartbeat. Too much digitalis can have significant side effects, but at the proper dose it's a very effective drug and, in the long run, contributes significantly to long-term survival.

A dog with some heart failure should be on a low-salt diet. That, along with diuretics, will control the fluid load and lessen the strain on the heart. There's a toll paid for high doses of diuretics, however, mostly in electrolyte imbalance and loss of potassium, sodium, and other minerals, so the smallest possible dose is advised.

Chronic valvular heart disease is genetic. Some Toy breeds have a higher incidence than others, but in general, it's fairly common in all the Toy and miniature breeds and less common in large dogs. It is difficult to eliminate from breeding lines because the onset of the disease often occurs after the dogs have been used for breeding and have already passed along their genes to the next generation. The best hope is to eventually identify the gene marker that indicates the disease, so that young dogs can be genetically tested and, if necessary, eliminated from a breeding program.

Congenital Heart Disease

Congenital heart disease is present at birth. Occasionally, small dogs are seen with patent ductus arteriosis (PDA), which is a congenital shunt (an abnormal connection) between the main artery leaving the heart (the aorta) and the pulmonary artery, which leads to the lungs. This shunt functions normally in the fetus, diverting blood from the lungs, but is supposed to

close at birth. When it doesn't, double and triple loads of blood are delivered to one side of the heart, eventually causing heart failure.

PDA is one of the few congenital cardiac defects that can be surgically corrected, if it's diagnosed before there is irreversible heart damage. It should be discovered while the puppy is still with the breeder, usually at the time of the first puppy shots.

If it's detected early and treated, the dog should have a normal life expectancy. If it's not, surgery and stabilizing medication can still buy the dog several years of life. PDA has been seen in Chihuahuas and Poodles.

A few breeds of Toy dogs have been seen with pulmonic stenosis, which is an obstruction of blood flowing out from the right ventricle. It may involve the heart valve or it may involve the little band below the valve, a condition called subvalvular pulmonic stenosis. Pulmonic stenosis should be diagnosed at the time of the first vaccinations. It has been seen in Pekingese.

The best correction is probably surgery. Balloon dilation, called angioplasty, has been used, but with less satisfactory results. Successful surgery results in a normal life expectancy.

Heartworm Disease

Wherever there are mosquitoes, there is the potential for heartworm disease. The disease is more prevalent in warmer climates, where the mosquito season is longer. Heartworms are parasites that spend a portion of their lifecycle within the mosquito. Their larvae are transferred to a dog's bloodstream when she's bitten. These heartworm larvae are carried in the bloodstream to the heart, where they mature into adult worms. The ensuing complications are complex and deadly.

Treating the infestation is far more expensive and dangerous than the preventive treatment, so puppies are routinely started on heartworm medication. There are daily and monthly preventive medications, and the monthly medications are currently more prevalent.

Intravenous injections of arsenic compounds have long been the recommended treatment for heartworm disease, and an intramuscular injectable form of the compound has come into use. It tends to kill the worms slowly, causing far fewer complications from the treatment. However, the treatment is still risky and prevention is strongly advised. While Toy dogs may spend less time outdoors, a mosquito can still slip through the window screen and leave its deadly parasites behind.

Gastroenterology

For most gastrointestinal diseases, Miniature and Toy breeds have the same degree of susceptibility as other dogs. However, common gastrointestinal upsets seem to crop up more often in smaller dogs, perhaps because a few table scraps can represent a fair-sized portion of the day's food for a little dog.

There are also a few more serious problems that are seen in Toy breeds.

Antropyloric Mucosal Hypertrophy

Also called antral hypertrophy, this disorder affects Oriental breeds such as Pekingese, Lhasa Apso, and Shih Tzu, and also occasionally occurs in Chihuahuas, Dachshunds, and Boston Terriers. The lining of part of the stomach grows abnormally, blocking the exit of food from the stomach to the small intestine. The blockage causes chronic vomiting and weight loss. Dogs may continue to vomit as many as ten to sixteen hours after eating, and may also appear bloated after a meal.

Gastritis and Ulcers

Helicobacter gastritis is an inflammation of the intestinal lining caused by the same organisms that cause ulcers in people. These organisms have been identified in the stomachs of dogs and cats—in some surveys in 60 to 100 percent of the animals examined.

Ulcers and chronic gastritis are sometimes seen in dogs and cats. If diagnosed early, they respond well to antibiotics. There's nothing definitive yet on the extent to which Toy dogs are affected, but it is an emerging problem.

Inflammatory Bowel Disease

This is a common cause of vomiting and diarrhea in dogs. It's a poorly understood disorder in which there is a presumed sensitivity to some type of protein. The body has an immune reaction to the protein, which, among other consequences, inflames the little projections called villi in the small intestine that aid in nutrient absorption. Nutrients can't be absorbed

and chronic diarrhea often results. The inflammation may also fool the body into thinking it needs to rid itself of food, triggering excessive vomiting.

Lymph Disease

The lymphatic system filters and removes debris from the body. Small circular glands called lymph nodes are connected by a series of vessels called lymphatics. The liquid they carry is called lymph. The lymph is carried to the dog's chest, where the cellular wastes and foreign materials it gathered enter the bloodstream for excretion.

Lymphangiectasia is a disease in which the lymph that carries material away from the intestines is obstructed. As a result, the small hairlike structures (called villi) that line the intestines and aid in nutrient absorption become dilated. An afflicted dog will not be able to absorb enough protein, will have chronic diarrhea, and may collect fluid in the abdomen.

The cause of this disease is not really known. It occurs in many breeds, but most often in Yorkshire Terriers.

Portosystemic Shunt

Yorkies are also predisposed to portosystemic shunt, more commonly called liver shunt, and it is the most common liver problem seen in young puppies. Normally, blood flows from the intestines to the liver, where the by-products of digestion are metabolized. But when there is a shunt, blood bypasses the liver, with disastrous and often fatal consequences.

Symptoms can be dramatic, including stunted growth, persistent vomiting and diarrhea, weight loss, and seizures. But they can also be subtle—increased urination, thirst, and salivation. Sometimes the first sign will be a urinary tract obstruction, because minerals in the bloodstream are not being metabolized and therefore can form urate calculi (small stones).

Detecting a shunt is not easy. Veterinarians have a saying, "To diagnose a disease, you have to think of it." Veterinarians in general practice who are unaccustomed to seeing the more unusual diseases may not be thinking about the uncommon diagnoses. If a dog has both excessive thirst and excessive urination, what looks like diabetes could, in fact, be a liver shunt.

Liver shunts are operable, but not always successfully. The errant blood vessels may be inside or outside of the liver, and the ones inside the liver are much more difficult to repair.

Pyloric Hypertrophy

Most brachycephalic breeds, especially the Boston Terrier and including the French Bulldog, have a propensity to develop this disorder. The pyloric sphincter is the muscular valve that separates the stomach from the small intestine, and when it gets very thick, the stomach can't empty very well.

This condition is similar to antral hypertrophy, and symptoms are also similar. If you see a Boston Terrier vomiting long after a meal, these two diseases should come to mind first.

Geriatrics

Aging is a progressive, irreversible change that goes on over time. Since Toys tend to live longer, that process is drawn out more slowly for them. It's not unusual now to see Toys from 20 to 26 years old. Small dogs become geriatric at around 12 years of age, a time when many giant breeds have come to the end of their lives.

According to one geriatric specialist, the number-one cause of death in geriatric Toys is cancer, followed by heart failure, kidney failure, liver failure, and gastrointestinal tract failure.

Veterinarians should carefully examine geriatric Toys for evidence of cancer. Laboratory screening should be done to evaluate kidney and liver function, and the chest should be listened to very closely for heart murmurs. Additional testing should be done to evaluate the heart if there's any question about heart function, because left heart failure is fairly common in older dogs.

As long as the dog is doing well, maintaining her weight, and is happy and seemingly very healthy, geriatric blood screening should be started when a Toy is 9 years old. This routine blood screen is invaluable for spotting organ problems because it gives a veterinarian a sense of what is normal for the individual dog and makes any abnormality easier to spot. The veterinarian should monitor trends in blood test values, rather than focusing on the results of a single test.

Signs of Illness

In fact, you should take your senior dog to the veterinarian twice a year. That way, if any disease process is starting, it can be caught and treated more quickly. Anything else would be "penny wise and pound foolish." Your veterinarian can do a complete geriatric exam to get baseline values, which will make it easier to spot any differences as time passes.

The geriatric Toy, like all older dogs, should be monitored for signs of illness. One of the most sensitive indicators that a geriatric dog isn't doing well is weight loss. This is almost always followed by breathing problems, or vomiting and diarrhea.

Toys tend to have trouble with their teeth (see chapter 9) and need regular periodontal disease management. If periodontal disease can be controlled, in some cases treating it can also slow the progression of kidney, liver, or gastrointestinal problems.

Sleeping more or grumpiness when getting off a favorite pillow or blanket are often observed in older dogs, but that's not necessarily a consequence of age; it can also be a sign of disease, such as arthritis, liver trouble, or an undetected cancer. It is not acceptable for a dog to be very lethargic just because she's old; there is usually an underlying reason for the inactivity.

Vaccinations

Geriatric specialist Dr. Johnny Hoskins does not recommend vaccinations for dogs older than 15. Given what we know about the immune system and vaccinations, he does not believe it is necessary. In areas where an annual rabies vaccine is required, he believes that veterinarians can work with local health officials. He suggests the veterinarian write a letter saying that because of the age of the animal and the controlled environment where the dog is kept, the exposure rate and risk are nil, and the vaccine is not recommended. The veterinarian should then sign and date the letter.

Internal Medicine

Because they're small, Toys will come down with a lot of syndromes more often seen in humans. The conditions listed here involve the various glands of the body; when the production of hormones is out of balance, a wide variety of disease can result.

Addison's Disease

Addison's disease occurs when the adrenal glands fail to produce enough cortisol, a natural steroid hormone. Cortisol controls the electrolyte levels in the blood, which maintains metabolism in the body's cells. With a deficiency, the sodium level lowers and the potassium level is raised. Sodium is responsible for maintaining blood volume and blood pressure, so when the sodium level lowers, the dog has very low blood pressure and goes into shock. High potassium causes weakness and also affects the contractility of the heart, predisposing the dog to irregular heartbeat (arrhythmia) and heart attacks. The digestive system is also affected.

Addison's disease usually occurs in young female dogs. It can happen at any age, but usually the diagnosis is made in dogs who are from 1 to 3 years old.

Treatment is very effective; it involves replacing the needed hormones either orally or by injection. There's an excellent long-term prognosis. The treatments are expensive, but Toy dogs need a lot less of the hormone mixture than larger breeds do, so that helps a bit.

Cushing's Disease

Cushing's disease results when the adrenal glands produce too much cortisol. It's the opposite of Addison's disease. It is rare in dogs under 5 years old. In about 80 percent of dogs, the disease is caused by a lesion in the pituitary gland at the base of the brain that overstimulates the adrenals, while in about 20 percent of cases one of the adrenal glands itself will have a tumor that excretes cortisol independent of what else is happening in the body. About half of these tumors are malignant and spread, and about half are benign and generally tend to stay small.

The typical signs of Cushing's disease are increased thirst and urination, panting, hair loss (usually on the trunk), and weakness.

The symptoms of Cushing's disease can also appear if a dog is taking steroids for a medical condition and ends up with too much in her system. Steroids are found in a lot of creams, eye ointments, and ear ointments, and if you get overzealous with their administration, that can cause these signs as well. When you stop using the products, the symptoms will go away.

The benign adrenal tumor is the easiest to treat. It is simply removed surgically. Not surprisingly, the worst form is a malignant adrenal tumor. It almost always ends up being fatal, because it has usually spread by the time it's seen. Surgery isn't going to cure these tumors,

and the effectiveness of medications varies. Animals who are helped by medication must take high doses, and the control is not very good. Eventually, the malignancy spreads and the dog succumbs to the resulting problems and the fact that a large tumor occupies a lot of space in the body, putting pressure on other organs.

The pituitary form of Cushing's disease is typically treated with medicine designed to suppress the secretion of cortisol by the adrenal gland. It has recently been found that 40 to 50 percent of dogs with the pituitary form of the disease actually have a very large tumor on their brain stem. The efficacy of radiation therapy is being evaluated to deal with the tumor.

The prognosis for the pituitary form of Cushing's disease has been studied at both the Animal Medical Center in New York and the University of California-Davis. Both showed an average survival of 1 to 2 years from the time of diagnosis. Since the average age of onset is 10 years, that means afflicted dogs can live to 12, which enters the range of expected canine longevity.

Cushing's disease is common in all breeds of dogs, although Dachshunds, Miniature and Toy Poodles, and Boston Terriers are among those with the highest incidence.

Diabetes

Diabetes mellitus in dogs is very similar to juvenile onset diabetes in people. It occurs when a lesion in the pancreas destroys the ability to secrete insulin, a vital hormone that enables the body to metabolize carbohydrates. High blood sugar results, and when the sugar starts to spill into the urine, clinical signs begin to appear.

Classic signs are an increase in water consumption, urination, and appetite, and weight loss. Left unchecked, diabetes can be fatal. Poor long-term management can also lead to complications such as blindness and loss of limbs.

Diabetes is a disease of older dogs, which is why it shows up more in Toys, since they tend to live longer. The average age at onset is 8 to 10 years, and it's uncommon to see it in dogs under 5.

In certain breeds with a predisposition for the disease, the dogs will have an earlier age of onset, sometimes as early as 4 years old. Among the breeds at high risk for diabetes is the Miniature Pinscher, where researchers suspect there's a genetic component. Poodles are also frequently affected. Miniature Schnauzers also have a higher incidence of diabetes because of their predisposition to pancreatitis.

The prognosis for a diabetic dog depends upon the owner's willingness to manage the disease, how well the dog responds to insulin therapy, and the development and severity of other illnesses. A study presented in 1997 showed that, on average, dogs lived three years from the time of diagnosis.

Treatment involves insulin injections, usually administered twice a day, a regimented high-fiber diet, and regular exercise. There are different types of insulin on the market and each dog requires a different dose, so the therapy has to be adjusted for the individual dog. Smaller dogs tend to require a slightly higher dose per pound of body weight than larger dogs. It's important to try to avoid concurrent diseases and infections, since they can interfere with insulin requirements.

Hypothyroidism

Hypothyroidism is a thyroid deficiency that, in most cases, is due to destruction of the thyroid gland. The thyroid fails to produce sufficient hormones, causing lethargy, weight gain, hair loss, seborrhea, and bacterial infections of the skin. You can also see neurological signs such as weakness, dragging the feet, head tilts, and even seizures.

There are genetic implications with some forms of the disease, so there are definite breed predispositions. The list of breeds that are affected is quite long, and it varies quite a bit from family to family within breeds. Some breeders have been more successful at breeding out this problem than others.

Hypothyroidism usually develops in younger dogs, with the average age of onset around 2 to 5 years. If it occurs in puppies, they fail to grow properly. This very short stature is called cretinism. (A cretin is basically a dwarf.)

Daily treatment with thyroid hormone replacement is very easy and the long-term prognosis is excellent.

Pancreatitis

Pancreatitis is inflammation of the pancreas, an elongated gland that serves many functions in the processes of digestion and metabolism. When digestive enzymes that normally are excreted into the intestinal tract are activated in the pancreas instead, they cause inflammation.

Pancreatitis occurs most often in middle-aged, overweight, female dogs, usually in Toys and other small breeds. There is some evidence that it's genetic in Miniature Schnauzers and Yorkshire Terriers, but that hasn't been absolutely proven. While uncommon, fatal pancreatitis has been seen in 3-month-old pups.

A diet that's high in fat or that includes a lot of greasy table scraps tends to trigger pancreatitis.

This is a serious, potentially life-threatening disease. Mortality is upward of 20 to 25 percent. Affected animals will have severe abdominal pain, loss of appetite, lethargy, depression, vomiting, and diarrhea. Dehydration is also a danger.

There are two forms of pancreatitis. Acute pancreatitis can be instantly fatal, with death resulting within twelve to twenty-four hours. The other form is chronic pancreatitis. If you can get the dog back on her feet and eating normally, she can still suffer from recurrent but occasional inflammations, so she's in and out of the disease and in and out of the hospital. Long-term chronic pancreatitis can lead to diabetes or a total loss of digestive enzymes, in which case the dog can't absorb food anymore and gets pancreatic exocrine insufficiency. That results in diarrhea and emaciation, because the dog can't digest and absorb nutrients.

In general, it's very difficult to distinguish between pancreatic disease and gastrointestinal disease. There are no definitive tests for either. There is increasing awareness that traditional blood enzyme tests used to diagnose pancreatitis are limited in their scope. So when you've got an animal with suspected pancreatitis or suspected chronic gastrointestinal disease, your veterinarian should think about doing Serum TLI, Cabolamin, and Folate tests. These tests are not perfect, but they're significant, and any veterinarian anywhere can send blood off for those analyses.

The better diagnosis results from a combination of the lab tests that are now available, plus ultrasound, which is slowly becoming an important diagnostic aid. There are now better tests to distinguish between chronic intestinal disease and pancreatic disease, which clinically look the same and can be easily confused. That's why it's important to do the lab tests *and* the ultrasound for a precise diagnosis.

Treatment of pancreatitis depends on the severity of the signs. In all cases, food is withheld so the enzyme-producing cells in the pancreas remain unstimulated. At worst, the dog may be in the hospital for one or two weeks on intravenous fluids and possibly antibiotics.

The dog may need blood transfusions and intravenous feeding, and plasma is very important in keeping her alive. While plasma is expensive, only a small amount is needed for a small dog. In the past, some animals would suddenly die in their hospital pens of acute pancreatitis; plasma seems to be a major lifesaver.

Treatment includes a low-fat diet, a weight-reduction plan, and sometimes oral pancreatic enzymes, which may allow the pancreas to rest and reduce the discomfort. Pain medication may also be given. Enzyme therapy has been controversial in both people and dogs, because it has not been clinically tested. But there is a lot of anecdotal evidence that it may reduce the discomfort. It's very safe, so there's no reason not to try it.

Diet is the key—it must consist of foods that are highly digestible, very low in fat, and be fed in small, frequent meals. Some dogs have lived five to ten years following a diagnosis of pancreatitis.

Neurology

If things go awry in your little dog's nervous system, the results can be devastating. Here are some of the neurological problems found in little dogs.

Encephalitis

Encephalitis is an inflammation of the brain. There is a moderately rare form called Pug encephalitis, and Maltese have now been identified as having a very similar disease. Pug and Maltese encephalitides occur in fairly young dogs, on up to age 4 or 5. The onset is very abrupt, with severe brain inflammation and rapid destruction of brain cells.

It is not known what causes these particular types of encephalitis, so there is no effective treatment. Initial treatment with extremely high doses of steroids can sometimes reverse the signs and get the dog back to normal, but high doses compromise the dog's immune system and can't be given for long.

Fortunately, this disease is very rare. There's probably a genetic factor that makes these breeds more susceptible.

Epilepsy

Epilepsy is a common disease; all breeds of dogs may develop seizures of unknown cause. There are probably twenty or thirty different types of epilepsy, and probably that many different defects of the brain, but they all express themselves as seizures. Normally, the neurons of the brain transmit impulses in a coordinated fashion, allowing controlled behavior and movements. But during a seizure the neurons fire at random and the body and mind are out of control.

While some seizures may be the result of trauma or disease, most are thought to stem from an inherited condition. Fortunately, epilepsy in most Toy breeds is relatively easy to control. Why epilepsy is easier to control in Toys is unknown, but it's presumed that they're inheriting a different type of epilepsy.

Epilepsy is more common in male dogs, and the average age of onset is between 1 and 5 years.

Granulomatous Meningoencephalitis

This condition, abbreviated GME, is somewhat similar to Pug encephalitis but offers a more hopeful prognosis. A rare autoimmune disease affecting Toy breeds, it's also seen in all the Poodle varieties. GME attacks the brain or spinal cord, eventually destroying it. The dog can have a variety of symptoms, although often the first sign is an abrupt loss of balance and frequent falling.

Unlike dogs with Pug encephalitis, dogs with GME generally respond well to immune suppressive therapy. High doses of steroids are given to start, and then are gradually reduced over about four months. About 75 to 80 percent of dogs end up in permanent remission. If the dog goes into remission, her life span can be quite normal.

Hepatic Encephalopathy

Hepatic encephalopathy begins as a liver disorder but ends up with neurological consequences. It occurs when the dog has an abnormal blood supply to her liver at birth and the liver never forms properly. Toxins build up in the blood that mainly affect the brain, and a neurological specialist will generally be the one to treat the disease.

Any breed of dog can have this disorder, but it's most often seen in Toys. Maltese and Yorkshire Terriers are the breeds more commonly affected.

Hydrocephalus

Hydrocephalus is a condition in which the fluid-filled spaces around the brain, called ventricles, contain too much fluid. This is a common condition in most Toy breeds. For example, there are almost no Chihuahuas who aren't hydrocephalic to some degree, because Chihuahuas generally have larger ventricular spaces in their brain. Maltese, Yorkshire Terriers, and Pomeranians also have a very high incidence of hydrocephalus. Most mildly hydrocephalic dogs have no problem. If the condition is serious, pressure on the brain damages brain tissue, leading to blindness, seizures, and, eventually, death.

This condition is definitely inherited, and affected dogs should never be bred. In breeds in which a mild form of the condition is accepted as normal, dogs who show any signs of illness, including epilepsy or other neurological problems, should not be bred.

White Dog Shaker Syndrome

This disease got its name because the first dogs identified with it were small white breeds—the Maltese was one. It affects Toys more often than other breeds.

The condition is probably a form of GME; treatments and outcomes are similar. It affects the part of the brain called the cerebellum, which coordinates muscle movement. Sudden trembling is the main symptom. The dog won't shake when she's sleeping, but the more she tries to move, the worse the tremor gets.

Initially, a dog with white dog shaker syndrome might be mistaken for a nervous little dog, because in the mild form it does resemble the nervous shaking often seen in Toys. A small dog with a tremor that began suddenly and seems to get worse should be seen by a neurologist.

Narcolepsy

Narcolepsy isn't unique to Toys, but Poodles (of all sizes) are one breed known to inherit it. Affected dogs tend to fall asleep abruptly while walking around, particularly when they're excited. Food almost always stimulates the condition in affected dogs—at the sight of food they will fall asleep at the bowl.

Certain medications will make the attacks much less common.

Occipital Dysplasia

Occipital dysplasia, seen in Chihuahuas, Pekingese, Pomeranians, and several other Toy breeds, is an opening at the back of the skull. By itself it doesn't cause a problem, and on skull X-rays many dogs are shown to have it. A small hole won't allow the brain to shift or be damaged. If the hole is large, or if the dog has significant hydrocephalus and occipital dysplasia, however, there can be serious problems.

One unusual sign of occipital dysplasia is that an affected dog will lower her front end to the ground and walk backwards. There's probably some type of discomfort when the brain presses against the hole in the skull and down on the spinal cord, and that posture may be an attempt to relieve the pressure.

Occipital dysplasia generally can be managed. The veterinarian treats the underlying problem that's causing the brain to shift. For example, if the problem is hydrocephalus, the vet will treat that by surgically shunting the fluid or using low doses of steroids to temporarily decrease fluid production.

Storage Diseases

Storage diseases are a group of very rare degenerative disorders. There are probably about twenty storage disorders and all are inherited. In most cases, they're caused by an autosomal recessive gene (both parents must carry the defective gene) that results in the absence of a specific lysosomal enzyme. This leads to excess accumulation (storage) of unusable material within the cells of the nervous system, causing gradual, progressive neurological degeneration. There are no effective treatments and symptoms can be quite varied, depending on the specific disorder.

Oncology

The same cancers seen in large dogs are seen in small breeds. There's no one type of tumor that is more common in Toys, but remember that cancer is often a geriatric disease and Toys are long-lived.

Oncologists see about forty to fifty types of tumors that are relatively common. Some are malignant, but when they're removed or successfully treated, the dog lives a long and

healthy life. Others are malignant or inoperable and cannot be removed. Dogs may receive chemotherapy or radiation, with varying degrees of effectiveness.

There are also little benign tumors that appear as lumps and bumps on the skin. There are about twenty or thirty different types of skin tumors that are relatively harmless. But only a biopsy (looking at a small piece of the tumor under a microscope) can tell the difference. If you see a lump on your dog, remember that masses usually don't go away, they only get bigger. Have the dog seen by a veterinarian as soon as possible.

When tumors are diagnosed, there are a lot of treatment options. Veterinarians usually worry most about quality of life. Some dogs live an average of one to two years after they've been diagnosed with cancer. Others go downhill rapidly, presenting some hard choices for their owners.

While owners and breeders say they see more cancer now than they did before, that's doubtful. It's more likely veterinarians today are better able to recognize, diagnose, and treat various cancers. Today, more dogs survive and the perspective is changing.

There are currently three treatment options for cancer. Surgery uses a scalpel to cut out the tumor. It's very effective for tumors that are localized and easy to remove without affecting vital organs.

The second option, radiation, uses a machine that delivers a beam of radiation that kills the cancer cells. The radiation is delivered in small doses to minimize the adverse effects to normal tissue. In typical radiation therapy, dogs are treated Monday through Friday for three to four weeks. This requires general anesthesia, because the beam has to be put in the exact same spot each time and the dog can't be kept still long enough. The treatment itself takes only five to ten minutes.

With chemotherapy, the third option, various drugs are given either orally or by injection. Sometimes drugs that will kill rapidly dividing tissues, including cancer cells, are injected directly into the tumor. Typical doses will spare the normal cells but kill the cancer. Depending upon the type of tumor being treated, chemotherapy is sometimes used for the dog's entire lifetime. Other times it is discontinued after a course of treatment lasting perhaps three or four months. Dogs generally do not experience the same severe side effects from chemotherapy that humans do.

Different states have different regulations about who may administer chemotherapy to animals. Some states may allow the owner to do it while wearing gloves; the drugs must then be sold with a sticker stating that gloves must be worn. At issue is the risk of handling these powerful drugs. It has yet to be proven conclusively that handling chemotherapy drugs puts you at risk for any disease, but it does require both care and common sense.

Hemangiopericytoma

Hemangiopericytoma is a malignant tumor. It's a soft, almost rubbery growth, typically in the legs, although these tumors also turn up in the chest wall and the abdominal wall. They're tumors that don't spread but are very damaging locally. They wrap around the nerves, blood vessels, and tendons, making surgical removal difficult. These tumors must be treated aggressively with surgery and radiation.

Lymphosarcoma

Lymphosarcoma is cancer of the lymphatic system. The lymph glands will become swollen and big lumps and bumps will appear on the body. The internal organs also become enlarged, giving the dog a swollen abdomen.

Lymphosarcoma spreads rapidly. If left untreated, typically within three to five weeks the dog is in a condition that requires euthanasia.

Mammary Tumors

Mammary tumors occur almost exclusively in unspayed female dogs. Little nodules or sores are seen along the mammary glands.

The first rise in estrogen in the body increases susceptibility to the disease. Therefore, if the female is spayed before her first heat, the probability of her getting mammary tumors is close to zero. If she's spayed after the second heat, her chances of developing them are two-thirds less than those of an intact female. Spaying later in life still reduces the risk somewhat.

Mast Cell Tumors

Mast cell tumors are seen in such small breeds as French Bulldogs, Boston Terriers, and Pugs. They are also fairly common in the other brachycephalic breeds and in many older dogs.

These tumors usually appear on the outer surface of the skin, and surgical removal is the first line of therapy. Depending upon the malignancy, surgery may be all that's needed. Some tumors may also require chemotherapy or radiation, as they tend to spread.

Testicular Tumors

Testicular tumors are very common in older intact dogs, but fortunately, most of them are benign. The best way to avoid them is to neuter all pet dogs when they're young. When the testicles are removed, there is no chance of developing testicular tumors.

Ophthalmology

When it comes to the eyes, purebred dogs have it hard. Many breeds and lines have a genetic tendency to develop eye disease. And many of the physical features people like in purebred dogs end up adversely affecting their eyes. Breeders can breed away from lines with health problems. But breeding away from physical features that are characteristic of a breed, such as prominent nasal folds, is not as easy, if this is the style required for the show ring.

Cataracts

A cataract is an opacity of the lens of the eye or its capsule. It is an inherited disease, and the age of onset varies, although cataracts are more commonly associated with older animals.

If the retinas are normal, then when cataracts progress to the point where the dog is blind, they should be surgically removed. The prognosis is good.

A diabetic dog may develop diabetic cataracts. The treatment is the same.

Cataracts are a problem in most purebred dogs. Especially susceptible breeds include the Cavalier King Charles Spaniel, Toy Poodle, Papillon, and Yorkie.

Conjunctivitis

An inflammation of the lining of the eyelid, conjunctivitis is fairly common in the heavily coated Toys, probably aggravated by the amount of hair they have around the eyes. It can be caused by chemicals such as grooming talcum powder, soap, dust, and aerosols. It's important to protect the eyes of your little companions when they're being groomed.

Conjunctivitis can also be bacterial, or it can be triggered by an allergic reaction. Occasionally, there are some viruses that cause it. The treatment depends on the cause.

Conjunctivitis is very contagious and a dog can be reinfected, so precautions must be taken. All grooming tools should be thoroughly cleaned.

Corneal Ulcers

Corneal ulcers occur in dogs of all ages when the top layer of the cornea is missing, either as a result of a bacterial infection or because it's been abraded off.

Breeds with prominent, bulging eyes, such as Pugs, Shih Tzu, and Chihuahuas, are at greater risk of developing these ulcers, and the ulcers tend to be more serious. It is thought that these breeds have diminished sensation across the center of their cornea. Consequently, they may not blink as often or as quickly if something touches the cornea. They also may not protect the cornea as well with their tears.

These dogs must be treated more aggressively for corneal ulcers, often with surgery, because they are more prone to corneal perforation once the corneas are exposed. The prognosis depends on how bad the ulcers are. If they are superficial, the prognosis is quite good; if they are perforating ulcers, blindness is likely.

Dry Eye

Dry eye, in which the tear glands don't produce enough watery tears, is common in small dogs. If left untreated, chronic eye infections and corneal ulcers result. The age of onset varies, but it is more common in older dogs.

A tear stimulant, cyclosporin, is the treatment of choice. In dogs who respond to the drug, tear production increases dramatically. Dogs can stay on the drug for years with no discernible side effects. Before 1987, when cyclosporin was introduced, owners had to put artificial tears into their dogs' eyes several times a day.

Certain breeds, including Lhasa Apsos, are predisposed to dry eye.

Veterinarians also see changes in the cornea called pigmentary keratitis, which are sometimes associated with dry eye. With this condition, a growth of blood vessels and/or pigment covers the surface of the eye. This is the end result of unchecked irritation, such as is found in dry eye.

Probably because their eyes are so exposed, the small breed dogs are more likely to have this condition. It is especially common in Pekingese, in which the hair of the nasal skin folds rubs on the surface of the eye. Pugs are also very susceptible.

When the primary cause of the irritation is treated, the cornea often clears. When the condition is serious, the pigmented membrane may have to be removed surgically.

Dystrophy of the Cornea

Dystrophy of the cornea, a degenerative weakness, can occur in the top layer of the cornea (the epithelium), the middle layer (the stroma), or the deep layer (the endothelium). For example, in Chihuahuas it affects the endothelium; their corneas become very cloudy and opaque as a result. Other breeds, such as Cavalier King Charles Spaniels and English Toy Spaniels, have stromal dystrophy. Epithelial dystrophy isn't seen much in Toys.

There is no effective treatment, but most of the time the condition does not interfere too much with vision.

Entropion

In this condition, the eyelid rolls inward so that the eyelashes rub against the cornea. Corneal abrasions are the result.

The problem is caused by the normal structure of the eye in certain breeds such as Yorkshire Terriers and Toy Poodles, and also in the brachycephalic breeds, such as Pugs and Pekingese. In addition, the hair closest to the eye often wicks the tears away from the eye's surface, leaving it dry and exacerbating the problem. Hair around the eyes should be carefully trimmed away.

Entropion is treated with lubricants and often requires surgery.

Glaucoma

Glaucoma, a group of eye diseases characterized by increased pressure inside the eye that causes changes in the optic disk, has been seen in Japanese Chin and Poodles. The age of onset varies, but it usually appears in adulthood and the prognosis is always guarded. There are several approaches to treating glaucoma, including surgery, all of which have to be individually monitored. Nevertheless, some dogs may go blind from this painful eye condition.

Geriatric Eye Changes

Geriatric eye changes are seen more often in Toys than in larger dogs, probably because Toys live so long. These changes include eyelid tumors, which are easily removed. A progressive clouding of the lens called nuclear sclerosis also comes on with age. There's no treatment. In senile retinal degeneration, the retina, a delicate light-sensitive membrane lining the inner eyeball and connected by the optic nerve to the brain, simply wears out as the dog gets older.

Another condition is asteroid hyalosis, in which the dog sees hundreds of tiny particles floating before him, as if he were in a snowstorm. These particles are actually suspended in the vitreous cavity in the back of the eye, seriously clouding vision.

All of these geriatric changes mean older Toys simply don't see well. It's important to consider this when you're thinking about rearranging the furniture with an old dog in the house.

Lens Luxation

In this condition, the lens in the eye gets freed from its moorings and starts to move around inside the eye. The Terriers, including Toy Terriers such as the Toy Manchester and the Min Pin, are especially prone to lens luxation. The treatment is to remove the lens.

Macroocular Fissure

When the eyelid opening is too large and you see lots of white around the eye, the condition is called macroocular fissure. Common in Pugs, it can lead to dryness, infection, and irritation of the eyes. The lids can be surgically narrowed so that they fit the dog better. Breeders should try to breed away from this inherited feature.

Multiple Ocular Defects

Some abnormalities of the eye as a whole are sometimes seen in Toy breeds. Any of the breeds that have white on their head are prone to multiple ocular defects. This is because the same gene that controls white color is also associated with multiple congenital defects of the eye. Affected breeds include Cavalier King Charles Spaniels, Maltese, and Papillons. The more white in the coat, the more likely they are to have these problems.

One of the problems that shows up is micropthalmia, which means "small eye." In dogs with this condition, the eyes are not well-formed. Micropthalmia can affect one eye or both. It may be a developmental problem that begins during pregnancy. There's no treatment.

Optic Nerve Hypoplasia

Optic nerve hypoplasia is underdevelopment of the optic nerve. Many Toy Poodles are particularly prone to this problem, as are Pekingese. There's no treatment for this birth defect.

Persistent Pupillary Membranes

When a puppy is in the womb, a spider web of tissue covers the pupils of her eyes. At birth this tissue normally disintegrates, leaving the pupil clear. Persistent pupillary membranes are little remnants of tissue that do not break down. These strands can cloud the cornea wherever they touch it.

There is no treatment for this condition. If it is mild, vision is not really affected.

Persistent pupillary membrane is inherited, but it is not known whether a dominant or recessive gene is the culprit.

Progressive Retinal Atrophy

Progressive retinal atrophy (PRA), a blinding disorder, is the most common inherited disease of the retina. In some breeds it appears when the dog is quite young, while other affected dogs appear normal when they're puppies but develop PRA as adults.

In PRA Type I, retinal degeneration is progressive. Night blindness is often the first symptom, progressing over several years to day blindness as well. In Type II, affected dogs lose the ability to see directly ahead of them but retain their peripheral vision. The degeneration stabilizes before complete blindness occurs. There is no treatment for either form of PRA.

PRA is seen in the Toy Poodle, Yorkie, Papillon, and Havanese, among many other breeds. The diagnosis is usually made by indirect ophthalmoscopic examination. Since it is an inherited trait (controlled by an autosomal recessive gene), dogs with PRA should not be bred. A veterinary ophthalmic examination can confirm the presence or absence of this condition even before symptoms are obvious, and many breeders have their dogs certified free

of PRA before breeding. (These certifications are monitored by the Canine Eye Registry Foundation, CERF. Dogs must be recertified every year.)

A genetic marker for PRA has been found for a number of breeds, including the Poodle, so the breeder can also send off a blood sample to determine whether a dog is a PRA carrier.

Retinal Dysplasia

Retinal dysplasia is an inherited birth defect of the retina occasionally seen in Yorkies and Cavaliers, among other breeds. Symptoms can begin at 6 to 8 weeks old. Night blindness is followed by gradual total blindness. There's no treatment.

Trauma

Eye trauma is a particular problem for breeds in which the eyes are prominent, such as Pugs, Brussels Griffons, and Pekes. It doesn't matter whether the injury comes from a branch, a cat scratch, another dog, somebody's foot, or a thrown toy. Chances are that a little dog with big eyes will eventually get hurt. All eye injuries require prompt veterinary attention.

The flatter heads on many Toy breeds mean they don't have deep eye sockets, so the eye is only protected by the eyelid. The fact that Toys don't have bone riding over the front of the eye means any time a little dog–big dog altercation takes place, there's a tendency for the eye to pop forward and the lid to get caught behind it. This is called traumatic proptosis and it is a major problem in small dogs, especially the ones with flat faces.

If the eye does proptose, it's a surgical emergency. The veterinarian must decide whether to replace the eye in the socket and temporarily sew the lid closed or remove the eye. The prognosis for vision is always poor, although sometimes an eye can be saved and look normal, even though the dog will be blind in that eye.

Reproduction

Toys, as a rule, mate normally, so they shouldn't need much assistance in that regard. Still, as with many breeds, there are some dogs who just don't get it. Whether or not to breed them anyway is the subject of some debate. Some fanciers say any dog who lacks the mating

instinct ought not to be bred, while others say there's no reason not to breed physically and mentally sound dogs, even if they need a little help.

Artificial insemination has long been used as an option, either with a fresh sample from a male on hand, or via frozen semen or fresh chilled semen. Frozen semen enables breeders to breed back to an excellent but now deceased dog. Results with frozen semen vary widely, depending upon the dog's fertility and the person who freezes the semen. Chilled fresh semen will stay viable for about six days, but the maximum time for fertility is only about forty-eight hours.

Toys have small litters, which causes two major problems. First, because the puppies don't have many neighbors in the uterus, they tend to grow bigger, making the birthing process difficult. Second, hormones from unborn puppies trigger a mother's labor, and sometimes a small litter will not release enough hormones. This is especially a danger for a singleton pup. You'll see the mother's temperature drop and expect her to deliver, but then nothing happens. A puppy can die this way.

Because of these problems, some Toys will require a caesarian section. The best thing for mother and pups is to anesthetize her without using preanesthetic tranquilizers. The dog should be masked or, if she's very small, the entire dog can be put in an environment in which the anesthesia can be pumped in (such as an empty aquarium tank).

New Toy mothers are especially predisposed to eclampsia, an upset in the calcium regulatory mechanism that leads to low calcium levels in the blood. Severe eclampsia leads to convulsions and death. Breeders must familiarize themselves with the signs and have a veterinarian on board ready to administer intravenous calcium.

Respiratory Diseases

Little dogs face some big problems when it comes to the respiratory system. Collapsing trachea is perhaps the biggest problem they face, and is one of the most common health problems in Toy dogs.

Collapsing Trachea

The trachea is a long tube that carries air from the neck to the chest. It is reinforced with rings of cartilage that help keep it rigid as air moves in and out of the tube. When the cartilage weakens, the trachea may collapse while the dog is breathing.

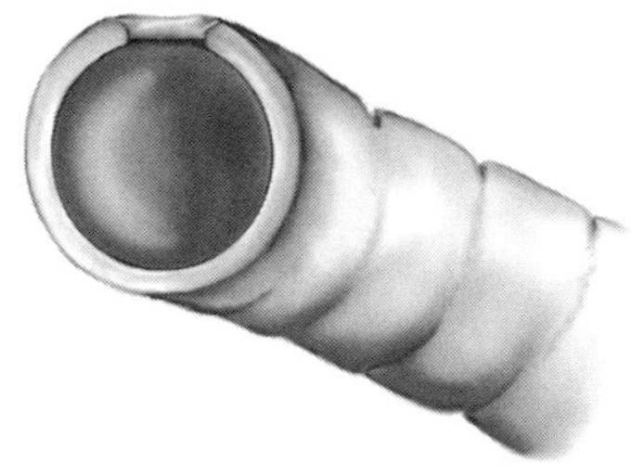

Normal Trachea

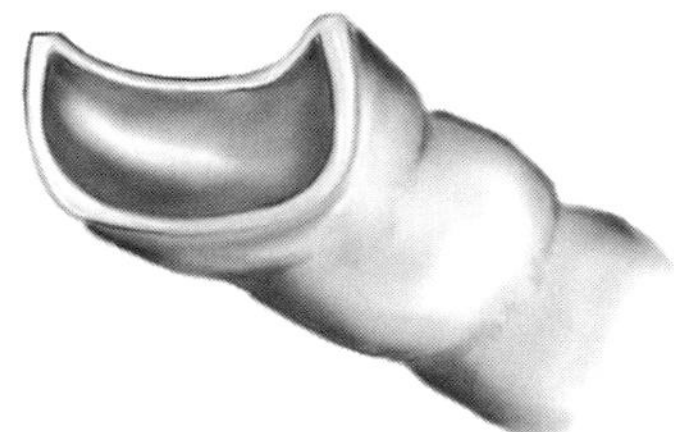

Collapsing Trachea

Collapsing trachea is a problem in Toys. It has always been a problem for the Toy Poodle, Maltese, Pomeranian, Chihuahua, Italian Greyhound, and Yorkie. It's seen from line to line and is passed from generation to generation. While the exact mechanism of genetic transmission is not yet known, there is no doubt that it's inherited.

While many affected dogs do fine, this isn't always the case. The normally round cartilage rings may flatten, forcing the dog to try to breathe through an extremely narrow opening.

The symptoms of the condition—shortness of breath, coughing, fatigue—usually appear after the age of 5, although they can begin as early as birth. Generally, young dogs tolerate collapsing trachea pretty well until they get older.

Normal geriatric changes in the lower airways and lungs of older dogs contribute to the problem. So does secondhand smoke. Dr. Richard Ford of North Carolina State University College of Veterinary Medicine has documented the fact that dogs experience secondhand smoke disease. Particulate matter, which is what smoke is, tends to settle low to the ground, which is where a dog tends to be, so there's a relatively high concentration of this matter at the dog's level. When this particulate matter accumulates over months and years, the membranes in the lower airways thicken. This thickening makes it even more difficult for the dog to draw breath.

Once the airway integrity is compromised deep in the lungs, as the dog tries to exhale, turbulence develops. The air flow dynamics change, making the pressure inside the pleural space greater than the pressure inside the trachea. The trachea then collapses. And the harder the dog coughs, trying to clear her airway, the worse it gets.

The dog with weakened cartilage due to a congenital defect now develops chronic bronchitis, coughs more, and the cycle goes on. The harder she coughs, the greater the collapse; the greater the collapse, the greater the tendency to cough.

The bronchitis can be treated with antibiotics. And the trachea condition can be medically managed with drugs to help dilate the airways and suppress the cough. A strict diet and restricted activity are also part of the plan.

The awkward question the veterinarian must ask is whether the owner smokes. Many owners don't want to accept the fact that they might be contributing to their dog's problem. Some won't give up smoking but will smoke outside the house, and some have added a room onto their house or screened in the porch for the dog. Remember that a little bit of smoke is a lot for a tiny dog.

Oral Nasal Fistula

It might surprise you to learn that the biggest respiratory health problem seen in Toys starts with their teeth. Toys have a much greater propensity for periodontal disease (more about that in chapter 9) and, as a consequence, the upper canine teeth tend to develop periodontal pockets. This loosens the tooth in the socket, inviting infection. The upper canine is a big tooth, even in a little dog, and its roots extend very close to the nasal cavity. As the infection in the tooth progresses, it can invade the nasal cavity. This usually begins on one side and progresses to both sides.

Episodes of severe sneezing in a middle-aged to older Toy are usually the first sign. Frequently, little specks of blood will be seen in the expelled mucous.

This is a stubborn infection that's not easy to treat. Veterinarians often go after the tooth infection first. It will appear to be resolved during a course of antibiotics, but the sneezing will reappear when the dog comes off the antibiotics. Once the oral nasal fistula has been diagnosed, the definitive treatment is to remove the canine tooth.

Soft Palate Problems

Occasionally Pomeranians and many brachycephalic Toy breeds are seen with an elongated soft palate, an anatomical anomaly. The hard palate is the roof of the mouth; the soft palate is the looser tissue behind this soft roof. At the very back of the throat is a valve called the

epiglottis that closes the opening of the trachea when food is being swallowed. When the soft palate is unusually long, food gets trapped in the airway; as the dog breathes in, the food is literally flapping in the breeze, which causes the dog to snort. This is called stertorous breathing.

A burst of snorting may be heard when the dog exhales (expiratory) or when she inhales (inspiratory). When it is expiratory, the dog may be responding to an allergic reaction or attempting to eject something that has been inhaled and ended up in the nasal passage. When it is inspiratory (sometimes called reverse sneezing), it may be due to an overlong soft palate. A surgical procedure can shorten the soft palate and resolve the problem.

Urology

Small dogs certainly have their fair share of the same sort of urologic problems that affect people.

Incontinence

Incontinence isn't a big problem for the small breeds. However, as they age, normal geriatric changes do make incontinence more likely. Muscle tone of the sphincters and the urethra may not be as great as it was. In most cases this is easily treatable, either with estrogen replacements or medication that increases the muscle tone of the urethra. Rarely does incontinence require a lot of intervention. For dogs who aren't controlled by those medications or owners who don't want to try them, little dogs are easily put in diapers.

As dogs get older, their kidneys are also reaching the end of their lives—just as the dogs are. The kidneys can't clear waste products and concentrate urine as well, so the dogs have to urinate more often. The best way to manage kidney failure is to detect it early, because early intervention increases the chance of correcting the underlying problem, or at least making it easier on the kidneys through diet, plenty of water, and medication.

The kidneys go on functioning for a long time after damage has begun, which means the earlier the damage is detected, the easier and more effective it is to treat. If kidney failure is first detected when the dog is vomiting, not eating, and losing weight, it's likely the damage started two to four years earlier. Routine blood screening will only reveal kidney problems

after more than three-quarters of the kidney has failed. That's why regular serum chemistry profiles and a geriatric profile are important for older dogs.

Stones

Dogs develop different types of stones that can obstruct the urinary tract. The two most common are struvite and calcium oxalate. While they're relatively easy to treat, urinary tract obstructions can become serious. If you see changes in your dog's urine, or if she's straining to urinate, it's time to see your veterinarian.

Struvite stones, seen mainly in female dogs, are the result of a urinary tract infection. This is primarily a young dog's disease, usually occurring in dogs 1 to 5 years old. Struvite stones may be dissolved by feeding a special veterinary diet, thus avoiding surgery. Antibiotics must be given throughout the entire period of dissolution, because as stones form, they trap bacteria in them. As they start to dissolve, the bacteria will be released in the urine and re-establish an infection unless antibiotics are continued.

Struvite recurs only if there's a recurrence of the urinary tract infection. Follow-up urine cultures can help head off recurrences. Every four months after an initial attack is a good idea, eventually tapering off. Urine cultures should also be done whenever the owner notices the dog either licking the vulva or urinating more frequently.

The other common type of stone is calcium oxalate. These are primarily seen in male dogs ages 7 to 9. Unfortunately, these stones cannot be medically dissolved because once they form, they're quite stable.

Calcium oxalate stones are primarily seen in Shih Tzu and Yorkies. Lhasa Apsos can form them at a younger age, between 3 and 5. They are rarely found in big dogs.

The reason these stones form is not known, but there do seem to be some dietary associations. Table food and excessive treats correlate with stone formation, so owners need to find other ways to express their love for their dogs. It hasn't been proven that there's a genetic predisposition, but it's likely familial.

Calcium oxalate stones must be physically removed. One method is surgical, but it's not the only option. A very expensive procedure called lithotripsy uses a shock wave to break the stones up. The tiny pieces are then voided in the urine.

Another nonsurgical method for removing stones is called voiding urohydropropulsion. The stones must be small enough to pass through the urethra. The urologist distends the

bladder and then positions the dog so that his spine is vertical—very similar to the way humans stand. The stones drop into the urethral opening, and then the urologist expresses the bladder, which voids the urine and the stones at the same time. The whole thing takes about five minutes and the dog has to be sedated, but there's no surgical incision. This procedure can also work with female dogs.

After the stones are removed, there are special diets to minimize their recurrence. They minimize protein and calcium intake and make the urine more alkaline. The healthy dog can stay on one of these special urinary tract diets for life.

Formation of stones is a chemical reaction in the bladder; the urine is too concentrated with these minerals for them to remain a fluid, so they precipitate out. The best way to avoid any stone is by providing your dog with plenty of clean, fresh water. The dog will form a more dilute urine, the concentration of minerals will be reduced, and stones will not get the chance to form.

Since you can't make your dog drink more, another way to add water to your dog's diet is to feed canned food instead of dry. Canned diets are usually about 70 percent water. While dry food is good for a dog's teeth, a dog who tends to get stones is probably better off with canned food. You can brush the dog's teeth more often to compensate.

Urinary Tract Infections

A dog who is unexpectedly urinating in the house, asking to go out more frequently, licking her genitals, or has red urine may have a urinary tract infection. Most routine antibiotics will take care of it, but for repeated infections, a urine culture is necessary to isolate the bacterial culprit.

If these infections recur frequently, the veterinarian should look for an underlying cause. The normal host defense systems have been disrupted in some way whenever there is a urinary tract infection. They can be disrupted by stones, renal failure, tumors, or other causes, and it's important to get to the root of the problem.

Chapter 9

Skin and Bones (and Teeth)

Little dogs have some big problems. Larger dogs aren't likely to have their hair tied up in a topknot, which could lead to permanent hair loss. They're unlikely to break a bone while flying off a grooming table. And they certainly don't have the periodontal problems for which Toys are infamous.

Dermatology

When it comes to skin problems, Toys seem to have a few advantages. Many people believe that tiny dogs have fewer bacterial infections of the skin. And because Toys tend to spend less time outside and with other dogs, they get fewer contagious skin diseases. This includes ringworm and canine scabies or canine sarcoptic acariasis, both contagious skin conditions caused by mites. The exception is dogs who come from pet shops and commercial breeders, who are prone to fungal infections because many dogs are kept close together. Ringworm is common in these dogs, and is transferred from one to another.

On the negative side, a few syndromes may be seen more frequently in small dogs, and we'll discuss those here. Skin diseases can be complex, and they often go hand in hand (or paw in paw) with allergies. If your dog has an allergy or a skin problem, your veterinarian

can refer you to one of the more than one hundred board-certified veterinary dermatologists in North America.

Alopecia

Alopecia is a general medical term used to describe hair loss. Toys are predisposed to the symmetric alopecias, with hair loss on the surface of their ears, behind the ears, and sometimes symmetrically in other areas. This disease is much like male pattern baldness in humans, and the hair follicles look similar on a skin biopsy.

The problem is seen most frequently in Miniature Dachshunds and a variety of short-coated breeds. It's believed to be genetic.

Congenital Hypotrichosis (Hairlessness)

The Chinese Crested and the Mexican Hairless are two examples of breeds developed to exploit a genetic defect. They are both examples of a syndrome that occurs rarely, but naturally, called congenital hypotrichosis, or congenital lack of hair.

Chinese Cresteds

Courtesy of Amy Fernandez

Any breed has the potential to end up with a hairless variety. Many years ago veterinarians at the University of California–Davis saw a Rottweiler brought in with congenital hypotrichosis. His only hair was a tuft on the top of his head, just like the tuft that crowns a Chinese Crested. They neutered the dog and placed him in a good home, not wanting to imagine the outcome should someone decide to develop the Hairless Rottweiler.

Basically, hairless breeds develop when a puppy with a faulty gene that causes congenital hair loss is viewed as desirable. The dog is bred, and eventually a breed is

formed. This is also how Sphinx cats were developed. From a dermatologist's point of view, however, these are animals with a genetic defect.

Hairless dogs have many skin problems, because dogs are meant to have hair. Those without hair still have little rudimentary hair follicles that get easily plugged or infected, leading to blackheads and acne, especially on their backs. You can head off some problems by bathing the dog regularly with a hypoallergenic shampoo, but it depends on the individual dog. Some dogs are very high-maintenance, others are not. As soon as there's a real problem, the dog should be taken to the veterinarian and treated with medicated shampoos or antibiotics.

Hair also protects an animal, and hairless dogs are more susceptible to scratches and cuts. In response, hairless dogs have developed thicker skin that heals very quickly if scratched or cut. But they still need extra protection from their surroundings.

Hairless dogs also need extra protection from the sun. Their skin burns easily, and they need sunblock and shade, much the way a young child would.

Dandruff

Dandruff is a complex medical topic. The cells of the outer layer of skin are being shed all the time by animals and people alike. Usually these are just washed or brushed away. But if they become visible as dandruff, larger numbers of cells are being shed. There are a variety of syndromes that could cause this. Any time a dog has dandruff that isn't removed by a gentle shampoo and keeps coming back, he should be evaluated by a veterinarian for potential underlying problems.

Dermatosis

Small dogs are prone to dermatosis, which means any skin lesion or group of lesions, including inflamed areas. It may include blackheads and whiteheads; these are commonly seen in Chinese Cresteds, but they crop up on other breeds as well. Look under the dog's chin, on the abdomen, and other places where hair growth is thinner for blackheads. In most cases, peroxide applied with a cotton ball twice a day will clear up this condition.

Dry Skin

It's important to take preventive measures so that a dog's skin does not dry out. Use the shampoo made specifically for dogs, preferably a hypoallergenic shampoo, especially for those breeds prone to skin disease. There are also humectant products on the market that are applied after a bath to replenish moisture in the skin. Every dog should be combed and brushed regularly to distribute the natural oils in his coat and remove bits of dead skin and hair.

How often should you bathe your dog? The specialist's advice is that dogs should be bathed as often as necessary, which varies tremendously from dog to dog. As long as you're using a gentle product, there's nothing wrong with shampooing a dog once a week or even more often. If you're seeing excessive dryness or skin irritation, the product you're using is not right for your dog. Talk with your veterinarian about choosing an appropriate shampoo.

Follicular Dysfunction

Until a few years ago, this dysfunction of the hair follicles didn't even have a name. Researchers at the University of California-Davis now call it follicular dysfunction in plush-coated breeds, although not much is known about it even now.

This syndrome, which causes symmetrical hair loss and increased skin pigmentation, mainly affects Pomeranians. It is seen in conjunction with abnormalities in growth-hormone-related diseases, and is very likely genetic. In the show ring, judges are looking for very plush, fuzzy coats, so breeders are selecting dogs for breeding who have that type of coat. But some endocrine abnormalities have been shown in Pomeranians who have very plush coats, and these dogs develop skin disease, so the gene for plush coat may carry with it a hidden defect. This theory is still controversial, however, and more research is needed.

Other than the hair loss and extra pigmentation, dogs with follicular dysfunction are healthy, so one choice is to simply care for their skin and leave the condition untreated.

Since endocrine abnormality is the underlying cause, growth hormone injections do help the dog regrow hair. They are given subcutaneously, every other day over a number of weeks. The problem is that after anywhere from 8 months to 2 years, the hair falls out again and the dog needs more injections. Treatment with growth hormone is both expensive and risky. While the newer products have so far proven safer, older treatments caused diabetes in some dogs.

Matting

Another skin problem occurs when long-coated breeds mat, usually because the owner has stopped grooming the dog regularly. Mats are tangled hairs that form clumps—something like dreadlocks. Once a mat forms, it will get bigger and bigger as more hair is drawn into the tangle. Small mats can be combed out, but large ones must be cut out.

Matting leads to skin problems because the mat ends up being so close to the skin and so tight that it pulls the hair out. Dogs can get superficial infections under areas of matted hair, so mats should always be carefully removed. The infections can be treated either with antibacterial shampoos or antibiotics.

Mats also hurt all the time, and brushing them out can be so painful that it's better to cut them out. Just a few minutes of daily brushing will spare your dog this pain.

Otitis Externa

This inflammation of the external ear canal is a problem in many breeds and may be the most common infection in dogs. The infection can extend from the skin circling the inside of the ear all the way to the eardrum. Dogs with floppy ears or excessive hair growing in the ear canals are especially prone to otitis externa, because less air circulates in the ear canals, making them havens for bacteria, fungus, yeast, and ear mites. Among Toys, Poodles have a particular problem with these infections.

Long-term otitis externa can cause deafness. It is also extremely uncomfortable for the dog. Once an ear becomes inflamed, the tissues of the ear thicken and more earwax is produced. The extra earwax causes inflammation in its own right, making the condition even worse.

At the very first sign of external ear inflammation or an unpleasant odor from the ears, the dog should be evaluated by a veterinarian. Ear checks should also be a part of any routine veterinary exam. Aggressive early management and long-term vigilance are the keys to coping with this condition. In breeds with lots of hair growing in the ear canal, clipping or plucking the hair should be part of their regular grooming routine.

Overgrown Nails

Overgrowth of the nails is another problem that can be avoided with regular grooming. When a nail is not regularly trimmed, it can grow so long that it curls under and pierces the foot pad.

Skin infections are a likely result. The nail must be cut and removed like a foreign body, and the skin treated with an antiseptic. Because Toys tend to spend less time outside, where their nails would be naturally worn down, regular nail trimming is especially important.

In addition, when a dog has been walking in wooded or grassy areas it's important to check his feet, especially between the toes. Tiny burrs and seeds can be major irritations for a small dog. Barbed seeds can work their way under the skin, especially around the nail openings, so be extra careful.

Sun Damage

A lot of the short-haired Toys have relatively thin haircoats, putting their skin at extra risk for all kinds of sun damage, from sunburn to skin cancer.

The most commonly seen sun-induced skin cancer is squamous cell carcinoma. This skin tumor can spread and cause considerable damage. Surgical removal is the first line of treatment, sometimes followed by radiation or chemotherapy.

The Italian Greyhound, a confirmed sun worshipper, is one of the breeds most at risk for this and other sun-related skin disorders. Owners should limit the amount of time their short-haired dogs spend basking in the sun. Dogs who prefer to lie in the sun should have sunscreen applied before they go out. Any case of sunburn can be serious and should be evaluated by a veterinarian. And remember that sunlight streaming in through a window is still sunlight.

Traction Alopecia

This skin problem is caused by the topknot in breeds such as the Maltese, Shih Tzu, Yorkshire Terrier, Silky Terrier, and Toy Poodle. The elastic or barrette used to hold the topknot in place pulls the skin and hair and eventually causes traction alopecia, which is permanent hair loss in that area.

It's important to be gentle and sensitive when tying up a dog's topknot. Dogs, unlike people, can't tell you if the elastic or barrette is too tight. Certainly, any time the skin around the eyes is pulled as well, the topknot needs to be loosened.

Dermatologists recommend not keeping the hair in a topknot all the time, no matter how loose or tight. The topknot should also be put up loosely and its location on the head

changed daily, so there isn't constant pressure and pulling on one spot. This is a regimen even show dogs can follow.

Allergies

As I mentioned earlier, many skin problems actually stem from allergies. Among the most common allergies are those to foods or parasites. For instance, canine scabies is caused not just by the presence of mites crawling around in the surface layers of the skin, but also by a hypersensitivity to the by-products of those mites.

Dogs develop three major allergic diseases and a number of minor ones. Allergies cannot be cured, but they can be treated. And sometimes the diagnostic process takes longer than the treatment.

Flea Allergy Dermatitis

The major allergic disease among dogs all over the world is flea allergy dermatitis, a complex disorder involving at least four different allergic mechanisms. It occurs in all breeds. As with all allergies, itching is the major clinical sign.

Many people are under the impression that all dogs have fleas. This is definitely not the case. It is also not true that all dogs have flea allergies. Many stray dogs have a large number of fleas and do not have any hypersensitive reaction to them. Ironically, a well-cared-for pet who has only occasionally encountered a flea is more likely to develop a hypersensitivity to flea bites.

When a flea bites a dog, it injects saliva into the skin to keep the dog's blood from coagulating. Agents in this saliva, some of which remain on the skin, are what trigger the allergic reaction. The dog can mount an immunological response in various ways. The majority of dogs will feel itchy on the rear half of their body. The most common sites of flea allergy are the rump (where the tail joins the body), the back legs, and the groin or stomach. If a dog is scratching a lot on the rear half of his body, even if you haven't seen fleas, a dermatologist will consider it to be flea allergy dermatitis until proven otherwise.

The irritation and scratching produce lesions. Treatment isn't easy, but many new products are available that are far more effective and much safer than previous treatment options. Most of these products are available only through veterinarians.

Effective flea control, for all animals in the family plus inside the house and in the yard, must also be part of the treatment plan. Flea control products have also come a long way in their safety and effectiveness. And your vacuum cleaner will become a tool in the fight against fleas. Work with your veterinarian to develop a plan that will be effective for your dog and for you.

Canine Atopic Dermatitis

The second most common allergy is canine atopic dermatitis. Humans with a similar disease have the upper respiratory symptoms of hay fever. When dogs are exposed to the same allergens (the major ones are tree, grass, and weed pollens, mold spores, and the ubiquitous dust mite), they itch. They itch predominantly on their face, feet, ears, and hindquarters, but itching can be more generalized on the body. The problem can be seasonal or year round.

Although atopic dermatitis is seen in all breeds of dogs, it's believed Terriers are at increased risk for developing this inherited problem. It's also seen in many small, hairy breeds. If a dog is rubbing his face or chewing on his paws, canine atopic dermatitis should be suspected. Affected dogs should be referred to a veterinary dermatologist for long-term treatment and management.

Food Intolerance

Food intolerance, also called food hypersensitivity, is the least common of the three major canine allergies. Most of the time a true allergic reaction is never established. The itchy symptoms are similar to those seen in canine atopic dermatitis.

Lamb and rice diets have become popular for dogs with food allergies, but there is nothing that makes a particular food inherently allergenic or hypoallergenic. The critical feature for food intolerance in dogs is habituation and long-term exposure; novel foods–foods the dog has never eaten before–therefore do not trigger the allergic reaction. Since lamb and rice were not commonly used in commercial dog foods until recently, they were better

choices for allergic dogs. But now that lamb and rice are often among the ingredients in dog food, they are no longer novel.

Dogs are usually tested for food allergies by using an elimination diet, which means feeding them a very few ingredients and then gradually adding more, to see which ingredient causes the reaction. Lamb and rice were therefore also chosen for elimination diets. But since they have become a common ingredient in many commercial dog foods, they are not really useful in managing food allergies. Veterinarians now suggest various home-cooked foods, and there are a number of commercial diets available only through veterinarians that use other novel protein and carbohydrate sources, such as duck and venison. Hopefully, those won't be co-opted by the pet food industry as well.

An elimination diet is usually followed for ten to twelve weeks. Once the dog's allergies are established, you and your veterinarian should work out a balanced, long-term diet for your dog.

Orthopedics

There aren't a lot of orthopedic diseases specific to Toy dogs. Toys seldom have hip dysplasia, although it does occur in some breeds, such as the Affenpinscher. But there are a few orthopedic problems they do tend to have, and these can be quite serious.

Broken Bones

Obviously, broken bones can be a problem for any dog. But Toys' bones break more easily than those of bigger dogs, because they're light and fine and because these tiny animals are living in a world of (to them) giants. It's very common for Italian Greyhounds to jump out of their owner's arms and break their front legs (usually the distal radius, one of the long bones between the elbow and the wrist). It's so common that the dogs can break both legs simultaneously. Repeated breaks are also not uncommon.

Using a small metal bone plate to add rigidity to a weakened spot carries its own set of problems. If the plate is removed, the remaining screw holes leave the bone weakened and the leg has to be splinted until the holes fill in. Leaving the plate in often results in osteoporosis under the plate.

Unfortunately, front limb fractures are common in many Toy breeds, including Chihuahuas, Papillons, Japanese Chin, and Min Pins. When these little dogs leap, their fine bones just aren't prepared for the jolt of landing.

Legg-Calve-Perthes Disease

Legg-Calve-Perthes disease, sometimes called simply Legg-Perthes, is one of the most common orthopedic problems of Toys. It is an inherited condition that affects dogs under fifty pounds, most often males.

The disease attacks the hip, a ball-and-socket joint. The ball is the head of the long thigh bone called the femur. In a process that's still not well understood, the blood supply to the femur head shuts down, and the bone dies. This is called avascular necrosis. Pain, stiffening, and frequent hip dislocations are the result.

The symptoms of Legg-Perthes start at about 6 months of age. The dog will limp or hop, walk stiffly, and cry out in pain when his hips are manipulated. Unfortunately, by the time the veterinarian sees the patient the degenerative changes in the hip joint are generally irreversible. While there is some sketchy evidence that putting a dog in a protective brace during the very early stages of the disease enables the degenerative bone to renew itself, there aren't enough cases seen that early to really evaluate this treatment.

Orthopedists usually see the dog and confirm the diagnosis between 8 and 10 months of age. If it's mild, it can be managed with analgesics and anti-inflammatory medications. But when the surrounding muscles have already atrophied, the head and neck of the femur are degenerated and the cartilage over the femoral head is gone, surgery is required.

This is the same surgery used to treat hip dysplasia, but it's much more successful in smaller dogs. In the surgery, called excision arthroplasty, the head and neck of the femur are removed. A false joint of fibrous tissue will eventually form at the hip. Although the dog will probably limp on this joint, it will be smoother than the degenerated one and he will be pain free.

Luxating Patella

An all too common hereditary problem in Toys is luxating patella, a kind of trick knee. With this condition, the patella, or kneecap, tends to pop out of the joint. Toys more often have

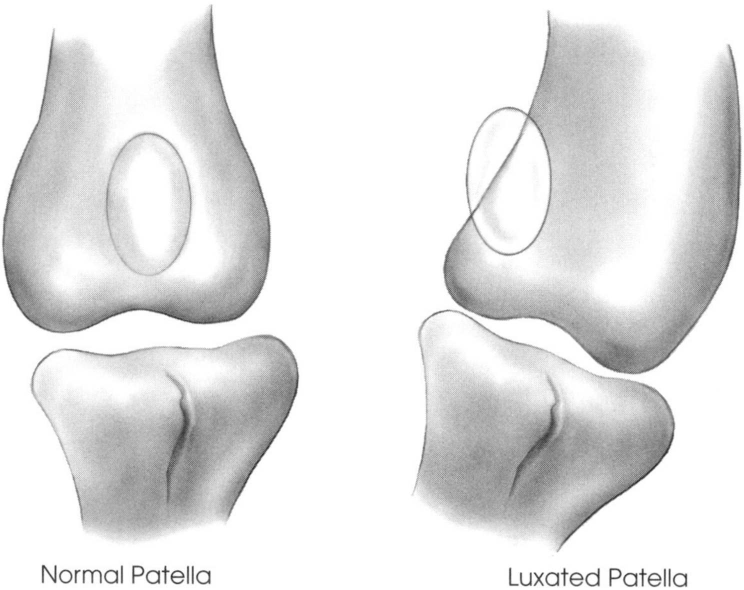

Normal Patella   Luxated Patella

medial luxating patella, which means the kneecap pops toward the inside of the leg. The patella sits in a groove at the lower end of the femur (the large bone in the thigh) and glides up and down when the knee is bent. If the groove is too shallow, the patella will pop out when the knee bends.

Researcher Robert William Putnam put forward a theory in 1968 suggesting the hip joint is also involved. Putnam's thesis was never published because he died prematurely, and his data group was not large enough to be statistically significant. However, his theory does have a following among veterinarians.

Putnam said a bad angle in the hip joint exerts force down the entire leg, so that as the leg grows, the kneecap is pulled out of place and a normal groove fails to develop. A tendon joins the patella to the quadriceps, the thigh muscle, and if the quadriceps is misaligned the kneecap will not be situated properly either. If the kneecap is out of place and resting on the side of the joint, when the muscle contracts it will flex the joint instead of extending it.

In the early stages luxating patella is not painful, but it can become progressively more painful as the shallow grooves are polished even smoother and arthritis develops.

Dogs can be affected in one or both hind legs. When both knees are affected (which is common), the dog may lift both rear legs off the ground and walk by balancing on his front legs.

Patella luxation is seen in four clinical grades, which are, more than anything else, a way for veterinarians to communicate with one another. Grade 1 is a kneecap that's usually in place naturally but that the examiner can push out of place. Occasional hopping may be the only sign of the condition. The significance of this mild form of the disease is that the dog's breeder should be told and his parents should not be bred again.

With Grade 2, the patella will pop in and out. When it does pop, the dog can extend and flex his leg and bounce it back into place. Dogs with Grade 2 patella luxation may intermittently hop and limp. Surgery is often necessary for these dogs.

The Grade 3 patella is always out of place, although weight bearing is still possible and the kneecap can still be pushed back into place manually. Surgery is always necessary and should not be delayed. This is especially true if the condition is found in a young, growing dog.

Grade 4 is when the patella is permanently out of joint. It cannot be replaced and the dog cannot put any weight on the affected leg. Surgery is recommended but is not always successful.

A Grade 1 luxation may never progress beyond that stage. Some veterinarians will want to operate right away, but the knee doesn't have to be repaired unless there are clinical signs. Mild patella luxation doesn't inevitably lead to arthritis, either. The level of treatment should depend on the level of discomfort to the dog.

Open Fontanel

The fontanel is the area at the top of the skull where the three bone plates come together. Usually they fuse when a puppy is about 4 weeks old, but sometimes they never completely fuse, leaving a hole in the top of the skull.

Congenital open fontanel is seen primarily in Chihuahuas, but all Toys, especially those with a high incidence of hydrocephalus, are susceptible to the problem. Many Chihuahua breeders expect this to occur to a certain degree and find it acceptable. However, since it's probably hereditary, the pair that produced a puppy with open fontanel should not be bred again.

Special care must be taken with a dog who has an open fontanel. But no treatment is needed and most dogs do just fine.

Rheumatoid Arthritis

While arthritis, in general, is more common in large dogs, rheumatoid arthritis shows up primarily in Toys, most often in Yorkshire Terriers and Chihuahuas. Part of a generalized disease of the body's connective tissue, the cause is suspected to be an autoimmune response.

Usually, several joints are involved, most often wrists, ankles, and feet. As the disease progresses, the cartilage between joints erodes. The joint space is shortened, and eventually bone spurs and lesions develop.

Rheumatoid arthritis can't be cured, but it can be managed with immune suppressants, corticosteroids, and pain relievers such as aspirin. Sometimes gold salts can also help with the pain. These can slow down the process of bone changes, but not stop them. If the joints completely break down, surgical fusion relieves pain and restores some movement.

Dentistry

Dogs get virtually every dental problem that humans get. Toys also have problems particular to them. One is that many Toy breeds lack full dentition. The average adult dog has forty-two permanent teeth, but many Toys have fewer. This is especially a problem in Chinese Cresteds, where the gene for hairlessness seems to be linked to partial dentition.

Toys require professional dental cleaning twice a year, whereas most larger dogs can probably get by having it done once every year or two. An interesting study done at the University of Pennsylvania School of Veterinary Medicine looked at dental disease and behavior in twenty geriatric small dogs. All the dogs in the study were videotaped eating and playing before and after they had their teeth cleaned, over the course of several years. The researchers wanted to see how regular cleanings affect the personalities of the dogs.

Anecdotally, dog owners say they have seen a difference after their older dogs' teeth were cleaned—the dogs seemed livelier, indicting that they felt better, especially if a tooth needed to be removed. Regular dental care can often relieve pain when the owner is unaware that a stoic dog has dental problems. It's also important for owners to brush their dogs' teeth every day using a toothpaste made just for dogs.

Baby Teeth

Around 4 weeks of age, puppies get their baby teeth, also known as deciduous teeth. By about 6 months, these baby teeth fall out and are replaced by permanent teeth—or at least they should be. If the deciduous teeth don't fall out, an extra tooth will be present when the permanent teeth start to grow in. Retention of the deciduous teeth is a particular problem in Toy breeds.

This can create a host of problems. First of all, the adult tooth and the deciduous tooth are going to be quite close together, creating a haven for bacteria and plaque. More serious are the orthodontic problems. The permanent teeth may erupt in the wrong place or grow at odd angles. The abnormal placement of teeth can impair the normal development of the bones in the jaw. The retained deciduous teeth can also die and develop abscesses.

Before the advent of veterinary dentistry, veterinarians would wait until a puppy was 9 months or older to pull any remaining deciduous teeth. They now realize that's too late, because by then the permanent tooth has already been diverted. You should never have two teeth of the same kind in the same dog at the same time.

Now, any deciduous teeth are usually pulled at 6 months; earlier if the permanent tooth is growing in crooked. The empty socket that's left behind will create negative pressure and suck the adult tooth back into its normal pattern of eruption.

Broken deciduous teeth can also be a problem, even though the teeth will be shed after a few months. Serious cracks expose the roots to bacteria, and a deep infection can invade the permanent teeth that are developing below the gum line. If these permanent teeth die, they may never erupt or may simply appear and then fall out. Dogs with seriously broken teeth should be on antibiotics to prevent infection.

Some unscrupulous breeders clip the teeth of their puppies to avoid dealing with those needle-sharp deciduous teeth. This is a painful, dangerous practice.

Periodontal Disease

Periodontal disease is an infection of the supporting structures surrounding the teeth. It begins when plaque and calculus stick to the teeth near the gum line. The subsequent gum infection is called gingivitis. If left unchecked, this progresses to periodontitis, in which the teeth loosen and may fall out.

This is a particular problem among Toys, for a number of reasons. Many of the smaller dogs tend to eat canned foods, which appears to facilitate the formation of plaque. Plaque, a clear, slick substance that forms daily, is 80 percent bacteria. The bacteria love to hide inside the sulcus, a little ditch around the teeth that's formed by the gum as it comes up, folds over the bone, comes back down, and attaches to the top of the bone supporting the tooth. A tooth is suspended in its socket by many little fibers, and the inflammation caused by this bacteria eats away until deep sulcus pockets form and there's no support left.

Toys, with their little mouths, tend to have crowded, uneven teeth, making lots of hiding places for plaque. The supporting bone around the teeth is also much thinner and more fragile in a Toy, so it degenerates faster. All small dogs are prone to this problem, especially the brachycephalic breeds, as well as Toy Poodles, Italian Greyhounds, and Yorkshire Terriers.

Good dental hygiene will prevent gingivitis and periodontal disease. If the disease is caught early, a thorough cleaning and a course of antibiotics may help. Many teeth will reattach themselves to the supporting bone if the infection is eliminated early enough.

The Spine

Diseases of the spine fall into two categories: orthopedic and neurologic. In other words, some only affect the bones of the spine—the vertebrae—while others also have neurological consequences.

Herniated Disc

One of the most common diseases of the spine in small dogs is herniated discs. The vertebrae are separated from one another by flexible cartilage discs that cushion the neck and spine and enable it to bend. Above the discs is the spinal cord. If a disc weakens, it will protrude up between the vertebrae, putting pressure on the spinal cord. The result is pain and partial or total immobility, depending on how much pressure there is on the spinal cord.

Treatment should begin right away. It consists of either anti-inflammatory drugs and rest or surgery to remove the disc. Surgery has the best results if it is done within twenty-four hours of an injury.

Discs can herniate from an injury or simply because they have weakened. This happens with age, but there may also be an inherent weakness in the disc. Toys more commonly suffer from an inherent weakness, called Hansen's Type I. Degeneration occurs in the discs shortly after birth and herniated discs are usually seen by 2 to 3 years of age.

Because the Dachshund is the primary breed affected, it was believed that a long back contributes to this type of disc disease. But the French Bulldog, which has a very short body, has almost as high an incidence of this disease as the Dachshund. In fact, there is evidence that this disc disease, especially in younger dogs, has a genetic component.

Small dogs with short, angulated limbs also have the worst forms of herniated discs and tend to have an earlier onset of the problem. These include Pekingese and Shih Tzu, but a herniated disc problem can strike any small dog. The problem also shows up in Miniature Poodles, Cocker Spaniels, and Beagles, whose herniated discs tend to be in the neck area.

Vertebra Abnormalities

There are congenital problems associated with the cervical vertebrae, which are the ones in the neck. The very first vertebra is called the atlas and the second is the axis. The axis has a little protrusion sticking off the front called the dens, which fits into a slot above it. Ligaments grow over it and attach the two vertebrae. If the connection between the two is unstable, the condition is called atlantoaxial subluxation.

The instability can result because the ligaments are not attached to the dens, because the two vertebrae are dislocated, or because the dens is missing. When any of those things happen, every time the dog moves his head up and down the vertebrae press directly on the spinal cord.

Atlantoaxial subluxation can occur as the result of an injury, but in Toy and Miniature breeds it's usually a congenital malformation. The problem first presents itself some time in the dog's first year. An early sign is a reluctance to be patted on the head. Some affected dogs will cry in pain or just collapse.

Mild cases can be treated with anti-inflammatories, a neck brace, and crate rest. This allows fibrous tissue to form and stabilize the joint. Therapy may have to be continued intermittently for the dog's life. More serious cases can be life-threatening and need surgery to stabilize the joint with pins and wires. Unfortunately, the surgery does not have a high

degree of success. And if the spinal cord has been damaged by the bones, that damage cannot be reversed.

This problem is most commonly seen in Yorkies, Maltese, and several other breeds, and is almost certainly inherited.

Another vertebra malformation is hemivertebra, in which a vertebra will be somewhat flattened into a shape resembling a butterfly. This weak link in the spine can be like a silent time bomb. A mild back trauma may push that vertebra out of position, paralyzing the dog.

Chapter 10

Surgery and Anesthesia

There's concern whenever any dog needs critical care, must have anesthesia, or must undergo surgery. When the dog is very small, additional concerns come into play. Fluid levels are critical in these little dogs, as is keeping them warm, because when they're sick, their body temperature will drop rapidly. Little dogs can go into shock during surgery, and they require smaller instruments and smaller incisions. Surgeons face a variety of challenges with their small patients.

Critical Care

At some point your small dog may require major surgery or may have a health crisis and require critical care (also called intensive care). If that happens, it's important to remember that your Toy has special needs.

To begin with, small dogs are easily traumatized and can go into shock; because their blood volume is so small, it doesn't take a lot of trauma to put these animals into a major-league crisis. This is true of dogs who have been injured and dogs undergoing surgery.

Stress

The critical care unit (CCU) is a stressful place for a dog, and that's another factor in her recovery. It's an environment in which activity is going on full speed ahead, seven days a week, twenty-four hours a day, and the lights are never turned off. It's especially important to keep the little dog calm under these stressful conditions. In the CCU at Colorado State University, for example, one person, a nurse or a fourth-year veterinary student, is assigned to each dog to minimize stress as much as possible.

Some small dogs are robust and tough, while others seem to be extremely frail. That means greater care must be taken when handling them, a little more caution used when picking them up, and more reassurance offered in many cases.

Body Temperature

When small dogs are sick their body temperature drops rapidly, so keeping Toys warm is another concern in the CCU. When they come out of anesthesia they're kept warm and heat lamps are used, but it's a delicate balance between providing just enough heat and too much. Before long, half the body skin can be sloughing if there's too much heat, so post-surgical care has to be handled very carefully.

Fluids

Water is the principle need of dogs in the CCU. First, the dog is rehydrated with a fluid that contains certain required electrolytes. This is done using an intravenous catheter, and again, it's a delicate balance between too much and too little. Fluid overload, or giving fluids too quickly or too slowly, can cause problems. If fluid pumps are available, the right amount of fluid will be accurately administered.

Blood Sugar and Nutrition

Blood sugar levels are definitely going to be a problem in a small dog. The blood sugar of a Toy who has not eaten for a day may drop to a dangerous level, while a larger dog may go a few days without eating and still have normal blood sugar levels. No matter what the presenting

problem, the veterinary critical care specialist must make sure there are provisions to support the Toy's blood sugar level.

Nutrition is important because of the pathology that occurs with malnutrition. If any dog, Toys included, doesn't eat for five days or more, the veterinarian knows the dog's in trouble. One would think this problem would be worse for small dogs, but according to a study at Colorado State University this doesn't seem to be true. The study looked at the relationship between the nutritional needs and the water needs of dogs. Researchers found most of the material that's currently in the veterinary literature is derived from human and rat studies, but dogs are neither people nor rats. Instead of turning up their metabolic requirements during illness, dogs turn their metabolic requirements down. This gives them the reserves they need. Consistently, the dogs in the study showed a metabolism at or below normal rates. It's true that Toys go down fast, but often that's a reflection of the fact that they're not adequately hydrated.

For exploratory surgery, or if the dog has a disease requiring surgical intervention, the critical care veterinarian will very frequently use nutrition as part of the recovery process. As part of the operation, the surgeon will put in a tube that can be used for feeding. It's a very benign procedure with few complications. The tube is maintained for about 10 days. There are times when it's not used, but it is very helpful to have that tube in place because if the dog doesn't eat, it's easy to get food into her. The real advantage is that the staff can start to feed the dog within about twelve hours of surgery.

Another challenge arises when the dog starts eating again, because often the staff will have to cater to her whims. Frequently, the owner is invited to bring food from home and even the dog's food bowl—often an important requirement to get the dog to start eating. Familiar food, familiar dishes and, most of all, familiar people can make all the difference. Despite the fact that the critical care staff will usually develop a good rapport with the dogs in their care because they're handling them all the time, many dogs get lonesome and won't eat until their owner comes in—at which time they'll wolf down their food.

Toy dogs like to be pampered in the CCU, which means palatable food is important. A major pet food company's special low-salt diet for heart failure patients, called a CV or cardiovascular diet, has become Colorado State University's critical care unit anorectic diet because it's so palatable, especially after fifteen seconds in the microwave. It's very unusual to see a dog turn away from it. This could also be a good choice for a dog who needs a special cardiac or anorectic diet at home.

Obesity

Obesity creates the greatest number of complications seen in small dogs in critical care. Toys seem to outnumber large breeds when it comes to being seriously overweight. Obesity is a medical condition in and of itself, and it only compounds any other medical or surgical problem.

Colorado State University did a study looking at obesity and weight loss. Most of the obese dogs did not have high blood pressure the way people do; in fact, their blood pressure was normal or close to normal. But when those dogs were put on a weight-loss program, their blood pressure went down, which is a positive sign. As some dogs age, especially little dogs, the valve on the left side of the heart may develop a weakness that will increase its resistance to blood flow (particularly if the dog is obese), which can compound the heart problem. That's why it's imperative for owners to keep excess weight off their small dogs.

Problems such as diabetes mellitus and collapsing trachea are also compounded by obesity. The build-up of fat within the chest cavity just in front of the heart puts added strain on the heart and lungs.

Surgery

Small dogs can present some special challenges for the surgeon, especially the brachycephalic breeds, which sometimes have narrowed nostril openings. They can also have problems associated with the larynx, upper respiratory problems, hypoplastic trachea, or elongated soft palate. Although it's fairly uncommon, enlargement of the tonsils because of severe infection or inflammation or some other disease process such as tumors can compromise breathing and swallowing much more quickly in a small breed than in a larger dog.

Size alone presents some challenges to doing surgery on small animals. While there is something to be said for not having to deal with a one-hundred-pound dog, the opposite size extreme is not any easier. Some of the very small breeds have an extremely small head and short muzzle, so in nasal exploratory surgery, for example, there's often not a lot of room to really see the condition of the nasal cavity or to remove neoplastic tissue or tumors.

In the chest area the challenge, again, is size. Whether it's removing a lung tumor or doing heart surgery, operating on a very small animal is comparable to operating on a

human infant. Considering that a newborn baby or a Toy dog is usually from six to ten pounds, neither the pediatric nor the veterinary surgeon has much room to move around. In fact, the veterinary surgeon probably has more of a challenge, because little dogs can weigh four or five pounds—or even just a pound when they're puppies. For a congenital heart problem such as a persistent right aortic arch or PDA, the surgeon is dealing with very tiny areas, looking at size extremes.

Small dogs require the use of smaller instruments, and there's not a lot of latitude for errors. For example, in disc surgery if the surgeon is using a power instrument to remove the bone and expose the compressed spinal cord, the surgeon must always proceed very slowly and with great care. With a very large breed, there are six, seven, or even eight millimeters of bone to cut before reaching the spinal cord, but with a Toy there may only be two or three.

Shunts are the most common liver problem requiring surgical correction and here, too, extreme small size makes surgery a greater challenge. Most of the shunts in very small dogs are not that easy to find. If they're extremely small, they may not show up on ultrasound. And a surgeon can't simply go looking through the liver. Contrast studies, done by injecting a solution that's visible on a fluoroscope into one of the veins that runs through the liver, is often the only really effective diagnostic tool.

The challenge for the surgeon in fracture repairs is that the size of the joints and bones requires extreme care. Generally, a Toy's bones are much thinner than those of larger dogs, especially in the legs. These bones do not have robust circulation, and that can cause a lack of healing and collapse of the fracture site. Stabilizing them with internal plates and screws presents other problems, because the legs of Toys have limited bone substance and there's just not enough to support surgical appliances.

Size affects intestinal surgery, as well, although sometimes in a positive way. Doing exploratory surgery on a small dog is, in one sense, easier because the surgeon isn't making an eighteen-inch incision, as might be necessary with a Labrador Retriever. With a smaller incision, entering and exiting the abdominal cavity can be easier, and it takes less time to close the wound. However, once inside a small dog, the surgeon has much less room to examine and manipulate the organs and tissues.

For most experienced surgeons, most soft tissue procedures can be completed in less than an hour. Not all procedures, however, can be accomplished with one surgery. You may not

need a board-certified surgeon for every operation, but there are certain diseases and certain procedures for which it will be advisable to have someone with that level of expertise.

It's important to understand the problem and discuss the options with your veterinarian. It's also important to get a second opinion for a very serious problem, just as you would if the patient were human. If you have second thoughts or doubts, a third opinion is also advisable. A caring, professional veterinarian should not feel this is an affront.

Anesthesia

What makes surgery possible, in both humans and animals, is anesthesia. Appropriate anesthesia and the appropriate use of analgesics to relieve the pain of an injury and after an operation are all important considerations in the overall picture of healthcare. If anesthesia is maintained in an appropriate fashion, the animal's body temperature and fluid levels are maintained and the surgeon proceeds with the normal cautionary measures.

Toys cannot be said to be at significantly greater risk than the average dog. That does not mean size is not a factor. While size considerations are not so serious that a veterinarian would say a dog can't be anesthetized, because they are so small, Toys are prone to several problems. They are the same problems that must be addressed in critical care: hypothermia and low blood sugar. Other considerations are based on the dog's breed, what's wrong with the animal, and what surgical procedure is to be done.

There's no one anesthesia that's the best choice for every dog in every situation, because there are so many factors involved. The anesthetist must make their decision case by case, taking into account blood tests, X-ray results, the problem, how long the surgeon is going to be working, what type of surgery it's going to be, and the dog's age and temperament. The breed of dog is also a factor, because some breeds are more likely to have certain underlying diseases. For example, brachycephalic breeds (those with flat faces) of all sizes can have a problem with anesthesia because they have what anesthetists consider to be an anatomical abnormality of their respiratory system. They tend to have upper airway problems, and the anesthesiologist must control the airway by putting a tube into the windpipe to help the dog breathe. Some of these dogs are also prone to having very low heart rates, or they may have secondary heart disease because of their upper airway problems.

When the dog is under anesthesia and has an airway tube in, she's either breathing well on her own or the anesthesiologist is assisting her breathing. As with most animals, the biggest concern is the period when the animal is going under anesthesia and when she's waking up. If a dog is going to have problems, that's when they will occur.

If it's a very short procedure, there are some very short-acting injectable anesthetics that can be used. But gas is usually the choice for dogs. One reason is that it can be cut off quickly. Also, injected anesthetics can diminish the full expansion capabilities of the lungs, and in small dogs positive ventilation of the lungs while under anesthesia can be important in preventing hypoxia (a low level of oxygen in the blood) and possible adverse cardiac consequences.

Isoflurane is the main gas anesthetic used in veterinary medicine. However, while isoflurane, is very popular, it is absolutely contraindicated in some cases. If the dog wakes up too rapidly from anesthesia, she goes through a very pronounced excitement phase. Still, isoflurane is generally thought of as a safer anesthetic because the dog can be brought out of it more quickly.

A newer option is Propofol, an injectable anesthetic that is becoming more popular, especially in small dogs, and is showing good results. Propofol is short-acting, lighter in effect, and is eliminated from the system more quickly. Consequently, it offers a greater safety margin.

Gas is not always used by itself. However, gas anesthetic is still the standard, particularly because it is almost always administered with oxygen or some other hypnotics or anesthetics. Toys are often premedicated, because some go under struggling and wake up struggling. Toys tend to be more scared and agitated than larger breeds, possibly because they tend to be more spoiled or fearful. That's not to say that other breeds aren't scared, but small dogs display it more—although some Toys are quite stoic. A dog should be calm when going under anesthesia, which is why, very frequently, a sedative is used to relieve her pain and to calm her. Dogs may also be tranquilized rather than sedated. There are many pre-anesthetic drugs to choose from.

Acepromazine, which comes in injectable or tablet form, is a tranquilizer that is commonly used in veterinary clinics but is not right for a lot of Toy breeds because it lasts too long and the dog's body temperature drops too low, among other problems. Some veterinarians use it in a fractional dose as a pre-op tranquilizer, but I do not like it used at all on Toys.

In any case, anesthesia should be carefully chosen, and for major surgery it's best if it can be done at a major teaching hospital where there is a veterinary anesthesiologist on staff to formulate an anesthesia "cocktail" that is right for both the patient and the particular procedure.

Breeders often say that their breed is sensitive to a certain drug, but breed sensitivity to a particular drug is actually very rare. Very few breeds have documented problems with a specific drug. Some breeds that do, such as Greyhounds and Border Collies, tend to have extremely low percentages of body fat.

With anesthesia becoming so much more refined, veterinarians are aware that dosages are critical, and protocols have been much more finely developed. Additionally, preparatory blood tests are usually done to detect any hidden internal weaknesses that may influence the choice of anesthetic and the dosage to be given. If there is an anesthetic failure, it may be due to an individual reaction or sensitivity to the anesthetic, or to some innate weakness that the veterinarian may not be aware of—an idiosyncratic reaction.

Once a dog is under, there's more to worry about with a Toy. While it is not a standard practice, some surgeons may place their instruments on the animal's chest, but small dogs can't breathe out against the weight of surgical instruments and are more likely to stop breathing if there's pressure on their chest. The anesthetist must make sure the instruments are not inhibiting the rib cage so the small dog can breathe adequately.

Brussels Griffon

Courtesy of Sue Janson

The amount of fluids given to the Toy is also critical, because they can be more easily overloaded if the veterinarian isn't exact in the amount. A few cc's more or less isn't going to make much difference in a ninety-pound dog, but it makes a big difference in a one-pound dog.

Toys can become hypoglycemic from the stress of surgery, and blood sugar levels must be carefully monitored. And Toys can easily go into shock on the operating table because of their low blood volume. They must be kept hydrated and warm.

Any dog going under anesthesia should have a complete physical exam first. It's also important that the dog have pre-surgical

blood work, so her blood sugar levels and liver function are known. Any upper airway problems in brachycephalic breeds should be noted as well. A lot of older small dogs are prone to collapsing tracheas, which affects them when the airway tube is removed. All of these factors should be known before surgery so that possible problems can be anticipated.

Toy breeds can't be treated like big dogs because there are differences. Veterinarians treating Toys must know the medical problems each breed has, and each dog must be viewed as an individual. The problems with anesthesia occur not because these dogs are small, but because whatever the breed is, the veterinarian must know about any underlying diseases or problems to make informed decisions.

The best and most informed decisions generally come from anesthesiologists. If your veterinarian administers the anesthesia himself, ask him to call an anesthesiologist to get an idea of which drugs to use for your dog in those specific circumstances. Anesthesiologists also have more drugs available to them than the local veterinarian. Breeders and owners should take advantage of hospitals that have anesthesiologists when their dog is having surgery that may involve a long or complicated procedure.

Keep in mind that an American Animal Hospital Association (AAHA) accredited veterinary hospital will have a surgery much like that of a human hospital with the same procedures for sterilization, monitoring, and so forth, being followed. Additionally, an AAHA accredited hospital must have equipment for resuscitation.

Part IV

What Sets Them Apart

Affenpinscher and Doberman Pinscher

Courtesy of Mary Downey, ©Sean Downey

Chapter 11

Breed by Breed

Each of the small breeds is unique, with characteristics and personality traits that make them the interesting individuals they are today. Many of them were bred to do a specific job long before they were bred down in size to be companions, and much of what we see in their personalities and characteristics is rooted in their original purpose.

Not every breed is right for every person. Every dog has considerations such as activity level, temperament, coat care, and special health concerns that could be either negatives or positives for you.

All small dogs are house dogs, requiring a warm place to sleep. Generally, small dogs do better with older children who are less likely to accidentally injure them.

The health problems listed here are those that have been seen in the breed. Unfortunately, we seem to see more, not fewer, health problems with time. Whether they're being recognized more, are the result of breeding, or a combination of the two, it's still unfortunate both for the dog and the owner. The health chapters in this book explain more about most of these conditions. This does not mean every dog of a given breed will have a particular problem common to that breed. Do ask the breeder what they are doing to eliminate a particular health problem from their line. No living creature is completely free of defects. The difference is in trying to do something about it.

With the completion of the Canine Genome Project, which was funded in part by the AKC Canine Health Foundation (www.akcchf.org), there is hope of finding the genetic markers for most diseases; finding markers enables breeders to test their breeding stock for those diseases. Once tests are available, there is hope for eliminating just about all genetic health problems through careful breeding. Meanwhile, there are nongenetic tests available for problems such as hip and elbow dysplasia, among others. The responsible breeder makes use of all available tests to produce the healthiest puppies possible.

The breeds listed here are all small dogs, but not all are official members of the Toy Group in the American Kennel Club (AKC). Some are found in the Terrier Group or the Non-Sporting Group, and one is in the Hound Group. Obviously, it's impossible to list all of the small dogs—twenty pounds or under—who are Toys by biology, even if they're not members of any registry's Toy Group. But all small dogs will view the world from a different vantage point. If your little dog isn't listed here, please don't be upset. It's just that we didn't have room for all the dogs who fall into this category. And keep in mind that the term "teacup," when used to describe a particularly small dog, is a marketing term. There is no such thing as a "teacup" dog. Those particularly tiny dogs are anomalies and shouldn't be bred, because their tiny size leads to health and developmental problems.

Affenpinscher

The German word for monkey is *affe,* and *pinscher* means terrier, so the breed's name can be translated as Monkey Terrier. They certainly do resemble little monkeys with incredibly expressive faces. In France the breed has been described as the *diablotin moustachu,* or the mustachioed little devil.

Affenpinscher-type dogs go back to about 1600 in Germany. Coming from the same general line that produced the Miniature Schnauzer and the Miniature Pinscher, the Affenpinscher is not the result of any combination of those breeds.

Affens love to travel, readily adjusting to new circumstances. But many Affens hate to go out when it's wet or raining. They're clean and require minimal grooming; just regular brushing and stripping the coat of dead hair.

Affenpinschers
Courtesy of Rhonda Scott

Very intelligent and with a desire to please, Affens are considered tractable and obedient, and some have done well in Obedience competition. Still, they will exhibit Terrier stubbornness and can be very headstrong. The person who can't be a loving leader shouldn't have a dominant puppy.

These dogs can be hard to housetrain. Males tend to mark territory, which must be rectified when they're very young.

Affens bark enthusiastically when they become excited. Because they're fearless, they've been known to break their legs when jumping off furniture. And they'll challenge a large dog without hesitation.

Displaying characteristics seldom found in other breeds, Affens tend to invent their own games. They'll toss their toys in the air for long periods of time in a self-absorbing game of catch, walk on their hind legs just for fun, and sit on their spine, tail tucked and back legs extended, looking as if they're deep in thought.

Affenpinschers stand between nine and eleven and a half inches at the withers (the top of the shoulder), and their average life span is 10 to 14 years (some have reportedly reached 17). Among the health problems seen in the breed are luxating patellas, Legg-Calve-Perthes disease, kidney problems, heart murmurs, and hypothyroidism. Hip dysplasia has also been seen in this breed. They are brachycephalic and have the problems associated with it. There have also been some cases of juvenile cataracts and PDA.

Bichon Frise

Although the breed description likens them to a powderpuff, these adorable little dogs could also be said to resemble a marshmallow—puffy, white, and very sweet. The gentle, sensitive little dogs are also incredible characters. It doesn't take them very long to wrap a human around their little paws.

The breed originated in the Mediterranean, a descendent of the Barbet (Water Spaniel). The Poodle and Maltese were also descended from the Barbet. Ultimately, these fluffy dogs were brought to the Canary Island of Tenerife. In the early 1500s they were brought to France, where they were groomed like little lions—but they should in no way be confused with the Lowchen.

The French Kennel Club admitted the Bichon in 1934. A few of the dogs made their way to the United States at the end of World War I, but it wasn't until 1971 that they were allowed to compete in AKC shows.

Bichons are between nine and twelve inches tall at the withers and should live 15 to 16 years. Among the health problems that are seen in this breed are cataracts, immotile celia syndrome, bladder and kidney stones, and luxating patellas.

Border Terrier

First appearing in England and Scotland, where Terriers were prized for their abilities to hunt fox, otter, and various vermin, the Border Terrier is often referred to as a "purebred mutt." Interestingly, that's considered a compliment. Recognized by the Kennel Club in Britain in 1920, they received AKC recognition ten years later. They are less dog aggressive than other Terriers, but still retain the instincts of a hunter.

This adorable little dog has a jaunty expression and a very natural look about him. There is nothing fancy about the Border Terrier. Even his coat makes him look as if he comes in a plain brown wrapper. Grooming is rather straightforward: frequent brushing and twice-a-year hand-stripping to remove dead hair. (Clipping will not accomplish that goal.)

Like all dogs, the Border Terrier requires daily exercise, at the very least a daily walk. Dog sports will be an added delight and a great form of exercise for these active little dogs. They will get along with cats if introduced at a very young age and will do well with dogs of the opposite sex, since those of the same sex seem to squabble more.

A generally healthy breed, they do have some problems in some lines, including PRA, juvenile cataracts, seizures, allergies, bite malocclusion, hip dysplasia, and heart defects.

Males weigh between thirteen and fifteen and a half pounds; females weigh eleven and a half to fourteen pounds. You can expect a Border Terrier to live 12 to 15 years.

Boston Terrier

Native to the United States, the Boston Terrier originated in the late 1800s when an English Bulldog was crossed with a white English Terrier. Almost all Boston Terriers can trace their ancestry to Hooper's Judge, a dog who more closely resembled an English Bulldog. The Boston Terrier Club of America was established in 1891. Two years later, the breed was admitted to the AKC's stud book, and the breed club became an AKC member club.

Known as The American Gentleman, their distinctive black and white coat pattern has been likened to little men in tuxedos. Don't let that elegant look fool you, though–these are active little dogs who enjoy being kept busy, even if it's just with a rousing game of fetch. Bred to be companions, they will not let you forget it!

In the show ring, they are shown in three weight classes: under fifteen pounds, fifteen to twenty pounds, and twenty to twenty-five pounds. Their average life span is 10 to 12 years.

Among the problems seen in this breed are a variety of eye conditions, including corneal ulcers and all types of cataracts. Cardiac problems, patella luxation, hemivertibrae, and all of the problems associated with being brachycephalic have also been seen.

Brussels Griffon

Originating in Brussels, Belgium, this breed takes its name from that city. During the early 1800s coachmen kept small terrier-type dogs in the stables as ratters. In Belgium, these were Affenpinscher-type dogs known as Griffons d'Ecurie (wire-coated stable dogs). The Pug was bred to this native Belgian dog in the mid-1800s, and from this cross came a smooth-coated Griffon dubbed Brabancon in honor of the Belgian national anthem, *La brabanconne.*

Brussels Griffon

Courtesy Donna Vartanian

At about the same time, the black and tan King Charles Spaniel and Ruby varieties of the English Toy Spaniel were also crossed with the Belgian stable dogs. From these two crosses, two distinctive coat types and three color combinations emerged: the harsh coated, bewhiskered rough, and the smooth-coated Brabancon; and the rich red color, the black and tan, and the solid black. The Affenpinscher, Yorkshire Terrier, and Pekingese are also thought to be among the breeds that have contributed to the development of the Brussels Griffon we see today.

A charming, small companion with lustrous eyes and an almost human expression, weighing from six to twelve pounds, the Brussels Griffon's life span averages 10 to 15 years.

Lively, sturdy, and intelligent, they're also alert, very sensitive, and demand a lot of love and attention. They like the company of other dogs, as well as cats. They are active, hiking, romping, and playing with their human companions but will then lie quietly near their owner. However, if not well-socialized, the Brussels Griffons will withdraw into their shell.

Some are reportedly fairly easy to housetrain, while others seem never to be reliably housetrained. They do best with positive obedience training. Unless leash training is started early and made to be fun, the Brussels Griffon will stubbornly refuse to walk on a leash.

This is a brachycephalic (short-muzzled) breed; common sense should be used in hot weather. Among the problems that have been seen are patella luxation and PRA. Some are born with stenotic nares. The nares (nostrils) of those dogs should be opened, and they should be spayed or neutered to avoid passing on the problem to another generation.

Coat care of the smooth variety requires only regular bathing and brushing. The rough-coated variety should be hand plucked twice a year. A dog kept in show coat will require more frequent coat care.

Cairn Terrier

Named after the rock piles (cairns) in which they hunted vermin in their native Scottish Highlands and the Isle of Skye, Cairn Terriers are active little dogs. Two other breeds were also developed from the same original ancestors: the West Highland White Terrier and the Scottish Terrier. This lively, tenacious little dog is probably most like the original ancestors, who were true working Terriers. Recognized by the Kennel Club in Britain in 1910, the breed was granted AKC recognition in 1917.

Intelligent and playful into their teens, these little dogs live an average of 13 to 14 years. Males weigh about fourteen pounds and stand about ten inches at the withers; females average thirteen pounds and are approximately nine and a half inches at the withers.

Among the health problems that can be found in the breed are juvenile cataracts, craniomandibular osteopathy, globoid cell leukodystrophy, cardiac defects, hypothyroidism, Legg-Calve-Perthes disease, patella luxation, ocular melanosis/secondary glaucoma, portosystemic shunt, PRA, seizures and epilepsy, and von Willebrand's disease (a bleeding disorder).

These little dogs do very well at dog sports, including Canine Musical Freestyle.

Cavalier King Charles Spaniel

A very old breed, dogs of this type have been depicted in paintings dating back to the sixteenth century. A charming companion blessed with a sweet expression, the Cavalier is lovable, sensitive, and generally friendly toward strangers. However, Cavaliers must be properly socialized, or they'll become timid.

This breed doesn't mix with rowdy children. They require companionship, and don't do well if left alone all day. Active and trainable, Cavaliers do well in Obedience, Agility, Flyball, and field work. These little Spaniels still retain their hunting instincts and will express an interest in wildlife, yet they love to cuddle. They are easily housetrained.

Standing twelve to thirteen inches and weighing between thirteen and eighteen pounds, the Cavalier comes in a variety of colors and has a silky, flowing coat that requires regular brushing. The average life span is 11 years, although many Cavaliers live to 16.

Cavalier King Charles Spaniel

Courtesy of Bressler West ©

The health problems seen in this breed are mitral valve disease, patella luxation, retinal dysplasia, cataracts, hip dysplasia, deafness, epilepsy, allergies, and thyroid disease.

Most recently recognized is an hereditary neurological problem, syringomyelia. Syringomyelia is sometimes referred to as neck scratcher's disease because scratching in the air near the neck is a common sign of this painful disorder. The condition is caused by slowing of the flow of cerebrospinal fluid because the back of the brain extends downward through the hole at the back of the skull and obstructs the top of the spinal column. Best diagnosed with an MRI, drugs are used to control pain. Surgery for very painful cases is possible, but it is not always successful.

New research is under way to try to find a genetic marker for the disease, which would be very helpful to breeders trying to eliminate this problem.

Chihuahua

This smallest Toy's origins may not really be known, because there are so many conflicting theories. But Chihuahuas are commonly believed to have descended from a small dog called the Techichi, bred by the Toltecs, whose empire flourished in southern Mexico from the tenth to the twelfth centuries. Abundant relics of the breed have been found around Mexico City.

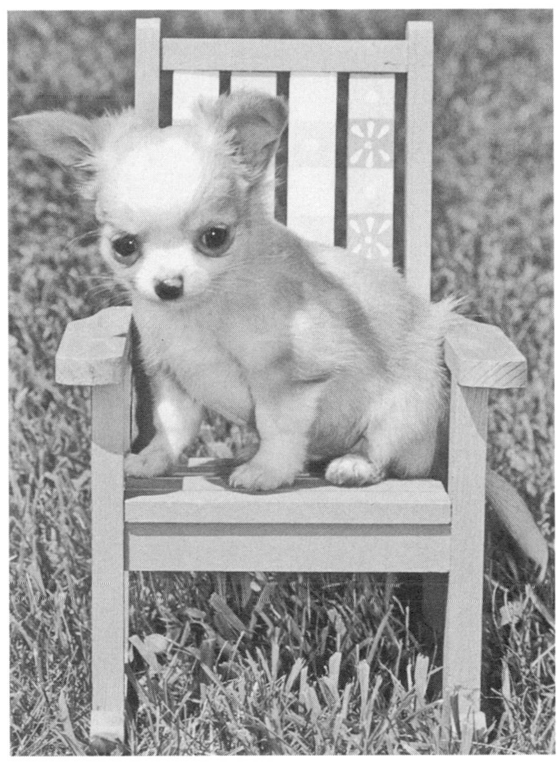

Chihuahua

Photo by Tara Darling ©, courtesy of Susan Payne

Weighing less than six pounds and easily injured, this is not a dog for the physically aggressive of any age. Partly because they are so small and vulnerable, some of these little dogs tend to be fearful. Timidity can also be a result of poor breeding.

Although they enjoy going out for a walk, a Chihuahua can get enough exercise romping through an apartment. He'll need a sweater or coat in winter and shouldn't spend too much time outdoors in cold climates.

Alert, playful little dogs who make good watchdogs, their breed standard describes them as "terrier-like." Chihuahuas adjust easily to a new home but can be shy if not properly socialized. They're intelligent and do very well in Obedience and Tracking. Chihuahuas also make good hearing dogs and therapy dogs but, like all dogs, need careful supervision so they're not inadvertently injured during a therapy visit.

The Chihuahua comes in two coat varieties: smooth and long. Obviously, the long coat will require more grooming.

Chihuahuas are relatively free of severe genetic problems and live 16 to 18 years on average. Some puppies are born with cleft palates and harelips. Other problems seen in the breed are patella luxation, heart murmur, collapsing trachea, and hydrocephalus. This breed has a soft spot on his head (the fontanel) that may never close, but Chihuahua breeders consider this normal in their breed.

The so-called "Teacup" Chihuahua is not a real variety, and reputable breeders consider them to be an anomaly. The very smallest dogs are not meant to be bred, but they do appear from time to time in a litter.

Chinese Crested

Many stories of origin surround these dogs. Some breeders say the breed was developed in China, but others disagree and add that before 1500 hairless dogs were never seen outside the New World, and that early explorers brought them to Europe. After 1500, however, references to hairless dogs are found all over the world.

It wasn't until the nineteenth century that British and American breeders tried to establish hairless breeds. The type of dog now called the Chinese Crested initially ranged from five to thirty pounds and varied in appearance. In the 1950s and 1960s, dogs who look like today's Chinese Cresteds began to be seen. They appeared first in the United States and later in Great Britain and Germany.

The Chinese Crested comes in two varieties: the Hairless, with tufts of hair only on his head, tail, and lower legs; and the Powderpuff, who is completely covered with long, silky hair. The Hairless has warm, soft, smooth skin that needs lots of protection from dryness and from the sun. These dogs will develop blackheads and whiteheads, so they should be bathed at least once a week. A unique feature of the Hairless dogs is that they have sweat glands in the skin (other dogs do not). Their skin is also thicker than that of a coated dog and heals very quickly if scratched or cut.

The Powderpuff doesn't shed excessively, but he does need a good daily brushing. Both varieties will need to wear a coat or sweater when going outdoors in chilly weather.

Chinese Cresteds

Courtesy of Amy Fernandez

Thought to have been used as bed warmers, these little dogs might also have been used for hunting, since they will chase rabbits and squirrels and have Houndlike characteristics. Standoffish with strangers, they adore their human family members, and sometimes the owner's trip to the mailbox is considered a long time away from home, to judge from the effusive greeting you'll receive upon returning!

Chinese Cresteds are generally healthy little dogs, living 15 or more years. The Hairless are often missing teeth and nails (factors related to the hairless gene), while the Powderpuffs have full dentition. Some have been seen with Legg-Calve-Perthes disease, patella luxation, detached retinas, and lens luxation.

Miniature Dachshund

The owners of Miniature Dachshunds are adamant that these dogs are true Hounds, not Toys. That's true, of course, but it's also true that the Minis are small dogs who have the same needs as other small dogs. At eleven pounds and under, they are Hounds by character but Toys by biology. And that means they deserve special consideration when it comes to training, nutrition, and their interactions in the great big world at large.

The breed name means "badger dog," which is indicative of their origins. Dachshunds were bred to hunt game in underground burrows–a job that requires a tough, tenacious dog. Dogs of a similar type are seen in illustrations as far back at the fifteenth century. The breed club has been a member of AKC since 1895. There is also a club in the United States for just Miniatures, which had been around for more than fifty years.

These long, low-slung German dogs come in three different coat varieties: Longhair, Smooth, and Wirehaired. They are playful little dogs and make charming companions. Having to endure being called Weiner Dogs, they display great good humor. These are often one-person dogs and will bond very closely to their human.

Not a very easy breed to housetrain, these little dogs are subject to disc problems. They can also have PRA and can bloat because they have deep chests, These little dogs can live to 15 years old.

English Toy Spaniel

The English Toy Spaniel, known in Britain as the King Charles Spaniel, is one of the oldest breeds. It is thought these darling little companions trace their roots back to Japan and possibly to ancient China, although they take their name from England's King Charles II (who reigned from 1660 to 1685).

These bred-down Spaniels come in four color varieties, each with their own powerful patron. The King Charles variety is black and tan. They were brought from France by the king's sister, Henrietta of Orleans. The Prince Charles is white, black, and tan, and the Ruby is chestnut red. The Blenheim is red and white and was developed by the first Duke of Marlborough. Their coat requires weekly brushing and combing.

English Toy Spaniels are affectionate, intelligent dogs weighing between nine and twelve pounds. Their life span is 10 to 12 years. A born and bred lapdog, happy to sit rather than romp, the English Toy Spaniel enjoys the company of other pets. They're cautious with strangers. Bright and willing to please, these dogs have still retained some of their hunting instincts.

English Toy Spaniels are somewhat independent, so obedience training will take a bit of time. They can get intimidated quite easily and must be raised with love and treated the same as any other dog, or they'll become timid.

This breed has few health problems, but patella luxation has been seen, as well as cataracts, inguinal hernias, and heart murmurs. Because of their very shortened faces, they tend to be especially sensitive to anesthesia.

Toy Fox Terrier

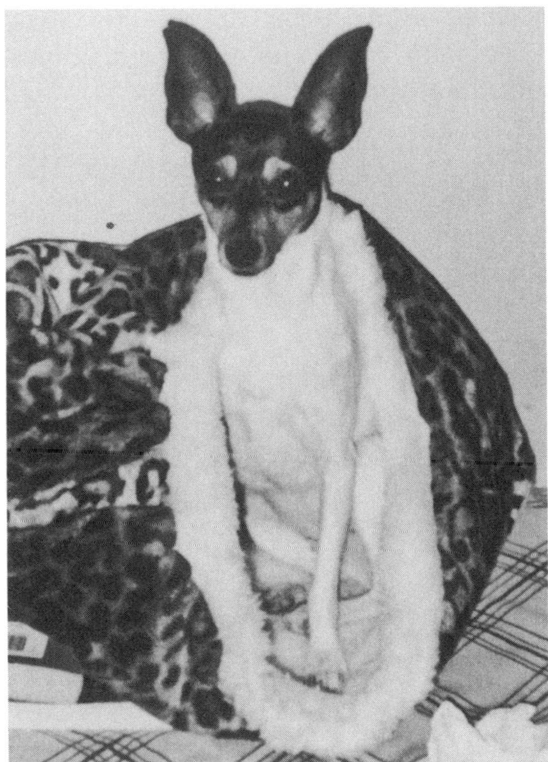

Toy Fox Terrier

Courtesy of Anne Gendron

Both a true Toy and a true Terrier, the Toy Fox Terrier is a small character who has no concept of his minuscule size. Friendly toward strangers, the Toy Fox Terrier is also fiercely loyal to family members and totally tuned in to his owners.

The result of crossing small Smooth Fox Terriers with several other breeds, including the Manchester Terrier, Miniature Pinschers, Italian Greyhounds, and Chihuahuas, Toy Fox Terriers were recognized by the United Kennel Club (UKC) in 1936, but it wasn't until 2003 that they received AKC recognition.

The breed really is a working Terrier in a tiny body. They will still tree a squirrel, displaying their prowess at hunting, which has never diminished. This is an active little dog suited for someone with an active lifestyle. They will enjoy Obedience trials as much as a good snuggle on the couch.

Toy Fox Terriers range from eight and a half to eleven and a half inches at the withers and live from 13 to 18 years. Among the health problems seen are demodectic mange, patellar luxation, Legg-Calve-Perthes, von Willebrand's disease, and congenital hypothyroidism with goiter.

Havanese

The Havanese is an old breed of the Bichon family, which includes the Bichon Frise, the Maltese, the Coton de Tulear, and the Bolognese. The earliest references to the ancestors of

Havanese

Courtesy of Nancy Dionne

the modern Havanese go back to Plinius (23 to 79 BCE) in the Mediterranean region, where they were reportedly placed on a person's stomach to cure stomach aches.

Both Spain and Italy played an integral part in bringing the Havanese to the New World. Also known as the Havana Silk Dog, today's Havanese descended from the dogs who found a permanent home in Cuba, where they were popular among the wealthy.

Sturdy and short-legged, their eyes are large and dark, with a soft expression. Havanese have a soft, profuse, untrimmed double coat that ranges from straight to curly in many colors and color combinations. It requires frequent brushing, but the dog doesn't shed much.

They do blow their coats occasionally—a major shed when almost all the hair is replaced—beginning at around 10 months of age. When they do, they'll require extra grooming, or the coat will quickly become tangled.

Havanese range from eight and a half to eleven and a half inches and weigh from seven to thirteen pounds. Their average life span is 12 years.

Happy dogs, Havanese thrive on affection and human companionship as full-fledged family members. They love to swim and play in the water. These outgoing little companions have a very calm, easygoing disposition. Havanese are sensitive to even an angry word and, like every dog, must never be hit or physically corrected. Dogs of the Bichon family can be difficult to completely housetrain and will have accidents.

They're agile and learn quickly, which makes them good Obedience candidates and probably accounts for reports that they were taught to do tricks for entertainment. They've been successfully used as therapy dogs.

When I wrote *The Irrepressible Toy Dog* in 1998, this breed was relatively free of genetic disorders beyond late-onset PRA. Sadly, this is no longer true. Havanese are now recognized to have cataracts, chondrodysplasia, patella luxation, Legg-Calve-Perthes, elbow dysplasia, portosystemic shunt, hepatic microvascular dysplasia, and some reportedly healthy dogs will have abnormal liver values. They are also seen with cardiac murmurs, deafness, and in lesser numbers there are Havanese who have seizures, kidney dysplasia, hypothyroidism, and skin problems that include sebaceous adenitis.

Italian Greyhound

An extremely old breed, believed to have originated more than two thousand years ago in what is today Greece and Turkey, Italian Greyhounds were probably among the first breeds to be developed exclusively as companions. They were found throughout southern Europe by the Middle Ages and became a favorite of the Italians in the sixteenth century.

The smallest of the Sighthounds, Italian Greyhounds range from five to fifteen pounds. Yet despite their small size, these are true Greyhounds. They have been royal favorites in

Britain, Denmark, Italy, Prussia, and Russia for centuries, and their elegance is widely admired.

Adaptable to both city and country living, happily residing in an apartment but enjoying exercise and outdoor activities, Italian Greyhounds prefer to be indoors most of the time and dislike the rain. This is not a breed that can be left alone to fend for himself in the backyard. (Actually, *no* small dog should be left alone in the backyard!) These loving little dogs require a lot of human interaction and prefer their family members, treating strangers with some reserve. If they're not properly socialized, they may become shy or hyperactive.

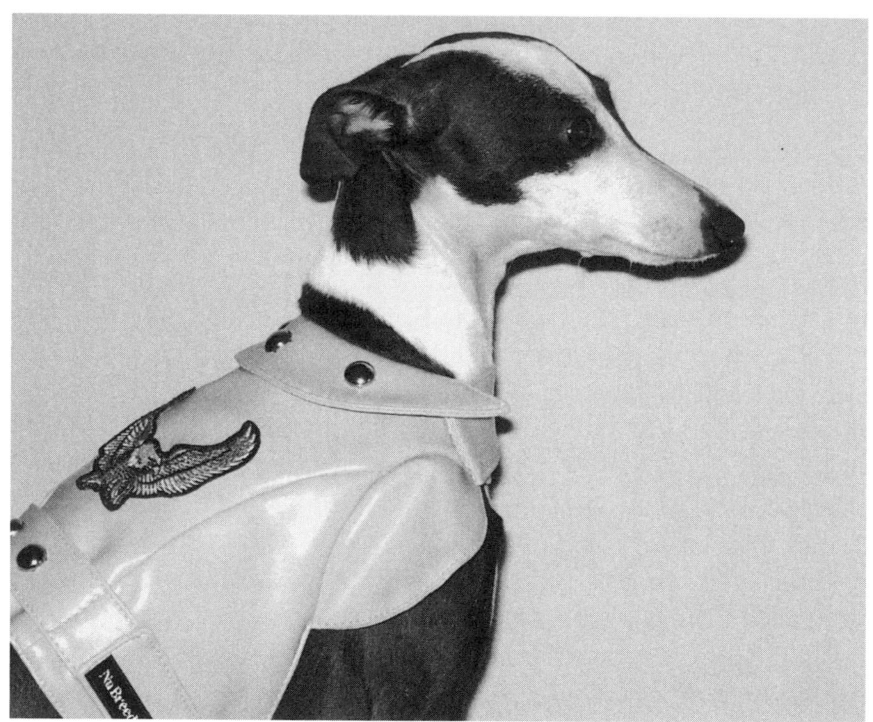

Italian Greyhound

Courtesy of Lilian Barber

Italian Greyhounds have a short, smooth coat with minimal shedding and require little grooming. But they will need a sweater or coat on chilly days and shouldn't be kept outside for very long when it's very cold or very hot. They're odorless and don't yap. In fact, the voice is rather deep for such a small dog.

Italian Greyhounds can easily be injured playing with a child. They get along with other animals in the household, especially if they've been raised together. They are also easily bored, which shortens their attention span. It is up to their trainer to keep them interested. Some have done well in Obedience, but most find the work too repetitive.

A fairly hardy little breed with a 12- to 14-year life span, many Italian Greyhounds live to be 16 or even 18. Hypothyroidism and other autoimmune problems, as well as PRA, some seizure disorders, Legg-Calve-Perthes, and subluxated patellas have shown up. A few bloodlines have a predisposition for leg fractures because they lack bone density. Von Willebrand's disease has also appeared in some lines.

Japanese Chin

It is likely this ancient breed originated in China and was then brought to Japan, probably as gifts from Chinese emperors to the Japanese royalty. In Japan there are *inu* (dogs), and there are Chin. In 1853, when Commodore Matthew Perry opened up Japan to international trade, he was given a pair of Japanese Chin that he later presented to Queen Victoria.

Intelligent, sensitive, lively, and aristocratic, the Japanese Chin has a distinctive Asian look. His straight, silky, particolor coat is draped over a small, compact body that's eight to eleven inches at the withers. Grooming is minimal but must be done regularly.

Reserved until they know you, Chin get along well with cats and other dogs, but they especially like other Chin. And like cats, they'll groom each other. Not exactly couch potatoes, they enjoy playing outside with their owners.

These intelligent little dogs have participated in Obedience, but they're not easily trained. The exercises must be made interesting for them; if they want to do something, they'll learn quickly.

Japanese Chin

Courtesy of Rose Marchetti

Chin are clean but, as with other Toys, housetraining must be consistent. They're also good therapy dogs. But they are far too delicate for small children.

Like other brachycephalic breeds, they suffer in the heat. These little dogs are long-lived, however, with some reaching 18 years. Health problems include luxating patellas, PRA, cataracts, gangliosidosis, dwarfism, seizures, breathing problems, and sensitivity to anesthesia.

Lhasa Apso

Native to Tibet, Lhasa Apsos have been mistaken for fluffy little lapdogs. Although they may enjoy a good cuddle, it would be wise to note that they were bred to be guard dogs with an innate ability to quickly distinguish friends from strangers and were known in their native land as the "Bark Lion Sentinel Dog."

They are one of three breeds from the area of the Tibetan lamaseries and villages (the others are the Tibetan Terrier and the Tibetan Spaniel). The Lhasa was the first of the three to receive AKC recognition, which came in 1935. Originally in the Terrier Group, they were moved to the Non-Sporting Group in 1959.

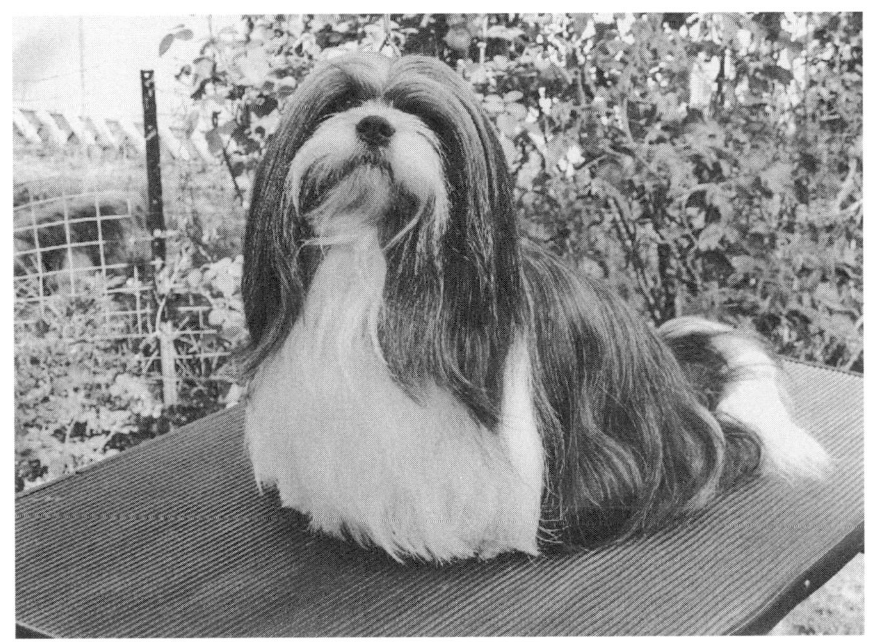

Lhasa Apso

Courtesy of Judith Lynn Laffoon

These little dogs are wary of strangers, as befits their origins, and are still watchful. They're independent and can be stubborn. They respond best to positive training.

The dense coat of the Lhasa requires regular grooming and regular baths. They stand about ten or eleven inches at the shoulder and weigh an average of twelve to eighteen pounds. Kidney disease is perhaps their most serious health problem. They live from 12 to 18 years.

Lowchen

Lowchen means "little lion" in German—an apt name for this delightful little character whose insouciance is utterly captivating. These small dogs have been a distinct breed for more than four hundred years and were companions in pre-Renaissance Europe, clipped even then to resemble small lions. Today, they are still shown with close-clipped hindquarters and a full, natural mane.

Lowchen

Courtesy of Karen Chisam

Intelligent and affectionate, these loveable little charmers make great companions and do very well in Agility and other dog sports. The have a positive, outgoing attitude and a strong, sturdy body to go with it.

Weighing from twelve to fifteen pounds, their average life span is 13 to 15 years. Among the health problems seen in Lowchen are PRA, cataracts, Legg-Calve-Perthes disease, and patella luxation.

Maltese

These charming, graceful, affectionate little dogs originated on the island of Malta thousands of years ago. The Greeks erected tombs for their Maltese, a breed gifted with intelligence and an outgoing personality. At the time of the Apostle Paul, Publius, the Roman governor of Malta, had a Maltese named Issa. The little dog was immortalized in a poem: "Issa is more frolicsome than Catulla's sparrow. Issa is purer than a dove's kiss."

Quiet and even-tempered, Maltese were bred to be true companions. Weighing under seven pounds, with four to six pounds preferred, they're ideal apartment dogs. They will sometimes bond with one special person, but without excluding the other family members.

Maltese enjoy playing, and many of them have a spirited nature beneath that gorgeous silky coat. The coat requires a lot of care, including daily brushing to keep it free from mats, and frequent bathing. Some Maltese's eyes tear and stain more than others; puppies are more likely to have tear stains when they're teething.

Older Maltese are adaptable and adjust well to a new home. They try to please their people, which makes them fairly easy to train. Maltese should never be allowed exclusive run of the house until you are certain they're completely housetrained. They're good watch-dogs, sounding an alarm when someone comes to the door, but they generally settle down once the visitor has entered.

When stressed, the Maltese can develop hypoglycemia, causing seizures and possible coma. Maltese puppies under 12 weeks old are also especially susceptible to hypoglycemia.

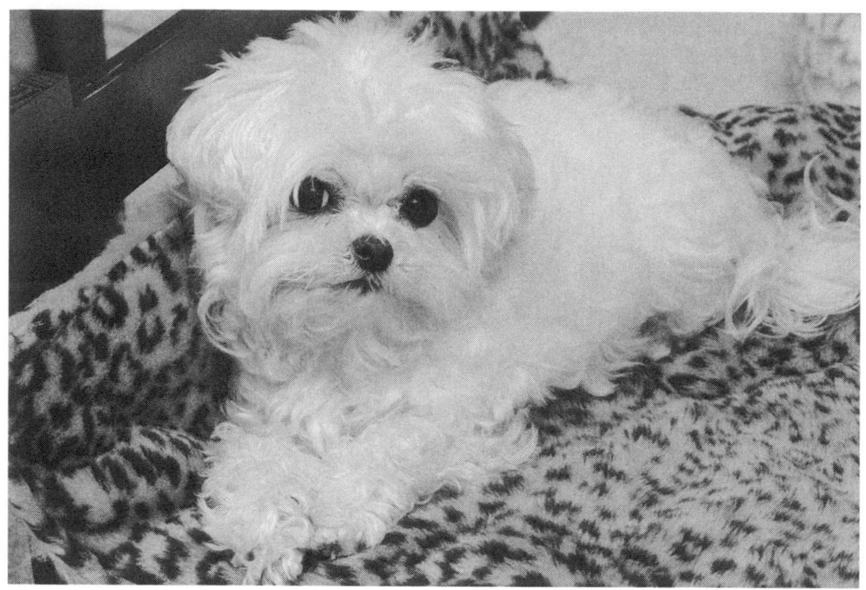

Maltese

Courtesy of Betty Wang

It's a fairly healthy little breed, although there have been occasional instances of PRA and heart problems, as well as patella luxation, entropion, glaucoma, hypothyroidism, collapsing trachea, and deafness. A healthy Maltese can live 12 years or more.

Toy Manchester Terrier

Weighing less than twelve pounds, this is a true Toy version of the Standard Manchester Terrier. The Manchester Terrier originated in Britain when dog fancier John Hulme crossed a

Whippet bitch with a noted rat-killing dog. The breed further developed in the 1880s, when poor sanitation led to plagues of rats. Small rat-killing dogs were much in demand, including the Toy Manchester, known at the time as the Black-and-Tan Terrier. The Toy Manchester is known in Britain as the English Toy Terrier.

These energetic little dogs will still go to ground (chase quarry in underground burrows), which means they'll enjoy participating in Earthdog tests. They're also good at Obedience, Tracking, and Flyball.

This is a Toy with a Terrier temperament. Cautious with strangers, preferring their owners, they will bond most closely with one member of the family even while they love everyone. Not a sparring breed, they're generally dog-friendly. The owner must be top dog, but gentle training methods should always be used.

Adventuresome little companions, they'll have no qualms about exploring on their own if not kept carefully supervised. They're good with senior citizens and enjoy carrying on a "conversation."

The smooth coat requires brushing. Toy Manchesters are very clean, and housetraining shouldn't be a problem.

Health problems are few, but watch for Legg-Calve-Perthes disease, PRA, von Willebrand's disease, hypothyroidism, and seizures.

Miniature Pinscher

This breed from Germany has been around for several centuries. He looks like a small Doberman Pinscher and certainly acts like a much larger dog, but the Min Pin is *not* a bred-down Doberman. In fact, the breed is older than the Doberman by centuries.

The Min Pin is a lively, intelligent, active companion and makes a good watchdog. The coat is solid red, black, or chocolate with red markings, and requires minimal grooming but should be brushed regularly.

These are very good Obedience and Agility dogs. Males may be more difficult to housetrain, but it can be done with patience and consistency. Min Pins like to express themselves vocally, and they can be master escape artists.

Miniature Pinscher

Courtesy of Barbara Zagrodnick

Min Pins stand ten to twelve and a half inches at the withers and live an average of 14 to 15 years. They're hardy, but watch for patella luxation, Legg-Calve-Perthes disease, PRA, cervical disc problems, cardiac defects, thyroid problems, cataracts, diabetes, osteopenia, and pannus.

Papillon

The Papillon we see today has been around since the thirteenth century, and the breed appears frequently in the paintings of the European old masters. Originally called the Dwarf Spaniel, later the Toy Spaniel or Continental Toy Spaniel, at first the breed had drop ears. Today, the drop-ear variety is known as the Phalene. They are always particolored or white with patches of color.

This breed was very popular in the French court and was a favorite of Marie Antoinette. Perhaps it was she who gave these charming dogs their name—*papillon* is French for butterfly.

The Papillon is a wonderful, fearless companion who excels at Obedience and Agility. Standing between eight and eleven inches at the withers, these are very active little dogs.

Papillon

Photo by Amber Grundman, courtesy of Judy Scott

When they're young, they may even be too active for some people, and they definitely need obedience training to channel that energy. Teaching them to lie down and stay on command will be invaluable. When they're a little older, Papillons are better able to adjust their energy to the owner's level. Papillons are adaptable, affectionate, and love to travel. A good dog for older people once he has outgrown that energetic puppy stage, he will lie down and relax near someone, but can also chase a ball or a toy all day.

Regular brushing is required or the hair will mat, especially behind the ears and elbows. Papillons can be seriously injured by young children or larger dogs, but they will get along well with dogs closer to their own size and with feline family members.

Health problems that have been found in the breed are patella luxation, PRA, portosystemic shunt, cataracts, entropion, hypoglycemia, collapsing trachea, PDA, and open fontanel. They're reportedly sensitive to certain drugs, and giving penicillin to a Papillon under anesthesia can be deadly. Papillons can live as long as 15 to 17 years. Death in old age is usually the result of kidney failure.

Parson Russell Terrier

The Parson Russell Terrier, originally called the Jack Russell Terrier when it was recognized by the AKC in 1997 (the name was changed in 2003), is a very active working Terrier and is commonly seen as a companion for horses. Interestingly, the companion of a recent Lassie was also a Parson Russell Terrier.

Developed in Britain by Parson John Russell (1795–1883), who was a founding member of the Kennel Club, this short-legged dog was bred to hunt red fox both above and below ground.

Living an average of 14 to 15 years and weighing between fourteen and seventeen pounds, these extremely active dogs need to have a job to do or they will choose something themselves that is hardly likely to make their owner happy. Plan to become very active in one of the more athletic dog sports if you want a Parson Russell Terrier.

A relatively healthy dog, some genetic problems have been seen, including deafness, patella luxation, PRA, lens luxation, and juvenile cataracts.

Pekingese

The origins of the Pekingese are as inscrutable as the country they come from. The earliest records of the breed date from the Tang Dynasty (618 to 907). Pekes were always palace dogs, treasured by emperors and forbidden to commoners. When the British looted the Imperial Palace in Beijing in 1860, five Pekingese were found behind some draperies. One ended up with Queen Victoria, and the West was introduced to these Little Lion Dogs.

The Peke standard says medium size is preferred, with a weight of not more than fourteen pounds. But the Chinese also kept Sleeve Dogs, carried in the long silk sleeves of imperial household members, who weighed less than six pounds.

The elegant coat comes in several colors. It has long, straight outer hairs and a thick undercoat. The coat requires a good deal of work—you can count on brushing a Pekingese at least an hour each week. Males shed annually; females shed with their heat cycles.

Pekingese

Courtesy of Rose Marchetti

A Pekingese lives 13 to 15 years, on average. The bowed front legs mean very long walks aren't part of the picture, and neither is energetic exercise!

Their personalities vary with the individual dog. Some co-exist with other pets; others don't. Some get along with large dogs, others want to fight with them. Some are quite territorial and want to chase away all visitors, while others are extremely welcoming. Some can make good therapy dogs.

Pekes can be quite stubborn and require a lot of patience during training. They generally do not like to walk on a leash, so they'll need early leash training. They only like children if raised with them. These are good little watchdogs, setting up a vocal alarm when strangers approach.

A brachycephalic breed with prominent eyes, they'll suffer in the heat, and their eyes must be protected from injury. They have also been known to have pastern or patella luxation, umbilical hernia, corneal ulceration, stenotic nares, Legg-Calve-Perthes disease, dry eye, and spinal problems.

Pomeranian

Pomeranians look like descendants of the large Northern breeds, as if they might be bred down from the sled dogs of Iceland or Lapland. But some examples of ancient Mediterranean earthenware vessels and mosaics depict small dogs with a strong resemblance to more modern Poms, so this may not be true.

The name comes from Pomerania, an area of northern Germany near modern Poland. The breed did not originate there, but that's where they may have been bred down to Toy size. As late as the middle of the nineteenth century there were larger Pomeranians, usually black or white, who were able sheep herders. In the eighteenth century a small red dog resembling the Pomeranian was known in France as the Loup-Loup (little wolf). That dog resembled today's American Eskimo Dog. But it's the Finnish Spitz that is thought to bear the closest relationship to today's Pom.

Queen Victoria maintained a show kennel of Poms she acquired while on a trip to Italy. When she was given a tiny red Loup-Loup whose color was greatly admired, he was introduced into the lines.

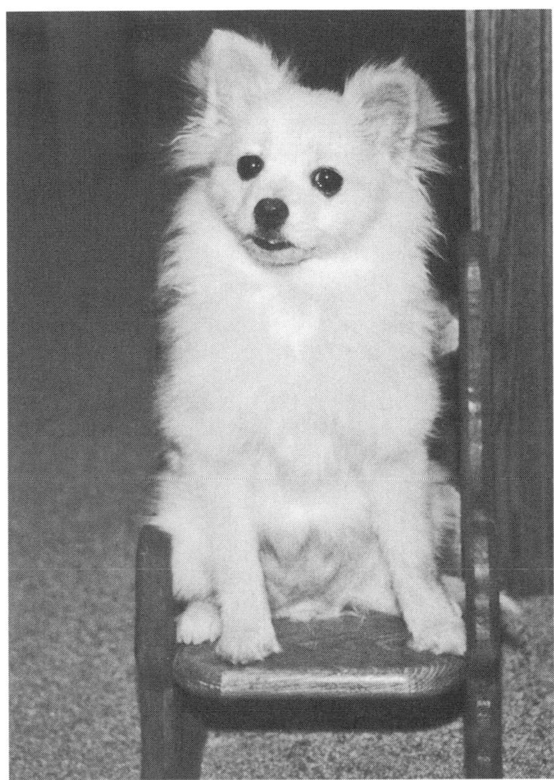

Pomeranian

Courtesy of Tracy Corso

An active, alert, intelligent, talkative little dog who loves his human family members and is defensive of his territory, the Pom is a good watchdog. Poms live well in a group and generally aren't aggressive toward each other, but will fearlessly defend against an approaching dog, no matter how large.

A daily walk will provide adequate exercise. The long, thick double coat with a short undercoat is protection against heat, cold, rain, and snow. It needs infrequent bathing but regular brushing. After the mature coat has developed, at about a year old, dust and other types of soil seem to slide off the smooth, straight hairs. Unless several Poms are playing and mouthing each other around the ears, their fur doesn't mat.

Weighing from three to seven pounds, the tiniest Poms will be more delicate. Pomeranians live 12 or more years.

Poms do very well in Obedience, since they learn quickly, are easily trained, and want to please their owners. They can be good therapy dogs. Ideal for adults and very gentle older children, Poms do not usually do well with young children.

Potential health problems include collapsing trachea, patella luxation, PRA, cataracts, dwarfism, entropian, hypoglycemia, and PDA.

Toy Poodle

This may well be the oldest of the three Poodle varieties (Toy, Miniature, and Standard). Germany, France, and Russia have all been thought to be countries of origin. Small dogs

resembling Poodles are depicted on monuments to Roman Emperor Augustus dating from about the year 30. Obviously an old breed, a white Poodle appears in a German painting circa 1620.

The term French Poodle (not actually a variety) probably stems from their popularity in that country. The French definitely contributed to the Poodle's look, adding decorative pompoms and rosettes to the show clip seen in the ring today. The French may also have introduced the Maltese and the Havanese into the breed.

These small dogs were once used to hunt truffles, because their delicate paws would not damage the mushrooms.

The Toy Poodle is a terrific little Obedience dog, and several have earned the coveted Obedience Trial Champion (OTCh.) title. The breed also does well in Agility, freestyle, and as therapy dogs. Despite his uncanny ability to look like a stuffed animal, the Toy Poodle is a very playful, intelligent companion.

This energetic little dog stands no more than ten inches at the withers. He comes in a variety of colors and scarcely sheds, but does require an incredible amount of grooming and will need regular clipping. The average life span of a Toy Poodle is 12 to 15 years.

The breed has its share of health concerns, including patella luxation, cataracts, PRA, epilepsy, collapsing trachea, Cushing's disease, and hypoglycemia.

Pug

A square, cobby, humorous little charmer, despite a dignified appearance, the Pug dates back to 400 BCE, originating in China. The breed was prized by the emperors; the Foo Dog was the ancient Pug. Dutch traders brought Pugs to the Netherlands, where they became favorites of William of Orange when a Pug's barking alerted the prince to invading Spaniards and saved his life. William's tomb contains a carving of the monarch with his Pug.

Pugs are loving, clean, intelligent, and sturdy, and they don't require extensive grooming time. The Pug's natural affinity for being near his owner also makes this a good breed for the elderly.

The Pug is even-tempered and playful. They exude charm. Anxious to please and anxious to learn, Pugs can do well in Obedience.

The adult Pug weighs between fourteen and eighteen pounds. Life span averages 12 to 14 years. A brachycephalic breed, the Pug will have all of the problems associated with this. Health problems can include Legg-Calve-Perthes disease, patella luxation, hip dysplasia, PRA, cataracts, entropion, eye injuries, corneal ulcers, epilepsy, liver disease, Pug dog encephalitis, and sensitivity to anesthesia.

Shih Tzu

Originating in the monasteries of Tibet, Shih Tzu were bred to resemble the heavenly lions that play a role in Tibetan Buddhism. The first Shih Tzu in China were probably gifts from the Tibetan Lamas to the Chinese emperors. In the Chinese court, these dogs were bred with great care. Many pictures of them were kept in *The Imperial Dog Book*.

Sturdy little characters who love long walks, Shih Tzu are at once playful and self-important. The least delicate of the Toys, they're shown in the Toy Group only in the United States and Bermuda. True companions with a sense of humor, they're outgoing and charming; a stranger is only a friend they haven't met, and that usually includes other pets.

The long coat, which comes in a variety of colors, will require extensive grooming, although the pet Shih Tzu's coat can be kept in a short trim.

Shih Tzu weigh between nine and sixteen pounds and stand eight to eleven inches at the withers. Like all dogs, the Shih Tzu should receive basic obedience training. These dogs are intelligent and gentle, but they tend not to do well in formal Obedience competition (although several have earned advanced titles). They do much better as therapy dogs.

Unfortunately, Shih Tzu puppies have a propensity to eat their own excrement, so you should clean up after them before they have a chance to!

Shih Tzu live 10 to 14 years, on average. This breed needs protection from heat. It is also notorious for inherited kidney problems. Potential health problems include patella luxation, dwarfism, renal cortical hypoplasia, juvenile renal dysplasia, autoimmune hemolytic anemia, von Willebrand's disease, and several genetic eye diseases.

Silky Terrier

This hardy little Terrier, native to Australia, is thought to have a number of different Terriers in his background. Many believe the likeliest origins to be a cross between an Australian Terrier and a Yorkshire Terrier. The breed emerged at the turn of the previous century, and the breed type stabilized by the 1930s.

Silky Terriers

Courtesy of Linda Hart

The Silky's odor-free blue and tan coat hardly sheds at all, but requires daily brushing to keep it free from mats and to give it the glossy sheen that earned the breed his name.

Silkies are active, affectionate, energetic, sociable, and hardy. These are real one-family dogs, and they make good watchdogs. They are wary of strangers until a family member has welcomed the newcomer. Some are not particularly dog-friendly; others are.

Weighing about ten pounds and standing nine to ten inches at the withers, these intelligent little dogs can do quite well in Obedience. Silkies are clean, so housetraining shouldn't be too difficult. They have a 15- to 16-year life span.

Health problems seen in this breed include patella luxation, Legg-Calve-Perthes disease, diabetes, epilepsy, and collapsing trachea.

Xoloitzcuintli

The Xoloitzcuintli (pronounced *show-low-its-queen-tlee*), familiarly called the Xolo (*show-low*), is an ancient hairless breed who has his roots firmly planted in Mexico, although one theory is that they first appeared in Ecuador. The name comes from the Aztec god Xolot, and *itzuintli,* which is the Aztec word for dog.

This is the national dog of Mexico, and they date back as artistic subjects more than 3,000 years to the Colima pottery dogs. From 1500 to 1700 the breed seemed to disappear, but in the mid-1800s there was a renaissance of the Xolo. It took time to truly establish the breed in the United States. The Xoloitzcuintli Club of America was formed in 1986 and incorporated in 1989.

These are intelligent, lively dogs. Moviegoers will remember seeing Xolos in the biographical movie of the life of Frieda Kahlo.

The breed comes in three sizes, including the Toy. There are also two varieties: hairless and coated. Average life span is 12 to 14 years, and they can be up to thirteen inches at the withers.

Among the genetic problems that have been seen in this breed are Legg-Calve-Perthes disease, sealed ear canals, patella luxation, acne, umbilical hernia, and, in the coated variety, demodectic mange.

Yorkshire Terrier

Native to Britain, the Yorkshire Terrier made his first appearance as the Broken-Haired Scotch Terrier in 1861. He has a mixed heritage, thought to include Clydesdale, Paisley, and Skye Terriers. These were bred with the dogs native to Lancashire and Yorkshire, including the Manchester Terrier, Black and Tan Terrier, and Halifax Fawn. Even the Maltese has been mentioned as having been bred with the Yorkie to improve coat quality and texture.

Peter Eden of Manchester is credited as owning the first entry of a Yorkshire Terrier, named Albert, in the Kennel Club Stud Book. Albert appears prominently in both sides of Huddersfield Ben's pedigree, and Ben is considered the father of the breed.

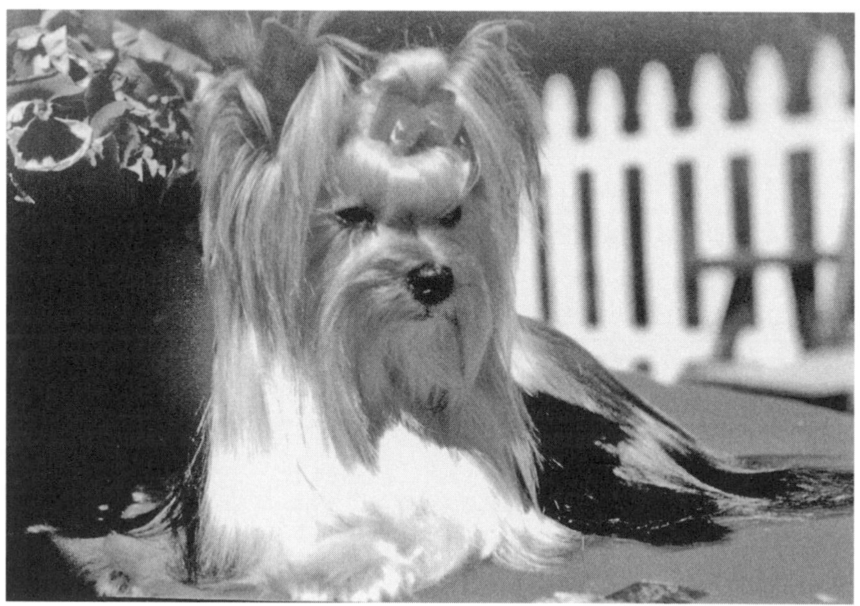

Yorkshire Terrier

Courtesy of Linda Grimm

With all of the stubbornness, courage, charisma, and intelligence of a Terrier, you can almost see the wheels turning in a Yorkie's head as he outsmarts you. This is a happy and active dog but, at less than seven pounds, he needs a gentle owner. The breed's many charming characteristics include an ability to smile with their mouth closed and, in some lines, to grin by deliberately showing their teeth in an unmistakable expression of silly pleasure.

Most are enthusiastic jumpers and must be carefully watched so that they don't injure themselves leaping up or down from high places. Yorkies, having no conception of their size, will often foolishly challenge a larger dog.

Their crowning glory is their long blue and tan coat, which doesn't shed but requires extensive brushing to keep it free from mats. Yorkies can do well in Obedience, and the quieter ones can make lovely therapy dogs. Life span averages 11 to 15 years.

Potential health problems include patella luxation, Legg-Calve-Perthes disease, collapsing trachea, lymphangiactasia, hypoglycemia, and a predisposition to pancreatitis. Unfortunately, there's also a high prevalence of liver shunt in this breed.

Appendix

Fun and Fabulous Ways to Pamper Your Little Dog

Your little go-everywhere dog adds joy to your life and fun to your home. Your dog does so much for your spirit, for your life, that you probably want to pamper him a bit. From the sublime to the—dare I say it?—ridiculous, there are many ways in which you can do exactly that. From clothes to carriers to fancy beds and dishes and more, the possibilities are seemingly endless. Here is just a small sample of the fabulous things you can do and buy to pamper your pint-size pup.

Have Dog, Will Travel

When you chose a small dog, you were guaranteed that you would have one who could go virtually everywhere with you. Yes, owners of larger dogs can take their dogs with them, but not with the same ease as a little one. Unless you're going on a transatlantic flight, your little dog can ride in a carrier in the cabin with you. There's nothing quite like a portable companion. Owners of larger dogs don't have that luxury.

Maltese

Courtesy of Betty Wang

A well-mannered little dog is an absolute delight, which is why small dogs are usually welcomed in far more places. And after all, that's why you got a dog in the first place—to have a companion. But there are some things that you should do whenever you take your dog on a trip.

You should have at least one form of identification on your dog; this can be either a collar and tag, a microchip, or a tattoo. If you opt for microchipping or tattooing, don't forget to register the number so you and your dog can be reunited if she gets away from you. Keep a current picture of your dog with you, also for identification. In fact, having two forms of identification is even better.

Carry some of your dog's food in a plastic bag—either enough for the entire trip or a small amount to tide you over until you can get to a pet supply store and buy a small bag of

food to last through your stay. This is no time to change your dog's food. Bring along bottled water, too. Water changes from one location to another, and you don't want to upset your dog's digestive tract.

Be sure to carry a first-aid kit. You can easily make one yourself, or you can buy a doggie first-aid kit that has been prepackaged. It's a good idea to have two of them; one for the car and one for the house. And don't forget to ask your veterinarian or a trusted friend for the name of a veterinarian in the area where you'll be traveling, in case there's an emergency. Your dog will also have to visit the veterinarian to get a health certificate within ten days before your trip.

Timely Tips

If you fly internationally, the airlines will insist that your little dog go in the baggage compartment. It hardly seems fair, but that's the rule at the present time. If you have to do that, use an airline-approved carrier, label it clearly in several places with the words "LIVE ANIMAL," fix your dog's identification and a photo to the top, and tie a small bag of food to it in case your dog needs feeding as soon as you arrive or she somehow gets put on the wrong connecting flight. In fact, you should try to book a nonstop flight whenever possible. Ask that the crate be situated near the door where there will be drafts of fresh air. And be sure to tell the flight attendant that you have a dog in the cargo compartment so that area will be kept pressurized. One trick used by Fresh Pond Travel (more about them soon) is to hand the flight attendant a note to give to the captain; use the note to introduce yourself and tell the captain that your dog is flying in the cargo hold and to please be sure it's pressurized and warm. If you can freeze water in the crate's metal dish before putting it into the crate, it will slowly melt, allowing your dog to have fresh water without much spillage.

If you're carrying your dog on board, be sure the carrier you use will fit under the seat without collapsing on your dog. It should conform to the space that's available. Some airlines now have frequent flyer programs for pets. This is a great idea, and you may want to consider supporting one of the airlines that are so accommodating to pet owners. Check with individual airlines to see who is offering these programs when you're ready to book your trip.

If you're traveling by car, be sure your dog is either in a crate or a safe car seat designed for dogs. Seat belts for dogs are also available, but little dogs do better in a car seat or crate.

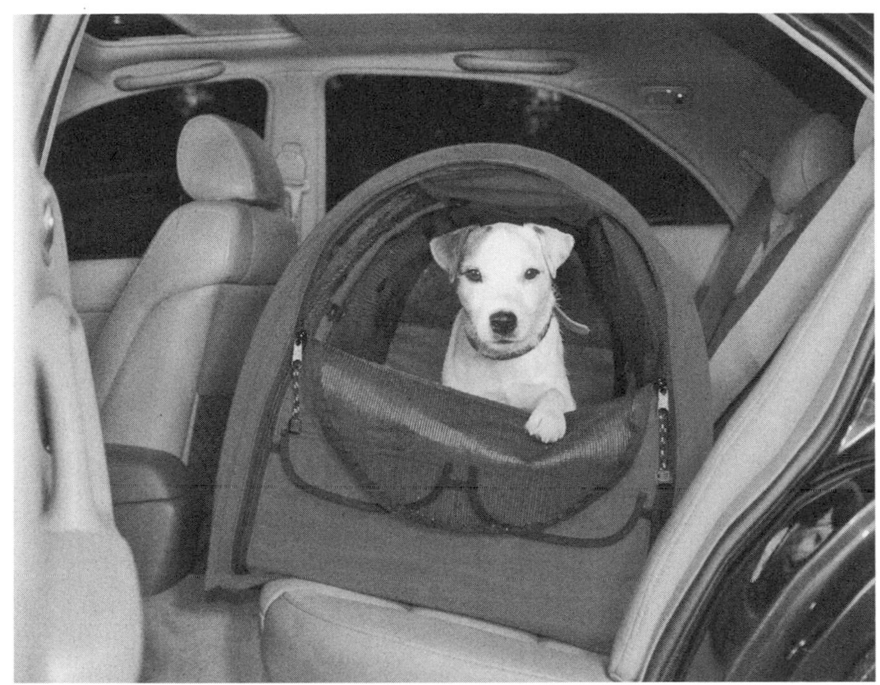

Parson Russell Terrier

Courtesy of Sturdi Products

You don't want your dog to go flying through the window if there's an accident, or become injured because you had to stop short. Be sure to stop for walks so your little companion can stretch her legs and take care of business.

Where in the World?

Where do you want to go? The sky's the limit. **Fresh Pond Travel** (www.freshpondtravel.com) is the travel agency that moves more dogs and owners than any other. They will not only help you plan your trip and book your dog's travel, but they also run dog show tours that you can take with or without your dog, in the company of other dog lovers. You can

e-mail this full-service travel agency at freshpondtravel@verizon.net or phone them toll free at (877) SHOWDOG. They have a mailing list for their dog show tours around the world, and you might want to ask to be added to the list.

Bring Your Pet.com (www.bringyourpet.com) is a web site with an e-mail newsletter. They specialize in listings of dog-friendly accommodations around the world. The newsletter gathers stories about animals from all over the globe.

Canine Couture

Dress your dog? Well, a warm sweater, a comfy T-shirt, or a snuggly coat will do wonders for your little dog, who loses body heat more rapidly than her larger cousins. There are a lot of owners who enjoy dressing their dogs up in cute outfits for nursing home or hospital visits, as well, or just for fun. There's an amazing array of clothing for little dogs, as well as fashion accessories. And everything seems to come in virtually every price range to suit every budget. One caveat: Those carriers that let the dog's feet hang out are not a good idea. Your dog should always be supported if you're going to hold her. She's not an accessory and shouldn't be toted around like that. You want your little dog to be safe and healthy. Just because some items are for sale doesn't mean they are a good idea. Think of your little dog's comfort and safety, and buyer beware.

Ajolie Yarn Motifs (www.ajolieyarnmotifs) is ideal for the person who wants to dress like their dog. Owner Jolie Stratton makes matching flings (scarves, boas, and the like) for people and their little dogs. Her Chihuahua, Diva, is the inspiration. The flings are custom made, and the ones for dogs are designed to stay in place. You can order through the web site or e-mail ajolieyarnmotifs@aol.com, or you can phone Stratton at (972) 579-0505.

It was a tiny Yorkshire Terrier who inspired **Cosette's Closet** (www.cosettescloset.com). Owner DebbieLynn was seriously injured in an accident, and Cosette, her under-two-pound Yorkie, serves as her service dog. The little sprite has saved her life numerous times by calling 911 on speed dial. Needing to work out of her home, she created Cosette's Closet, which specializes in clothing and accessories for little dogs and their people, plus such interesting items as a dog park for your apartment-dwelling dog and doggy car seats. You can e-mail her at deb@cosettescloset.com.

G.W. Little (gwlittle.com) is dedicated to clothing for little dogs, and they have a catalog as well as a web site. The name means The Great World of Little Dogs. Well, we know all about *that*! The owners of the company, based in California, donate a portion of their sales to support the programs of local animal rescue organizations and no-kill shelters. They offer a discount to those who join their Pet Fashion Club (for a membership fee). The company has a wide range of products for little dogs and their owners. If you don't have Internet access, you can request a catalog by calling (866) 495-4885.

Chi-wa-wa Ga-ga (chiwawagaga.com) calls itself "A small store for dinky dogs." The owners started their business in a storefront at 37 French Market Place in New Orleans' historic French Quarter. The shop was damaged by Hurricane Katrina but has since reopened. And you can always shop online. The "real" owners are two Chihuahuas, Angelo and Tweaky. Chi-wa-wa Ga-ga carries everything from clothing and costumes to bedding and rain gear, treats, toys, and more. You can phone them at (504) 581-GAGA (4242). You can also sign up for their online mailing list.

The Ritzy Rover Pet Boutique (theritzyrover.com), based in North Carolina, has quite an array of fashions for your little dog. They also have a large-breed department in case you also have a large dog or need a gift for someone who does. Their web site even has a Wish List. Their custom dog houses and beds are very elaborate, as are the canine fashions, hair bows, and more. The owner oversees all orders. Telephone help is available from 10 a.m. to 4 p.m. EST at (704) 573-1504. The Ritzy Rover also has an e-mail newsletter announcing special promotions, or you can e-mail them at info@theritzyrover.com.

Calypso's Choice (www.calypsoschoice.ca), also in Canada, has fashions for little dogs. This is another case of a Chihuahua being the inspiration for a canine clothing company. There are capes, bomber jackets, hoodies, and more. Each product is a limited edition. Hats and hoods are also available. E-mail Sara@calypsoschoice.ca.

Glamour Dog (www.glamourdog.com) is a Texas company with a flagship retail boutique in Frisco, in the northern Dallas–Fort Worth area. Owned by a husband and wife—he's a graphic designer; she's a fashion designer—and their little Maltese, Chanel, started them on the road to upscale canine fashion. Clothing, harnesses, beds, jewelry, carriers—it's all available here. Glamour Dog is also a sponsor of the SPCA of Texas. To contact customer service, you can either use their online e-mail form or phone (877) GlamDog (452-6364). You can sign up online for their mailing list announcing sales and special events.

Eloise, Inc., is named for the Coton de Tulear who inspired her owner to create this company. You'll recognize their dog beds from various films and television programs, as well as Starwood Hotels. They also carry fashionable collars and leashes, as well as a necklace for the owner that's personalized with the dog's name. Available in some stores around the United States, Canada, and Asia, you can find Eloise, Inc., online at www.EloiseInc.com. And you can phone (866) ELOISES (356-4737) or e-mail WagnerJOAT@aol.com.

Ruff Ruff and Meow Dog Clothes (www.ruffruffandmeow.com) is a California-based company with a wide range of hilarious tanks and T-shirts for your little dog, including some that are specific to various U.S. states. They also have doggy wristbands. Why? Good question! But if you want your dog to wear one, you can find it here. A catalog is available. You can call toll free (866) 742-RUFF (7833).

Modern Tails Luxury Pet Boutique (www.moderntails.com), which is based in New York City, has a range of sweaters, coats, furniture, accessories, and more for your little dog. You can phone toll free, (877) 399-4645, or e-mail help@moderntails.com.

Dazzling Dogs and Felines (www.dazzlingdogsandfelines.com), based in Arizona, was inspired by three active, adorable puppies. You can find coats, princess dresses, furniture, and more for your little dog. E-mail admin@dazzlingdogsandfelines.com.

Pawstigious Pups (www.pawstigiouspups.com) in New Jersey owes its origins to a little Maltese named Kodie, whose owner fell in love with the dog fashions she saw coming out of Asia. You'll find everything from hoodies to dresses, coats, tees, sweaters, pajamas, panties, harnesses, leashes, and collars to beds. Phone (609) 748-8241, or e-mail sales@pawstigiouspups.com.

Woof—The Small Dog Company (www.woofonline.com) is located on the New Jersey shore. The brainchild of two dog lovers, these friends got the idea for their company while walking their dogs. Their goal was to create high-quality dog fashions for less money. They will send out occasional e-mails announcing new products. Among the things you can find here for your little dog are dresses, raincoats, sweaters, jackets, tiaras, hairclips, collars, leashes, necklaces, and even wedding attire. Their toll free number is (888) 878-2160, or you can e-mail service@woofonline.com.

Pampered Puppy (www.pamperedpuppy.com), overseen by Merry the Princess Pug, provides Merry's evaluations of various products. The latest fashion finds for dogs are here, with more and more added each month. You can sign up for e-mail updates when there are

new reviews on the web site along with contests at Pampered Puppy; prizes include luxury dog services for your dog.

Inspired by the owner Jennifer Sankary's Chihuahua, Paris, **Bella Paris** (www.bellaparis.com) specializes in harness vests and dresses for little dogs. Both fashionable and practical, they provide a comfortable way for your little dog to wear a harness. A small dog carrier is also available. You can order online or by phone at (818) 823-3969. The website also has a list of retail shops that carry the Bella Paris line, and you can e-mail the company at info@bellaparis.com.

If you're dreaming of pajamas, a top hat, a golf shirt, or jeweled or beaded collars for your little dog, you'll find all of that and much more at **The Fashionable Pet** (www.thefashionablepet.com). They also carry pet steps and a toy box for your little darling. E-mail mbaker@thefashionablepet.com or call (248) 921-7681.

Lolawear (www.lolawear.com) specializes in clothing for particularly small dogs. Three-pound Lola the Yorkshire Terrier is president of the company. She's a go-everywhere companion to company owner Lynne Thomas. Lolawear carries everything from hair accessories to loungewear, and there's even a listing for "unmentionables." Most of the clothes and bows are custom made. Your dog's measurements are required for all clothing orders to ensure a proper fit. Five percent of sales are given to Puppy Mill Rescue. E-mail the company at barbiedog@lolawear.com.

Hip Doggie (www.hipdoggie.com), in Southern California, has a variety of clothing for small dogs: Everything from fashion-forward sweaters and T-shirts to sweatshirts, dresses, and suits. They also have a sale section on the website or call (818) 505-8599.

Roxy Hunt Couture (www.roxyhuntcouture). Canine couture takes on a whole new slant when the dog and her mom are both soap opera stars. Crystal Hunt, who plays Lizzie Spaulding on *The Guiding Light*, and her little dog, Roxy, are behind this line of clothing. A visit to the website will not only let you see the fashions but also a growing list of retailers who carry it. You can also order directly from the website or call (877) 476-9948.

Small Dog Supplies

It's a given that you will need supplies for your little dog—everything from dishes and a harness and leash to a safe carrier, grooming supplies, shampoo, conditioner, and lots more.

Premier Pet Products (www.premier.com) is the home of the Gentle Leader headcollar and the Easy Walk harness. Premier also carries Fido Fleece apparel and Busy Buddy toys, which are chew toys designed to keep your little one's mind (and mouth) occupied when she can't have your undivided attention. You can buy directly through their web site, or they can refer you to a distributor in your area. To contact them between 8 a.m. and 5 p.m. EST, Monday through Friday, call toll free (888) 640-8840.

SturdiProducts (www.PetCarrier.com) carries an assortment of products made in America for travel with your little dog. Their SturdiBag, which comes in a range of sizes, is an incredibly lightweight carrier that fits under the seat of a plane without collapsing on your dog. It has a nice pad inside and an extra pocket on the outside for a toy, small can, or plastic bag of food and comes in a variety of colors. Their CarGo is a double-sided carrier for the car that goes right into the hotel room. One side is for the dog; the other is where you can place food and water. There is a zippered barrier between them made of the same lightweight fabric. Or you can put a dog in each side, if you prefer. One side also has space for an optional hammock if your little dog wants to nap there while you're out of the room. The design cleverly has four zippered doors (two in front and one on each end) for easy entry, and there are seatbelt safety straps. Other travel products for you and your dog can be seen online. Phone toll free at (800) 779-8193 or order online.

Snuggle Puppies (www.snuggleme.com) is a wonderful toy for a new puppy. It has a battery operated "heartbeat," along with a heat pack that safely slips inside the soft toy. The heartbeat and the warmth help simulate the puppy's experience with her mother and littermates to make her transition to a new home easier. It's also useful for the responsible breeder who may have lost the pups' mother during whelping. If the new owner sends just the outer part of the toy along to the breeder to place with the mother and littermates a day or two before the pup goes home, it will also pick up familiar smells, which will further comfort the puppy in her new environment. The web site has links for various countries, so others around the world can easily purchase the toy in a variety of currencies. You can also reach the company through their toll free number in the United States, (800) 463-4107, or at (970) 920-9400, or e-mail info@snuggleme.com.

Mighty Mite Dog Gear (www.mightymitedoggear.com) specializes in agility equipment for little dogs as well as tents, books, videos, clickers, and more, including a message board. You can reach them at Rena@mightymitedoggear.com or 123 Hempstead Ave., Rockville Center, NY 11570.

Cherrybrook (www.cherrybrook.com) has an outlet store in New Jersey and big booths at dog shows in the eastern United States, as well as Ohio, Illinois, and Michigan, but you can also shop online quite easily. Everything from grooming equipment to show leads, dog books, toys, and more can be found here. To request a mail order catalog, call them toll free at (800) 524-0820.

ClickerTraining.com (www.clickertraining.com) is clicker training guru Karen Pryor's company, where you can purchase supplies for training your little dog using positive, effective training techniques. You can also write to Karen Pryor Clicker Training, 49 River St., #3, Waltham, MA 02453.

Pet Edge (www.petedge.com) is a catalog company based in Massachusetts and they, too, have an outlet store. Their web site has an assortment of basic dog supplies along with some dog clothing and lots of toys. To contact them toll free within the United States, call (800) 738-3343. Outside the United States, call (978) 887-2368, extension 7209, and ask to speak with the International Sales Department. The mailing address is PetEdge, P.O. Box 128, Topsfield, MA 01983-0228. Or you can place an e-mail order at order@petedge.com.

HelpYourPets.com (www.helpyourpets.com) has pet steps for your handicapped or elderly dog, to ease her access to those favored comfy spots on the bed or sofa. This company carries Mini Steps specially made for small dogs. Call toll free (888) 842-5230, or write to them at 3706 N. Walton Blvd., Bentonville, AR 72712.

Post Modern Pets (www.postmodernpets.com), located in Mountain View, California, offers beds and toys for owners who like modern and postmodern designs. Your dog can enjoy the same style furniture as the rest of the family members with a dog bed that's part of your home decor. E-mail the company at sales@postmodernpets.com or call (650) 331-3500.

A Pet's World (apetsworld.com) is the brainchild of Jane Knittle, who spent nearly three decades in the fashion industry manufacturing ladies, children's, and menswear for some of the finest stores in the United States. When a Maltese entered her life, she began to create things for small dogs. Her line of carriers, coats, collars, leashes, harnesses, small dog toys, beds, and distinctive gifts for pets and their special people can be found in some pet boutiques, as well as at her web site. Call (877) 738-8683 (802-366-1511 in Vermont). You can also write to A Pet's World, P.O. Box 1993, 204B Manchester Valley Road, Bldg. C, Manchester Center, VT 05255.

Golly Gear (www.gollygear.com) is owned by two sisters in Skokie, Illinois, who also own a brick-and-mortar bookstore. Their small dogs are the inspiration for the company, which was named after Golly, a Brussels Griffon. Golly Gear offers all sorts of things for little dogs, including clothing, toys, and treats, and 10 percent of their profits go to various rescue organizations for small dogs. You can e-mail them at manager@gollygear.com or call (800) 694-6531 (847-677-0680 in Illinois).

The Regal Dog (www.theregaldog.com) in Miami, Florida, carries everything from clothing and accessories to beds, dog dishes, and toys, and even has items it will personalize with your dog's name. Phone (305) 255-2126.

The company slogan of **Bailey & Wags** (www.baileyandwags.com) is The Rewards of Loyalty. They have all sorts of clothing and accessories for posh dogs and their owners. You can shop on the website by styles, such as Sporty or Preppy, or shop by theme, such as Strictly Couture and Spa Dog. This Florida company can also be reached toll free at (800) 887-5448.

Myuptownpooch.com (www.myuptownpooch.com) has a wide range of designer dog clothing, pet beds, pet jewelry, and more, including dog spa products. They specialize in custom designer dog clothing by Emma Rose Design. This Rhode Island company ships worldwide. E-mail sales@myuptownpooch.com or call (401) 624-3259.

While all small dogs should use their feet and walk, there are times when it's safer for them to be in an enclosed place. Strollers for pets are starting to be seen on dog show grounds to safely get the little dogs across the field while hauling along a grooming table, grooming equipment, and other gear. It's easier than carrying a crate and there's less jostling for the dog. They can also be practical on long hikes with a little dog, or when you want to jog, because your little one simply can't keep up. **Just Pet Strollers** (www.justpetstrollers.com) has a range of stroller types to suit you and your little dog(s). E-mail them at petlover@metropawlis.com or call, toll free, (877) 673-7387.

If you have a dog with arthritis or other joint problems, you may want to consider buying a **Gel-Pedic Pet Bed** (www.gelpedic.com), made by Splintek PPInc. The patented gel foam in the bed molds to your dog's body and keeps the dog warm in the winter and cool in the summer. The natural eucalyptus bars used in the bed repel fleas and mites. E-mail the company at sales@gelpedic.com or call (888) 738-7237 or (816) 531-1900.

PetaPotty (www.petapotty.com) is not a canine litterbox. It's more like bringing the outdoors indoors. The box uses either real or synthetic grass, so it's more like going outdoors

(making an easier transition to that substrate), but enables you to train your dog to go indoors if you live where blizzards might interfere with outdoor walks. It's also handy for the infirm owner who can't get out for regular walks or the owner who can't get home at lunch hour for a mid-day walk. The waste is gathered in a designated area for easier disposal. E-mail the company at info@petapotty.com or call toll free (866) 738-7297.

Pish Pad (www.pishpad.com) is for the person who needs a substrate for their dog or puppy to use when nature calls. Made of three materials that are bonded together, the "soaker" layer collects liquids and holds them away from your dog while the bottom layer protects the floor surface underneath. The top layer will not break the hair of a long-coated dog, nor will the hair be wet, nor will there be any stained hair, according to the company. While the pad sticks to any surface, it is also easy to remove and leaves behind no residue. Pish Pads are reusable and can be handy while traveling. They can be cut to size and they don't retain odor. E-mail pishpad@aol.com.

For readers in Canada, **NKConcepts** (www.nkconcepts.com) has a range of dog supplies, including obedience equipment, books, and more. You can e-mail owner Nancy Kitching at nkitch@videotron.ca or phone her at (450) 458-3165. You can also write to NKConcepts, 156 Fair Haven, Hudson, QC, J0P 1H0.

Across the pond in the U.K. is **Puddle Pat Care** (www.puddlepetcare.co.uk), with a range of supplies for your dog including some really clever toys to exercise your little dog's mental prowess. Their dog beds are as decorative as they are practical for your little dog's sleeping enjoyment. You can telephone them at 011 44 01243 601010, e-mail enquiries@puddlepetcare.co.uk, or write to Puddle Pet Care, P.O. Box 1010, Selsey, West Sussex, PO20 9JY. Unfortunately, they don't publish a paper catalog, so you will need Internet access to see their products.

Something Different

You're going to wonder why I'm sending you to a web site devoted to cats. Well, there's good reason. Sammy Clark is a woman with a passion for making things for small animals, and she has created something very special that much-loved little dogs will adore. It's a bed in the shape of a royal crown. Beautifully hand-crafted and reasonably priced, it will not only provide a comfy place for your dog to sleep but a nice fashion touch for your home. You can choose the fabric and color of the gemstones adorning the bed. Log on to **Sammy Kats** at

www.geocities.com/sammykatsaol/index.html, scroll past the cage curtains, and at the very end, like a pot of gold at the end of a rainbow, is the crown bed, fit for any little canine prince or princess. Along the way, you might want to look at the adorable bibs. Cats might wear them as bibs, but little dogs can wear them as fashionable collars on a therapy dog visit or any special occasion. You can e-mail Sammy at Sammykats@aol.com or phone her at (504) 738-9078. Her mailing address is 10408 Ware St., River Ridge, LA 70123.

Tasty Treats

Finding special treats for your little canine is easier than ever, because there are now so many bakeries dedicated to pets. Remember that these are treats, so break each one into tiny pieces and make them last. You don't want to overfeed your little companion, and you certainly don't want to create health problems caused by obesity.

Latka's Treats (www.delicioustreats.com) is the brainchild of Beth Goldberg, who named the bakery for her Polish Lowland Sheepdog, Latka. Latka's treats are many and creative. This New York City-based company has been featured on a variety of television programs and in magazines. Latka's treats can be found in stores around the United States or online. There are treats for all occasions, and many are ready for gift-giving in clever containers.

Bones Bakery (www.bonesbakery.com) was created by the owner of a rescue dog named Lola who is part Rottweiler and part Pointer. Their web site has links to local shopping information around the country as well as a way to shop for their special doggy treats. They have goodies for every occasion and for no occasion at all—just for the fun of a special treat. They even sell an all-natural soap for dogs. You can call toll free at (888) 899-7009 or write to them at info@bonesbakery.com.

Woof (www.woofbakery.com) is based in Rhode Island, but you don't have to live there. Woof ships its doggie goodies, including celebration baskets, via online shopping. Gifts and accessories are also available. Call (401) 253-5755 or visit the store 54 State St., Bristol, RI 02809. You can also e-mail deb@woofbakery.com.

Hard Bonez Barkery (www.hardbonezbarkery.com) has everything from treats to doggie birthday cakes and ice cream. You can order online, of course. The mailing address is P.O. Box 20336, Kalamazoo, MI 49019. Phone (269) 343-8801 or toll free (866) 385-8805, or e-mail Fido@hardbonezbarkery.com.

Just for You

B-Unique (www.bunique.com) has some really wonderful items for dog owners. You can find the ubiquitous T-shirts and sweatshirts, although theirs are anything but common, but of more interest are the really wonderful designer-type items they sell. Their clothing is often decorated with Swarovski Austrian Crystals and metallic nail heads. And there are hand-painted designs as well as wonderful appliqués. In fact, they have an appliqué design of the dogs in the Toy Group that's a real winner. They can even customize clothing with your logo on it. Based at 3165 S. Alma School Rd., Chandler, AZ 85248-3762, they are found at some of the biggest and best dog shows in the United States. You don't have to wait for a dog show to order from them, though; you can phone (888) 269-3639 or e-mail wendy@bunique.com to discuss ordering something special for yourself or a friend.

If you love to collect tchotchkas with your dog's breed, **Dog Collectibles** (www.dogcollectibles.com) is the place for you. The owner of this online store travels the world finding breed-specific items, and you won't be disappointed when you click on your favorite breed on the home page. You can order online or via e-mail (info@dogcollectibles.com) or write to Dog Collectibles, 365 Boston Post Road, #241, Sudbury, MA 01776. You can also phone (978) 443-8387.

Dogues Gallery (www.doguesgallery.com) is perfect for the person who loves wonderful dog art items featuring their breed. The creativity of owner Judith Sherburne Gates is clearly apparent. An alumna of the Rhode Island School of Design, she combines her skill as an artist with her deeply rooted love of dogs to create memorable items. She has gorgeous breed representations on everything from roof slates to ornaments, fabrics, and jewelry, as well as wooden gift boxes. You can contact Judith via e-mail at jgates8@cox.net or at (401) 434-4536 or write to her 1540 Pawtucket Ave., East Providence, RI 02916-1624.

Pampered Paws (www.pamperedpawsjewelry.com) features the gold and sterling silver fine jewelry made by talented artisans who also custom design and hand craft pieces in 10k, 14k, and 18k gold, if you're really in a mood to splurge. Whatever you can imagine, they will create. Each piece captures the essence of the individual breed. Their fine breed pieces are quite beautiful and can be seen online. They periodically travel to dog shows. Their mailing address is 2803 Aquarius Ave., Silver Spring, MD 20906. Or you can telephone (301) 438-0994 or e-mail pamprpaw@worldnet.att.net.

Walker Works features the artistry of Robert L. Walker, whose copper and pewter etchings are of particular note. (He also does photography, reverse glass, canine art, and pencil portraits.) You can contact Walker Works by telephone at (716) 688-7519, by mail at 1146 Dodge Rd., Getzville, NY 14068, or via e-mail at walkerworks@adelphia.net.

Are you interested in leather handbags and wallets, glass ornaments, ceramics, grooming bags, denim shirts, and jackets with your breed on them? Or perhaps with a custom portrait of your dog as the theme? Then you may want to check out the work of **Beth Babos.** This California artist also does note cards and pet portraits. You can contact her at (818) 597-9693, e-mail mail her at Beth.Babos@sbcglobal.net, or write to 31823 Langspur Court, Westlake Village, CA 91361.

Why am I including **Kockeyed Kandles** (www.kockeyedkandles.com)? Well, if you've ever turned to mush over the smell of puppy breath, then you'll want to surf over to their web site and find the Puppy's Breath scented candles. They'll even create special candles with that scent, including one that can be used as an invitation. You can also reach them by phone at (830) 885-6664 or by mail at P.O. Box 599, Spring Branch, TX 78070. E-mail information@kockeyedkandles.com.

Crazy Dog Lady (www.crazydoglady.com) is the place to go if you want a portrait of your special little dog done as a quilt, a quilted wall hanging, or a pillow. Jan Queijo works from photographs you supply. All hard copy photos will, of course, be returned. E-mail her at jan@crazydoglady.com

If you like soft sculpture you'll be enraptured by the work of Tammy Hendricks. Tammy is a teddy bear artist who has also turned her talents to designing and hand-making incredible little dogs. You can see some amazing examples at **Collectible Dogs** (www.tammybears.com/pooches.html). The page on her web site that leads to the dogs is called the Adoption Center. E-mail tammybears@pldi.net or call (405) 387-2638 (they're in the Central Time Zone).

Are you a do-it-yourself kind of person? If crafts are your thing, check out **Rhapsody Dolls** (www.rhapsodydolls.com/dog_patterns.htm), where you can buy patterns to make your own tiny soft dog sculptures. You will need some sewing skills, but these are mainly fabric sculpting projects. For those familiar with this craft form, the dolls are Intermediate to Advanced projects. Patterns come in a wide range of breeds. E-mail Rhonda@rhapsodydolls.com. Or write to R. Hagy, P.O. Box 2194, Ellijay, GA 30540.

Klay9 Kreations (klay9kreations.com) will create a clay sculpture of your dog using a photo as a model. Artist Lindsay Neely, who has a BA in Art and Design from Iowa State University, is the person behind this fun and whimsical way to celebrate your special companion, whether purebred or of mixed heritage. One dollar from each order is donated to various rescue organizations. E-mail info@klay9kreations.com or phone (612) 229-0228. The mailing address is Klay9Kreations, c/o Lindsay Neely, 3837 28th Ave. S., Minneapolis, MN 55406.

Dawn Secord (www.dawnsecord.com) is an award-winning artist who works in pastels. She's registered with the American Kennel Club's Museum of the Dog. She offers prints and greeting cards and also does commissioned portraits, so you can have a museum-quality portrait of your special little canine companion. You can phone her toll free at (866) 393-7111 or e-mail her at fff@linkline.com. Reach her by mail at Fur, Feathers, and Fins Studio, 3233 Grand Avenue, Suite N-123, Chino Hills, CA 91709.

Resources

Books

Arden, Darlene. *The Angell Memorial Animal Hospital Book of Wellness and Preventive Care for Dogs*. Contemporary Books/McGraw-Hill, 2002.

——. *Unbelievably Good Deals and Great Adventures That You Absolutely Can't Get Unless You're a Dog*. McGraw-Hill, 2004.

Book, Mandy, and Cheryl S. Smith. *Quick Clicks*. Hanalei, 2001.

Pryor, Karen. *Clicker Training for Dogs*. Sunshine Books, 2001.

——. *Don't Shoot the Dog*. Bantam Books, 1999.

Rubin, Sheldon. *First Aid for Your Dog*. LW Press, 2005.

Rugaas, Turid. *On Talking Terms with Dogs: Calming Signals*, 2nd edition. Dogwise, 2006.

Ryan, Terry. *The Bark Stops Here*. Legacy-by-Mail, 2000.

Smith, Cheryl S. *The Rosetta Bone*. Howell Book House, 2004.

Internet

AKC Canine Health Foundation

www.akcchf.org

Articles summarizing the research funded by the AKC Canine Health Foundation are available on this site. It also includes sample health surveys, lists of available genetic tests, and news about cutting-edge health discoveries.

American Animal Hospital Association

www.healthypet.com

On this site, you'll find the latest medical news and guidelines from the AAHA, a pet care library, pet FAQs, some coloring pages for kids, and a way to search for AAHA-accredited hospitals in your area.

American Kennel Club

www.akc.org

The largest pedigreed dog registry in the United States features canine care articles and breed standards for all the breeds it registers. You will also find breeder referral and rescue referral information, and a feature that helps you find dog clubs in your area.

American Veterinary Medical Association

www.avma.org

Click on the Public Resources section and you'll find animal health brochures, information about any animal health issues in the news, advice on disaster preparedness, fun pages for kids, advice for new pet owners, and a detailed reference section.

Canadian Kennel Club

www.ckc.ca

Breed standards, advice on choosing the right breed for you, canine legislation, local clubs in Canada, and a calendar of events are featured on this web site.

International Association of Animal Behavior Consultants
www.iaabc.org
This organization certifies animal behavior consultants. The web site will help you locate a certified consultant in your area.

The Kennel Club
www.the-kennel-club.org.uk
You don't need to be in Britain to use this web site. There is a wealth of information about training and health issues, and various breeds and their characteristics.

Merck Veterinary Manual Online
www.merckveterinarymanual.com
The *Merck Veterinary Manual* is a comprehensive reference book for veterinarians on every aspect of companion animal health. The whole book is available online.

Pet Diets
www.petdiets.com
You'll find a wealth of information from veterinary nutritionists on pet nutrition and advice about how to make a nutritious, balanced, homemade diet for your dog.

United Kennel Club
www.ukcdogs.com
The emphasis at UKC is on sporting and working dogs, including small dogs. The web site contains the breed standards for all the breeds recognized by the UKC, plus lists of dog events.

World Canine Freestyle Organization
www.worldcaninefreestyle.org
Learn more about the sport of dancing with dogs, including upcoming events, video clips, local clubs, and how to get started in training your dog.

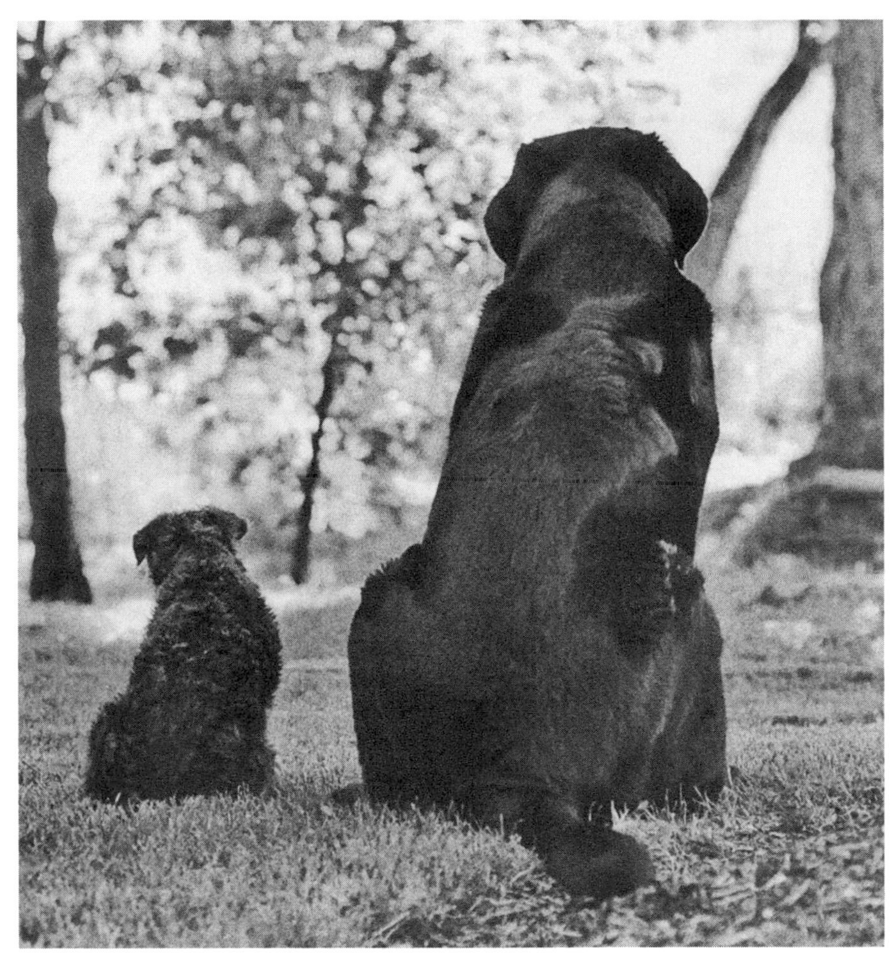

Border Terrier and Labrador Retriever

Courtesy of Deenie Galipeau

Index

G

H

I

J

K

L

R

S

T

U

V

W

X

Y

Yorkshire Terriers *(Courtesy of Jeanne Roushey)*

Affenpinscher *(Courtesy of Barry Kurth)*

Maltese *(Courtesy of Betty Wang)*

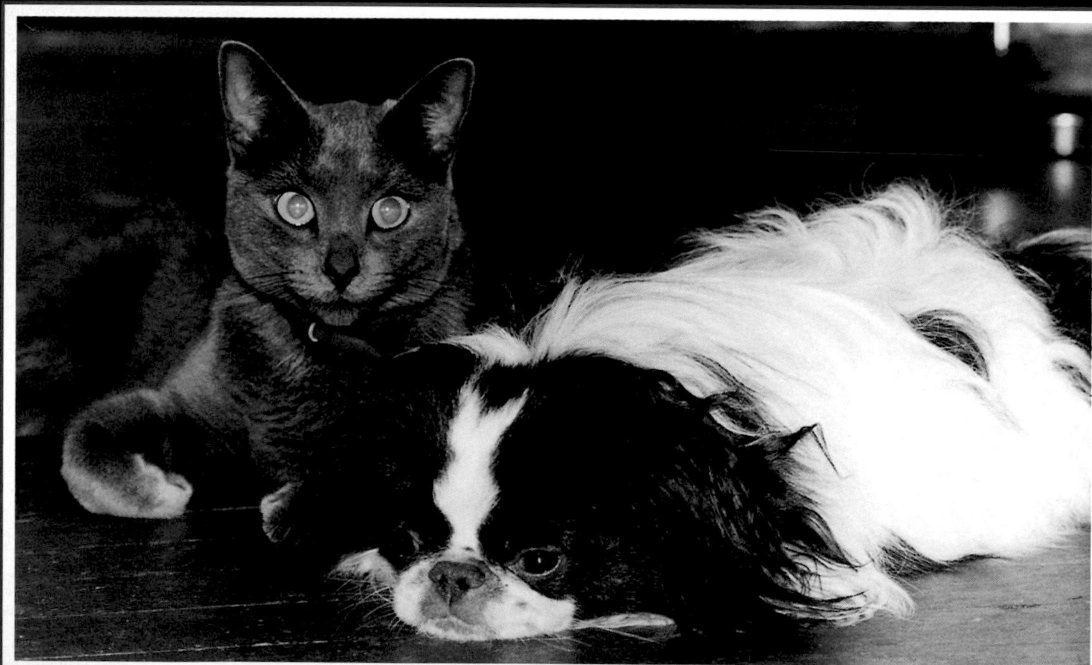

Japanese Chin and feline friend *(Courtesy of Rose Marchetti)*

Chihuahuas *(©Tara Darling, courtesy of Susan Payne)*

Pomeranian and ferret *(Courtesy of Susan R. Major)*

Mixed breed *(Courtesy of Pam Martin)*

Border Terrier and Labrador Retriever

Maltese *(Courtesy of Betty Wang)*

Pekingese and Scottish Deerhound *(Courtesy of Vanna Condax)*

Border Terriers *(Courtesy of Deenie Gallipeau)*

Lhasa Apsos *(Courtesy of Vickie Kuhlmann)*

Cavalier King Charles Spaniel *(Courtesy of Bressler West©)*

Mixed breed *(Courtesy of Cheryl S. Smith)*

Italian Greyhound *(Courtesy of Patricia Campbell)*

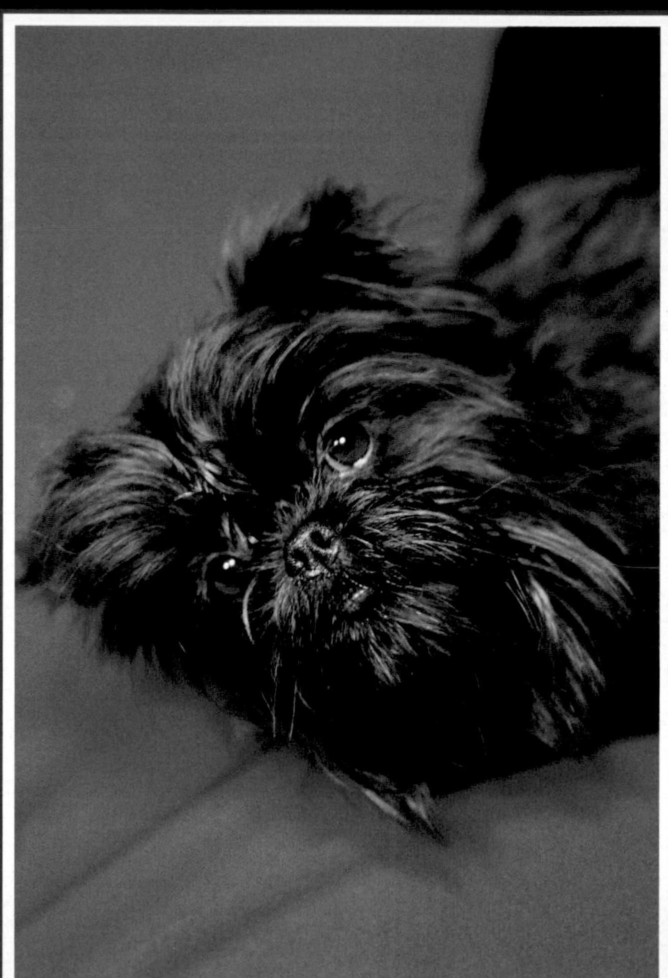

Affenpinscher *(Photo by Sean Downey, courtesy of Mary Downey*

Boston Terrier *(Courtesy of Stephanie Alford)*

Italian Greyhound *(Kathleen Schaffer©, courtesy of Patricia Campbell)*

Havanese *(Courtesy of Susan Bulanda)*

Papillons *(Amber Grundman©, courtesy of Judy Scott)*